BORDER PATROL EXAM: POWER PRACTICE

Copyright © 2012 LearningExpress, LLC.

All rights reserved under International and Pan American Copyright Conventions.
Published in the United States by LearningExpress, LLC, New York.

Library of Congress Cataloging-in-Publication Data:
Border patrol exam : power practice.—1st ed.
    p. cm.
   ISBN 978-1-57685-903-2 (pbk. : alk. paper)—ISBN 1-57685-903-7
  (pbk. : alk. paper)
   1. United States. Immigration Border Patrol—Examinations—Study
guides.   2. Border patrol agents—United States—Examinations—Study
guides.   I. LearningExpress (Organization)
    JV6483.B665   2012
    363.28'5076—dc23   2012015334

Printed in the United States of America

9 8 7 6 5 4 3 2 1

First Edition

ISBN-10: 1-57685-903-7
ISBN-13: 978-1-57685-903-2

For more information or to place an order, contact LearningExpress at:
    2 Rector Street
    26th Floor
    New York, NY 10006

Or visit us at:
    www.learningexpressllc.com

Editor: Marco A. Annunziata
Production Editor: Eric Titner
Assistant Editor: Lindsay Oliver

ABOUT THE CONTRIBUTORS

Ashleigh Martinez was born and raised in southern California. After graduating from the University of Southern California, she lived in Costa Rica for five years, where she taught, translated, and developed language curriculum. She now lives in San Diego, California, and is pursuing her certification as a Spanish-English translator and interpreter at UCSD.

Michele R. Wells has been a writer and editor for more than fifteen years. A senior editor at one of the world's largest entertainment companies, she specializes in nonfiction book and multimedia publishing. She is the Founding Chairperson of First Book-Brooklyn, a nonprofit organization that provides new books to children in need, and volunteers regularly with Everybody WINS Power Lunch, a NYC-based literacy and mentoring program for kids.

CONTENTS

CHAPTER 1	About the Border Patrol Exam	1
	Logical Reasoning Test	2
	Language Testing	2
CHAPTER 2	Border Patrol Study Skills and Test-Taking Strategies	5
	Study Skills	5
	Study Environment and Attitude	6
	Learn How You Learn	7
	Creating a Study Plan	8
	What You Know and What You Need to Know	8
	How Do You Know What You Know?	9
	Learning Strategies	9
	Border Patrol Exam-Specific Strategies	11
	Timing	12
	Multiple-Choice Test Strategies	12
	Almost There: Strategies for the Final Days before the Exam	13
	Handling and Preventing Test Stress	13
	A Healthy Mind and a Healthy Body	15
CHAPTER 3	Practice Test 1	17
	Logical Reasoning Test	21
	Spanish Language Proficiency Test	28
	Answers	34
	Practice Test 1: Scoring and Diagnostic Chart	46

CONTENTS

CHAPTER 4 Practice Test 2 — 47
Logical Reasoning Test — 51
Spanish Language Proficiency Test — 58
Answers — 65
Practice Test 2: Scoring and Diagnostic Chart — 78

CHAPTER 5 Practice Test 3 — 79
Logical Reasoning Test — 83
Spanish Language Proficiency Test — 89
Answers — 95
Practice Test 3: Scoring and Diagnostic Chart — 105

CHAPTER 6 Practice Test 4 — 107
Logical Reasoning Test — 111
Artifical Language Review — 118
Grammatical Rules for the Artificial Language — 120
Artificial Language — 122
Answers — 128
Practice Test 4: Scoring and Diagnostic Chart — 142

CHAPTER 7 Practice Test 5 — 143
Logical Reasoning Test — 147
Artificial Language Review — 153
Grammatical Rules for the Artificial Language — 155
Artificial Language — 157
Answers — 163
Practice Test 5: Scoring and Diagnostic Chart — 178

CHAPTER 8 Practice Test 6 — 179
Logical Reasoning Test — 183
Artificial Language Review — 191
Grammatical Rules for the Artificial Language — 192
Artificial Language — 194
Answers — 201
Practice Test 6: Scoring and Diagnostic Chart — 216

ADDITIONAL ONLINE PRACTICE — 217

CHAPTER 1 ▶ ABOUT THE BORDER PATROL EXAM

Each year, tens of thousands of people nationwide take the Border Patrol Exam, which is offered when current lists of eligible applicants are depleted and Congress authorizes additional hiring. Fewer than 800 of these candidates will be selected. Tests are normally scheduled at the nearest location to your home and could be administered in a federal building, civic hall, or library. You will be notified where to report for your written exam. When you receive the test notification packet, be sure to read all the material carefully!

You must pass a written exam like the practice tests contained in this book. The exam consists of the following sections: Logical Reasoning and a language test consisting of *either* the Spanish Language Proficiency Test *or* (if you don't speak Spanish) the Artificial Language Test (which tests your ability to learn languages). There is also an assessment of job-related activities and achievements.

The test takes about four and a half hours. Once you have taken the Border Patrol Agent test, you should receive a Notice of Results in the mail within four weeks following the test.

Logical Reasoning Test

The Logical Reasoning section of the test measures your vocabulary, reading comprehension, and critical thinking skills, which are necessary to prepare and perform the duties required of a Border Patrol Agent.

You should know that Border Patrol Agents are often called upon to testify in legal proceedings, and it is imperative to understand the legal reasoning process. The logical reasoning questions were designed with this application in mind. They are also designed to test your ability to understand complicated written material and derive conclusions. You will be required to come to logical conclusions based on various facts in the written material.

The questions in this test are different from regular reading comprehension questions that ask you to understand the meaning of a passage. Specifically, this is the kind of reading that will test your ability to draw conclusions and take action. Often, the situations presented in the questions can be quite complex. Careful reading and focused thinking are required to determine what *is* being asked and what *is not* being asked. The logical reading questions vary in level of difficulty from average to difficult.

Logical Reasoning Test Tips

1. When choosing a conclusion, always look for one that can be made based only on the information in the paragraph.
2. Assume all information in the paragraph is true. Do not use other factual information you may already know to reach your conclusion.
3. Focus on the key lead-in sentence and read the paragraph carefully. Consider all of the answer choices carefully before making your final answer selection.
4. Pay special attention to words such as *all, some, none, unless, except,* and *only*. These qualifying words help define the facts in the statement.
5. Keep in mind that negative prefixes such as *non-* or negative words such as *disorganized* or *unfasten* can be critical to an understanding of the information in the statement.
6. If for other tests you have been told to avoid answers that contain the word *all* or *none*, disregard that advice for the Logical Reasoning Exam. These words do not indicate an incorrect answer in this test. *All* and *none* can be in both the incorrect and the correct answers.
7. Answer every question on the test. Guess at an answer only after eliminating answers that you know to be false. While you are not penalized for guessing, your chances of picking a correct answer are greatly improved by using the process of elimination. You have a one in five chance of picking a right answer by blindly guessing. Your chances improve with every choice that is eliminated.
8. Do not pay attention to patterns made by **a, b, c, d,** or **e** on the answer sheet. Correct answer positions are selected randomly. You cannot improve your chances of guessing based on a pattern on the answer sheet. Trying to figure out a pattern is a poor test-taking strategy.
9. The best way to improve your chances on the exam is through practice. Take the tests found in this book and study their answer explanations. This will hone your logical reasoning ability. Remember that the time you put into preparing for the Logical Reasoning Exam is time well spent and will increase your chances of doing well on the test.

Language Testing

If you speak Spanish, you may take a proficiency test that measures that ability. However, if you do not speak Spanish, then you will take an Artificial Language Test that measures your ability to learn the Spanish language.

ABOUT THE BORDER PATROL EXAM

Spanish Language Test

There are four different kinds of questions on the Spanish Language Test.

1. **Part I—Vocabulary**

   The best way to prepare for the vocabulary part of the test is to memorize, memorize, memorize. Using flash cards or a book of vocabulary lists, spend time every day drilling your vocabulary. This is an effective way to increase your Spanish comprehension and reinforce what you have already learned.

   The surest way to do well on the test is to study your vocabulary as much as possible. However, even then, you may run across a key word or a choice you don't know. How do you proceed? A useful tip is to look not only for the meaning of the word but also for its part of speech. For example, is the word a noun, a pronoun, or a verb? Often, several choices can be eliminated just by observing that they are the wrong number and gender for the noun, the wrong pronoun, or the wrong form of the verb.

2. **Part II, Section I—Grammar**

   For this part of the test, the important thing to focus on is the grammar. Look for the combination of words that not only has an appropriate meaning but also matches grammatically. Look for obvious errors such as choices using the wrong number and gender or an incorrect verb form.

   When evaluating verbs, begin by looking for the one with a form that matches the subject, which may be either a noun or a pronoun. Then look for one that uses the appropriate tense. This will quickly eliminate several possibilities. Often, it may not even be necessary to know the meaning of the verb to be able to choose the correct answer using this technique.

3. **Part II, Section II—Grammar**

   This section requires you to put it all together. It tests your ability to recognize various language elements and incorporate them into a complete picture, the correct sentence. To do well on this portion of the Spanish Language exam, look for errors of grammar, sentence structure, or incorrect word usage.

4. **Part II, Section III—Comprehension**

   This section also tests your overall comprehension. It requires you to decide whether a selection is correct. If it is incorrect, you will need to choose an alternative to the italicized word.

   First, decide if the italicized word is used correctly in the sentence. Having a strong vocabulary will help you here! If the word seems to have an appropriate meaning, then look for the right grammatical structure. If the italicized word is a noun, look for matching number and gender; if it is a verb, look for correct form and tense. This is where the time you spend studying Spanish grammar will pay off! If the italicized word passes both of these tests, choice **e** is the right one—the sentence does not need any correction.

Artificial Language Test

In general, these test questions deal with an Artificial Language created to measure your ability to learn a language. Remember that *knowledge of a specific language other than English is not required to answer the questions correctly.*

In the actual test, you will be given a Supplemental Booklet containing all the vocabulary for this language, all the rules of the language, and a glossary of grammatical terms. It is in this Supplemental Booklet that you will find information necessary to answer the questions in the test.

CHAPTER 2 ▶ BORDER PATROL STUDY SKILLS AND TEST-TAKING STRATEGIES

The advice in this chapter will help you set up an effective learning environment and create a successful study plan. You will also learn important study strategies and test-taking tips.

Study Skills

You probably feel as though you have spent practically your entire life studying, so why do you need to learn how to study for the Border Patrol Exam? The Border Patrol Exam is different from any other test you have ever taken. Not only is it more important, but multi-subject, standardized tests require a unique form of preparation.

You certainly do not have to scrap all the good study habits you have already learned, but you will most likely need to adapt them to the specifics of the Border Patrol Exam. You may already be using some of the techniques found in this chapter, but now is a good time to reevaluate your study habits and tailor them specifically to the Border Patrol Exam.

While studying for the Border Patrol Exam, you will also learn which study habits do not work and be able to eliminate wasted study time. Remember that the more effective your study habits, the less time you will spend studying and the more free time you will have to do what you really enjoy.

Study Environment and Attitude

The Right Mood

It will probably be tough to carve out extra time to study for the Border Patrol Exam on top of your regular work, your extracurricular activities, and your social life. These reasons may even lead you to procrastinate, but procrastinating can cause lots of trouble at test time. If you procrastinate too much or for too long, you will not be prepared for the exam.

One of the best ways to beat procrastination is to use a reward system. We all like to be rewarded for a job well done. If we know there is going to be a reward at the end of our work, it is easier to get started. So promise yourself a small reward for each study session. For example, you might promise yourself an hour of watching TV or playing video games as a reward for an hour of study. You might promise to treat yourself to a movie or a new book after you finish a chapter in a test-prep book. Remember, your attitude is important. It can dramatically affect how much you learn and how well you learn it. Make sure that you have a positive attitude. You will study, you will learn, and you will do well. Your study time will be time well spent.

The Right Conditions

You can have the best attitude in the world, but if you are tired or distracted, you are going to have difficulty studying. To be at your best, you need to be focused, alert, and calm. That means you need to study under the right conditions.

Everyone is different, so you need to know what conditions work best for you. Here are eight questions to consider:

- What time of day do you work best—morning, afternoon, or evening? How early in the day or late in the night can you think clearly?
- Do you work best in total silence? Or do you prefer music or other noise in the background?
- If you prefer music, what kind? Classical music often helps people relax because the music is soft and there are no words. But you may prefer music that energizes you. Others work best with music that has special meaning to them and puts them in a positive state of mind.
- Where do you like to work? Do you feel most comfortable sitting at the kitchen counter? At the dining room table? At a desk in your bedroom? (Try to avoid studying in bed. You will probably be relaxed, but you may be too comfortable and fall asleep.) Or do you prefer to study out of the house, in the library, or a local coffee shop?
- What do you like to have around you when you work? Do you feel most comfortable in your favorite chair? Do you like to have pictures of family and friends around?
- What kind of lighting do you prefer? Does soft light make you sleepy? Do you need bright light? If it's too bright, you may feel uncomfortable. If it is too dark, you may feel sleepy. Remember that poor lighting can also strain your eyes and give you a headache.
- How does eating affect you? Do you feel most energized right after a meal? Or does eating tend to make you drowsy? Which foods give you a lot of energy? Which slow you down?
- Can you put problems or other pressing concerns out of your mind to focus on a different task? How can you minimize distractions so you can fully focus on your work?

Think carefully about each of these questions and be honest with yourself. You may like listening to music, but do you really study better in silence? Do you usually study in your room but are tempted by talking on the phone or using the computer? The more honestly you evaluate your study environment, the more effectively you will use your time, and the less time you will have to spend studying. Write down your answers so you can develop a good study plan.

Study Groups

The majority of your study time should be spent alone in the environment that is best for your study style. However, a good way to get motivated and add some variety to your studying is by forming or joining a study group. Studying with a group will not only be more fun than studying alone, but if you are stuck on a problem, someone in your group may be able to explain it to you. And do not underestimate the value of helping other people in your group. Explaining a difficult concept to someone else is a great way to reinforce what you know or help you decipher what you do not really understand. There are a few things to consider when you form your study group:

- Find an appropriate place with few distractions to study.
- Keep your group small; three or four people are best.
- Include only other students who are as serious about studying for the Border Patrol Exam as you are.
- Set an agenda for your meeting, keep it specific, and decide on one concrete goal for each meeting of your study group.

The Right Tools

Help make your study session successful by having the right learning tools. As you study for the Border Patrol Exam, have:

- a good English and Spanish language dictionary
- a calculator
- paper or legal pads
- pencils (and a pencil sharpener) or pens
- a highlighter, or several, in different colors
- index or other note cards
- folders or notebooks
- a calendar

Keep your personal preferences in mind. Perhaps you like to write with a certain kind of pen or on a certain kind of paper. If so, make sure you have that pen or paper with you when you study. It will help you feel more comfortable and relaxed as you work.

Learning How You Learn

Imagine that you need directions to a restaurant you have never been to before. Which of the following would you do?

- Look on a map.
- Ask someone to tell you how to get there.
- Draw a map or copy someone's written directions.
- List step-by-step directions.

Most people learn in a variety of ways. They learn by seeing, hearing, doing, and organizing information from the world around them. But most of us tend to use one of these ways more than the others. That's our *dominant* (strongest) learning style. How you would handle getting directions, for example, suggests which learning style you use most often:

- **Visual.** Visual learners learn best *by seeing*. If you would look at a map for directions, you are probably a visual learner. You understand ideas best when they are in pictures or graphs. You may learn better by using different colors as you take notes. Use a highlighter (or several, in different colors) as you read, to mark important ideas. Mapping and diagramming ideas are good learning strategies for visual learners.

- **Auditory.** Auditory learners learn best *by listening*. If you would ask someone to tell you directions, you are probably an auditory learner. You would probably rather listen to a lecture than read a textbook, and you may learn better by reading aloud. Try recording your notes on a tape player and listening to your tapes.
- **Kinesthetic.** Kinesthetic learners learn best *by doing*. (Kinesthetic means *feeling the movements of the body*.) They like to keep their hands and bodies moving. If you would draw a map or copy down directions, you are probably a kinesthetic learner. You will benefit from interacting with the material you are studying. Underline, take notes, and create note cards. Recopying material will help you remember it.
- **Sequential.** Sequential learners learn best *by putting things in order*. If you would create a step-by-step list of driving directions, you are probably a sequential learner. You may learn better by creating outlines and grouping ideas together into categories.

Think carefully about how you learn. Which is your dominant learning style?

Learning Styles and Finding the Methods Right for You

The best way to tackle the preparations involved in studying for the Border Patrol Exam is first to think about the way you study now. Do you set aside a specific time to do your homework? Is there a place that you always go to study? Do you take on all your subjects at once or start with the easiest? Once you have given some thought to your current study habits, it is time to honestly evaluate how well they work.

Creating a Study Plan

You will probably spend more time studying for the Border Patrol Exam than you have spent studying for any other test. So even with the best intentions, if you sit down with this book and say, "I'm going to master the Border Patrol Exam," you will most likely get discouraged and give up before you sharpen your No. 2 pencil. But if instead you create a study plan by breaking down your tasks into manageable parts and scheduling time to tackle them, you will almost certainly succeed.

The first step you should take is to make a list of everything you need to study in order to do well on the Border Patrol Exam. Make this list as detailed as possible. Instead of "study Spanish" or "practice logic," for example, appropriate tasks should be "take a practice Spanish Language test" or "go over missed questions on the last logical reasoning practice test." Make your list long. The smaller the tasks, the faster you will cross them off your list. The effort you put forth at the start will more than pay off in the end by eliminating wasted time.

What You Know and What You Need to Know

In order to make your list, you need to determine what you already know and what you need to learn. To create an effective study plan, you need a good sense of exactly what you need to study. Chances are you already know some of the test material well. Some of it you may need only to review, and some of it you may need to study in detail.

Take the Border Patrol Exam practice tests in each chapter of this book to find out how you would do on the exam. How did you score? What do you seem to know well? What do you need to review? What do you need to study in detail?

Scheduling Study Time

Next, you need to set a time frame. Once you have a good sense of how much studying is ahead, create a detailed study schedule. Use a calendar to set specific deadlines. If deadlines make you nervous, give yourself plenty of time for each task. Otherwise, you might have trouble keeping calm and staying on track.

To create a good schedule, break your studying into small tasks that move toward your learning goals. A study plan that says "Learn everything by May 1" isn't going to be helpful. However, a study plan that sets dates for learning specific material in March and April *will* enable you to learn everything by May 1.

As you set your deadlines, consider your day-to-day schedule. How much time can you spend on studying each week? Exactly when can you fit in the time to study? Be sure to be realistic about how much time you have and how much you can accomplish. Give yourself the study time you need to succeed.

Stick to Your Plan

Make sure you have your plan on paper and post your plan where you can see it. Do not just keep it in your head! Look at it regularly so you can remember what and when to study. Checking your plan regularly can also help you see how much progress you have made along the way.

It is important that you do not give up or get discouraged if you fall behind. Unexpected events may interrupt your plans. You may have a big test coming up at school or you may come down with the flu. Or it might just take you longer to complete a task than you planned. That's okay. Stick to your schedule as much as possible, but remember that sometimes life gets in the way. So, if you miss one of your deadlines, do not despair. Instead, just pick up where you left off. Try to squeeze in a little extra time in the next few weeks to catch up. If that does not seem possible, simply adjust your schedule. Change your deadlines so that they are more realistic. Just be sure you still have enough time to finish everything before the exam.

You will need to revisit your list often, allotting more time to areas with which you feel less comfortable and reducing the time needed on areas you have mastered.

How Do You Know What You Know?

One of the keys to successful studying is knowing what you know and knowing what you don't know. Practice tests are one effective way to measure this. But there are other ways.

One of the best ways to measure how well you know something is by assessing how well you can explain it to someone else. If you *really* know the material, you should be able to help someone else understand it. Use your learning style to explain a difficult question to someone in your study group. For example, if you are an auditory learner, talk it out. If you are a visual learner, create diagrams and tables to demonstrate your knowledge. Rewrite your notes or devise your own quizzes with questions and answers like those on the exam. Provide an explanation along with the correct answer.

How do you know what you *do not* know? If you feel uncertain or uncomfortable during a practice test or when you try to explain it to someone else, you probably need to study more. Write down all of your questions and uncertainties. If you write down what you do not know, you can focus on searching for answers. When you get the answers, you can write them next to the question and review them periodically. And notice how many questions you answer along the way—you will see yourself making steady progress.

If you are avoiding certain topics, it is a sign that you don't know those topics well enough for the exam. Make up your mind to tackle these areas at your next study session. Do not procrastinate!

Learning Strategies

How successful you are at studying usually has less to do with how much you know and how much you study than with *how* you study. That is because some study techniques are more effective than others. You can spend hours and hours doing practice tests, but if you do not carefully review your answers, much of your time will be wasted. You need to learn from your mistakes and study what you do not know. The best method is to use several of the following proven study techniques. You may already be using many of these study skills, but they can help you make the most of your learning style and store information in your long-term memory.

Asking Questions

Asking questions is a powerful study strategy because it forces you to get actively involved in the material you want to learn. That, in turn, helps you better understand and remember the material. And there is another important benefit—the process of asking and answering your own questions helps you become comfortable with the exam format.

Highlighting and Underlining

Whenever you read or study, have a pen, pencil, or highlighter in your hand. That way, as you read books, notes, or handouts that belong to you (not the school or library), you can mark the words and ideas that are most important to learn or remember. Highlighting or underlining helps make key ideas stand out. Important information is then easy to find when you need to take notes or review.

The key to effective highlighting or underlining is *to be selective*. Do not highlight or underline indiscriminately. If you highlight every other sentence, nothing will stand out for you on the page. Highlight only the key words and ideas or concepts you do not understand.

Taking Notes

Taking notes helps you understand, organize, and remember information. The secret to taking useful notes is knowing what you should write down. As with highlighting, the key is to be selective. Take notes about the same things you would underline, especially main ideas, rules, and other items you need to learn. Whenever possible, include examples so that you can see the concept clearly.

Making Notes

Making notes is often as important as *taking* notes. Making notes means that you *respond* to what you study. There are several ways you can respond (talk back) to the text:

- **Write questions.** If you see something you don't understand, write a question. *What does this mean? Why is this word used this way?* Then, answer all of your questions.
- **Make connections.** Any time you make connections between ideas, you improve your chances of remembering that material. For example, if you are trying to learn the definition of the word *demographic*, you may know that *democracy* refers to government by the *people*, while *graphic* refers to *information*, written or drawn. From that you can remember that *demographic* has to do with *information* about *people*.
- **Write your reactions.** Your reactions work much like connections, and they can help you remember information.

Outlining and Mapping Information

Outlines are great tools, especially for sequential learners. They help you focus on what is most important by making it easier to review key ideas and see relationships among those ideas. With an outline, you can see how supporting information is related to main ideas.

The basic outline structure is this:

I. Topic
  1. Main idea
    a. Major supporting idea
      i. Minor supporting idea

BORDER PATROL STUDY SKILLS AND TEST-TAKING STRATEGIES

Mapping information is similar to making an outline. The difference is that maps are less structured. You do not have to organize ideas from top to bottom. Instead, with a map, the ideas can go all over the page. The key is that you still show how the ideas are related.

Making Flash Cards

Flash cards are a simple but effective study tool. First, buy or cut out small pieces of paper (3 × 5 index cards work well). On one side, put a question or word you need to learn. On the back, put the answer. You can use different colors and pictures, especially if you are a visual learner.

Memorizing versus Remembering

It is true that repetition is the key to mastery. Try repeating a new phone number over and over, for example. Eventually you will remember it. But it may stay only in your *short-term* memory. In a few days (or maybe even a few hours), you are likely to forget the number. You need to use it to really learn it and store the information in your *long-term* memory.

Although there are some tricks you can use to help remember things in the short term, your best bet is to use what you are learning as much and as soon as possible. This is especially important when you are studying for the Border Patrol Exam, because much of the test focuses on your reasoning skills and not simple memorization. This means you really have to understand the material, because you will not be given the opportunity simply to recall information. This does not mean that you do not need to know basic information in all of the areas covered.

Here are some general strategies to help you remember information as you prepare for the Border Patrol Exam:

- **Learn information in small chunks.** Our brains process small chunks of information better than large ones. If you have a list of 20 grammar rules, break that list into four lists of five rules each.

- **Spread out your memory work.** Do not try to remember too much at one time. For example, if you break up those 20 rules into four lists, do not try to do all four lists, one after another. Instead, try studying one list each day in several short, spaced-out sessions. For example, spend 20 minutes in the morning getting familiar with the new rules. Review the rules again for 15 minutes at lunchtime. Take another 15 minutes while you are on the bus going home. Add another ten-minute review before bed. This kind of **distributed practice** is very effective. It is also a sneaky way to add more study time to your schedule. And it provides lots of repetition without tiring your brain.

- **Make connections.** You learn best when you make connections to things you already know.

- **Use visual aids,** especially if you are a visual learner. Help yourself see in your mind what you need to learn.

- **Use your voice,** especially if you are an auditory learner. Say aloud what you need to learn; you can even sing it if you like, especially if you can make a rhyme. Any time you are learning grammar and structure, say a sample sentence aloud several times. Try different variations, too.

Border Patrol Exam-Specific Strategies

The amount of material covered in the Border Patrol Exam may seem overwhelming at first. But keep in mind that there should be little new information for you to learn. The most important thing to do is identify your areas of weakness. Once you do that, you will realize that the few grammar rules and math problems you need to learn are entirely manageable.

Learn from Your Mistakes

Spend time reviewing your practice questions to determine exactly why you got an answer wrong. Did you misread the question? Are you unfamiliar with comma usage? Only when you pinpoint exactly why you answered something incorrectly can you learn to get it right.

Learn about the Test

One sure way to increase your chances of success is to find out as much as you can about the exam. If you do not know what to expect on the test, you will not know how to study. It is likely that you will be extra anxious about the exam, too. The more you know about the test, the better you can prepare—and the more relaxed you will be when the test comes.

Getting sample tests and working with skill builders like this book can help you in many ways. You will get used to the kind of questions asked and the level of difficulty of those questions. You will also become familiar with the format and comfortable with the length of the exam.

When you take your practice tests, try to re-create the actual testing conditions as closely as possible. Sit in a chair at a desk or table somewhere free from distractions. Time the test and use only the amount of time you would have on the real test. After you score your test, review your answers carefully. Ask yourself why you got the questions wrong that you did and add those concepts to your study schedule.

Timing

The more practice tests you take, the more comfortable you will feel regarding how long you have to answer each question. You should be able to spend less time answering the easier questions, and then come back to the harder ones with the time remaining.

Multiple-Choice Test Strategies

Multiple choice is the most popular question format for standardized tests like the Border Patrol Exam. Understandably so: multiple-choice questions are easy and fast to grade. They are also popular because they are generally considered *objective*. They are questions based solely on information and do not allow the test taker to express opinions.

Multiple-choice questions have two parts:

1. **Stem:** the question
2. **Options:** the answer choices

The incorrect answers are called **distracters**.

Here are six strategies to help you answer multiple-choice questions correctly:

1. Circle or underline key words in the stem.
2. Immediately cross out all answers you know are incorrect. This will help you find the correct answer. It is an especially important step if you have to guess the answer.
3. Beware of distracter techniques. Test developers will often put in look-alike choices, easily confused options, and silly options.
4. Read stems carefully: Be sure you understand exactly what is being asked. Watch for tricky wording such as "All of the following are true EXCEPT." You will find distracters that seem accurate and may sound right but do not apply to that stem.
5. Beware of absolutes. Read carefully any stem that includes words like *always, never, none,* or *all*. An answer may sound perfectly correct and the general principle may be correct. However, it may not be true in all circumstances.

Almost There: Strategies for the Final Days before the Exam

Your months of preparation will soon pay off. You have worked hard, and the test is just a week or two away. Here are some tips for making sure things go smoothly in the home stretch.

The Week before the Test:
- Be sure you know exactly where you are taking the test. Get detailed directions. Take a practice drive or mass transit trip so you know exactly how long it will take to get there.
- Review everything you have learned.
- Get quality sleep each night.
- Practice visualization—see yourself performing well on the Border Patrol Exam.

The Day before the Test:
- Get light exercise. Do not work out too hard. You do not want to be sore or physically exhausted the day of the exam.
- Get everything you will need ready: pencils/pens, a calculator, admission materials/documentation, and water or any mints or snacks you would like to have along.
- Make a list of everything you need to bring so you don't forget anything in the morning.
- Get to bed early.
- Make sure you set your alarm. Ask a family member to make sure you are up on time.

The Day of the Test:
- Get up early.
- Eat a light, healthy breakfast, such as yogurt and granola or a low-fat, low-sugar cereal and fruit.
- Dress comfortably. Wear layers so that you can take off a sweatshirt or sweater if you are too warm in the test room.
- Do not drastically alter your diet. For example, if you drink coffee every morning, do not skip it—you could get a headache. However, do not drink a second cup or super-sized portion. Too much caffeine can make you jittery during the exam, and you may crash when the caffeine wears off.

At the Test Site:
- Chat with others, but *not* about the test. That might only make you more nervous.
- Think positively. Remember, you are prepared.
- Avoid squeezing in a last-minute review. Instead, visualize your success and plan your reward for after the test is over.

After the Test:
- Celebrate!

Handling and Preventing Test Stress

Handling Test Stress

Test anxiety is like the common cold. Most people suffer from it periodically. It won't kill you, but it can make your life miserable for several days.

Like a cold, test anxiety can be mild or severe. You may just feel an underlying nervousness about the upcoming exam. Or you may be nearly paralyzed with worry, especially if there is a lot riding on the exam. Whatever the case, if you have test anxiety, you need to cope with it. Fortunately, many strategies help prevent and treat test anxiety.

Prevention

The best cure for test anxiety is to *prevent* it from happening in the first place. Test anxiety is often caused by a lack of preparation. If you learn all you can about the test and create and follow a study plan, you should be in good shape when it comes to exam time. Here are some other, more general strategies:

- **Establish and stick to a routine.** Routines help us feel more comfortable and in control. Whenever possible, study at the same time and in the same place. Make your test preparation a habit that is hard to break. Studying for the Border Patrol Exam will become easier as it becomes routine. You will be more likely to avoid distractions, and others will know not to disturb you during your Border Patrol Exam study time.
- **Keep your general stress level low.** If there are a lot of other stresses in your life, chances are a big test will make those other stresses seem more difficult to manage. Remember to keep things in perspective. If something is beyond your control, don't waste your energy worrying about it. Instead, think of how you can handle what is in your control.
- **Stay confident.** Remind yourself that you are smart and capable. You can take this test—and you can do well on it.
- **Stay healthy.** When your body is run down or ill, your brainpower will suffer, too. You are much more likely to be overtaken by worries. Take care of yourself throughout the test-preparation process.

Treatment

If it is too late to prevent test anxiety, don't panic. You can still treat it effectively. Here are some strategies to help reduce test stress:

- **Face your fears.** Admit that you are worried about the test, and examine the reasons. Your fears won't change the fact that you have to take the test, but they can paralyze you and keep you from studying and doing well on the exam. Acknowledge your fears, put them in perspective, and refuse to let your fears hurt you.

  One helpful strategy is to write down your fears. When you put your worries on paper, they seem more manageable than when they are bouncing around in your brain and keeping you awake at night. Once you write down your fears, you can then brainstorm solutions. For example, imagine you are worried about not being able to find enough time to get your work done and finish studying. Once you put this fear down on paper, you can begin to determine how to squeeze in the hours you need to get everything done, and you will feel more in control.
- **Keep things in perspective.** Yes, the Border Patrol Exam is a big deal; it is an important test. But even if you do poorly on the test, is it the end of the world? Will your family stop loving you? Will you be less of a person? Of course not. And if you really blow it, remember that you can take the test again. Perspective is important to performance. Of course you should be serious about succeeding. But don't lose sight of other important aspects of your life.
- **Be sufficiently prepared.** Anxiety often comes from feeling insecure in a new situation. But if you prepare well, using this and other books, the Border Patrol Exam will not be new to you. And if you follow your study plan, you will know how to answer the questions. If you have fallen behind, remember that it is not too late to catch up.
- **Stop making excuses.** Excuses may give you some comfort in the short term, but they do not take away test anxiety—and they will not help you do well on the exam. In fact, excuses often make things worse by making you feel guilty and powerless. Do not let yourself feel like a victim. You may have a lot of things happening in your life and many things may interfere with your studies, but you have the power to choose how you deal with your circumstances.
- **Imagine yourself succeeding.** Highly successful people will often tell you that one of their secrets is visualization. In their mind's eye, they *see* themselves succeeding. They imagine the situations they will face, and then imagine themselves handling those situations beautifully.

Visualization is a powerful tool. It is a way of telling yourself that *you believe you can do it.* The power of this kind of belief is amazing. If you believe you can accomplish something, you are far more likely to accomplish it. Likewise, if you believe you *can't* do something, you are far more likely to *fail*. Positive visualization will make it easier for you to study and manage your entire test-preparation process.

Anyone can use the power of visualization. Picture yourself sitting calmly through the exam, answering one question after another correctly. See yourself getting excellent test results in the mail. Imagine yourself telling family and friends how well you did on the exam.

- **Stick to your study plan.** Test anxiety can paralyze you if you let it. And before you know it, you have missed several deadlines on your study plan. Guess what? That only makes your test anxiety worse. As soon as you feel your stomach start to flutter with test anxiety, return to your study plan. Make an extra effort to stick to your schedule.

A Healthy Mind and a Healthy Body

It is difficult to do your best on a test when you are not feeling well. Your mind *and* body need to be in good shape for the test. If you let your body get run-down, you may become ill. That, in turn, sets you back on your study schedule. And that may lead to test anxiety, which can make you feel run-down again. You need to avoid this downward spiral. If you do feel run-down, take a day or two to rest and feel better. Maybe you will be two days behind your study schedule, but when you continue, your studying will be more effective. As long as it is not a constant problem for you and as long as you are not using illness to avoid studying, you will do yourself a favor by resting.

Take good care of yourself throughout the entire test-preparation process and especially in the week before the exam. Here are some specific suggestions for staying healthy:

- Get enough rest. Some of us need eight or more hours of sleep each night. Others are happy with just six. You know what your body needs for you to feel clear-headed and energized. Make sleep a priority, so that you are able to concentrate the day of the exam. If you have trouble sleeping, try one of the following strategies:
  - Get exercise during the day. A tired body will demand more sleep.
  - Get up and study. If you study in the night when you can't sleep, you can cut out study time from the next day so you can take a nap or get to bed earlier. (Of course, sometimes studying will help you fall asleep in the first place.)
  - Relax with a hot bath, a good book, or sleep-inducing foods. A glass of warm milk, for example, may help you fall back asleep.
  - Do some gentle stretching or seated forward bends. Try to touch your toes with your legs outstretched. This is a relaxing posture. Or practice a few relaxation poses from yoga: child's pose or cat stretch (see a website like www.yoga.com for details).
  - Spend a few minutes doing deep breathing. Fill your lungs slowly and completely. Hold for a few seconds and then release slowly and completely. You can practice deep breathing any time you need to relax or regain focus.
  - Write down your worries. Again, putting your fears on paper can help make them more manageable.
- **Eat well.** Keeping a healthy diet is often as hard as getting enough rest when you are busy preparing for a test. But how you eat can have a tremendous impact on how you study and how you perform on the exam. You may think you are saving time by eating fast food. But in reality, you are

depriving your body of the nutrition it needs to perform at its best. You may think that a couple of extra cups of coffee a day are a good thing because you can stay up later and study. But in reality, you are tricking your brain into thinking that it's awake and you are making yourself more dependent on caffeine.

Foods to avoid—especially at test time—include high-sugar, high-calorie, low-nutrition foods, such as doughnuts, chips, and cookies. Instead, find healthy substitutes.

CHAPTER

PRACTICE TEST 1

Like the official Border Patrol Exam, the practice test that follows tests your logical reasoning and Spanish-language abilities. For this exam, you should simulate the actual test-taking experience as closely as you can. Find a quiet place to work where you won't be disturbed. Tear out the answer sheet on the next page if you own this book, or photocopy it if not, and find some no. two pencils to fill in the circles. You should give yourself four and a half hours to complete the test. Set a timer or stopwatch for practice, but do not worry too much if you go over the allotted time on this practice exam. After the exam, use the answer explanations to see how you did, and to find out why the right answers are right and the wrong ones are wrong.

LEARNINGEXPRESS ANSWER SHEET

Logical Reasoning Test

1. In contrast to economic migrants, who generally do not receive legal admission to a country, refugees can receive legal status in two ways: by being designated a refugee while abroad, or by entering the United States and requesting and receiving asylum. In the years 2005 through 2007, the number of asylum seekers accepted into the United States for resettlement was about 40,000 per year. Approximately 30,000 were accepted per year in the U.K. and 25,000 were accepted per year in Canada. Japan accepted 41 refugees in 2007.

   From the information given here, it CANNOT be validly concluded that:
   a. there are two ways in which refugees can receive legal admission to a country.
   b. more refugees received asylum from the U.K. than from Canada in 2007.
   c. more refugees receive asylum each year from Canada than from Japan.
   d. economic migrants seldom receive legal status.
   e. none of the above

2. Approximately 560,000 immigrants were living in a small country in 2011. Most of these immigrants were not employed in professional occupations, but some of them were. For example, some of these immigrants were accountants and some of them were social workers. Pharmacists, another professional occupation, made up a smaller number of these immigrants.

   From the information given here, it can be validly concluded that:
   a. most immigrants were either accountants or social workers.
   b. none of the accountants were immigrants.
   c. it is not the case that some of the social workers were immigrants.
   d. most of those not employed in professional occupations were immigrants.
   e. some of the accountants were immigrants.

3. With the Secure Fence Act, the United States sought to construct fencing around 1,945 miles of border to deter individuals from entering the country illegally. However, the Act has met with opposition as environmental groups have expressed concern that the fence would negatively affect wildlife species, keeping them from available food and water. Landowners fear that they will have to surrender land to the government for the fence to be built. Other groups are concerned that plants would be uprooted to make room for the fence, and that bright lights, cameras, and motion sensors will adversely affect the quality of life in the area.

From the information given here, it CANNOT be validly concluded that:

a. animals may find it difficult to obtain food and water if the fence is built.
b. the government believes that constructing a fence may help deter those who would enter the country illegally.
c. landowners may need to give over land to the government for the construction of the fence to be possible.
d. the fence will not be constructed due to opposition from various groups.
e. lights and motion sensors may pose a negative effect on the quality of life of those who live near the proposed fence.

4. The popularity of handheld cellular phones has resulted in the growth of texting, or sending written text messages via cellular phone, as a form of communication. As texting becomes more prevalent, conflict may arise between the users' expectations of privacy and public access rights. In some investigations, access to all texts, including messages that fall outside the scope of the investigation, has been sought and granted. In spite of this, some people send messages through text that would never be said face-to-face or written formally.

From the information given here, it CANNOT be validly concluded that:

a. some messages that people would never say face-to-face are sent via text.
b. some text messages that have been requested as part of investigations have contained messages that would never have been said face-to-face.
c. some text messages have been requested as part of an investigation.
d. some text messages have not been exempted from investigations.
e. some text messages contain information that would not have been written formally.

5. The agent in charge needs his team to cover the north, south, west, and east entrances of a building. If Guard W can cover the south and north sides, Guard X can cover the north and west sides, Guard Y can cover the west and east sides, and Guard Z can cover the east side, which of the following arrangements can be accomplished?

From the information given here, it can be validly concluded that the guards can be positioned as follows:

a. Guard X: west, Guard W: south, Guard Y: north, Guard Z: east
b. Guard X: west, Guard W: north, Guard Y: south, Guard Z: east
c. Guard X: north, Guard W: south, Guard Y: west, Guard Z: east
d. Guard X: north, Guard W: south, Guard Y: east, Guard Z: west
e. none of the above

6. Recently the age limit to apply for entry into the Border Patrol was raised from 37 to 40. The primary reason for the change was to allow veterans of the U.S. Armed Forces to apply for the job after they have completed a 20-year career in the military. For example, an individual who joined the Armed Forces when she was 18 years old and served the full 20 years was too old to apply for a job as a Border Patrol Agent after retiring from the military when the Border Patrol age requirement was 37. With the age requirement changed to age 40, the Border Patrol can now benefit from the 20 years of military training and experience many veterans possess.

From the information given here, it can be validly concluded that:

a. the age limit for application into the Border Patrol was recently changed to 37.
b. all veterans possess 20 years of military training and experience.
c. some veterans possess 20 years of military training and experience.
d. no veterans possess 20 years of military training and experience.
e. many veterans of the U.S. Armed Forces retire at age 37.

7. Insurance companies often recommend alarm systems to improve the safety of a business. However, statistics in a particular state show that the break-in rate for businesses equipped with alarm systems is slightly higher than the break-in rate for businesses without these alarms. Some systems are easily set off by street noise or other stimuli, generating false alarms. Others do not come equipped with signs alerting passersby to the presence of an alarm.
From the information given here, it can be validly concluded that:
   a. alarm systems in this state are often installed in businesses in areas that are prone to break-ins.
   b. because these systems generate many false alarms, authorities are slow to respond to such alarms.
   c. without signs announcing the presence of an alarm, the system does little to deter theft.
   d. alarm systems offer little protection against break-ins.
   e. many business owners feel safer after purchasing an alarm system.

8. A border is a line that serves as the boundary between one political or geographical area and another. The Border Patrol uses specific equipment, such as electronic sensors placed at strategic locations, to help detect people or vehicles attempting to cross that line to enter a country illegally. Video monitors and night-vision scopes are also used to help identify and prevent illegal entry. Agents patrol the border on foot or in cars, trucks, boats, or helicopters. They may also patrol using ATVs or bicycles, or other forms of transportation.
From the information given here, it can be validly concluded that:
   a. agents never patrol on horseback.
   b. agents seldom patrol on snowmobiles.
   c. the Border Patrol detects more vehicles than people on foot using electronic sensors.
   d. the Border Patrol relies more on electronic sensors than on video monitors to detect potential illegal entry.
   e. the Border Patrol utilizes specialized equipment for effective detection of those attempting to enter the country illegally.

9. The computers in a certain field office must be updated at least once every five years, but not more than once every three years, to ensure effective communication. The replacement process is expensive, so resources need to be allocated according to greatest need. Up to ten computers can be updated each year, with the oldest ones being given priority, to avoid increasing the budget. There are fifty computers in the field office; four of them are five years old, twelve of them are four years old, and the rest are one year old.
From the information given here, it can be validly concluded that:
  a. if ten computers are updated this year, then in two years ten more updates will be needed.
  b. if four computers are updated this year, then next year's budget will need to be increased.
  c. if five computers are updated this year, then next year's budget will stay the same.
  d. if ten computers are updated this year, then only five will need to be updated next year.
  e. none of the above

10. Agent Jefferson needs to inspect the following sectors in a particular week: San Diego, El Centro, Yuma, and Tucson. El Centro must be inspected before San Diego. Yuma must be visited before San Diego but after Tucson. El Centro must not be inspected first.
From the information given here, it CANNOT be validly concluded that:
  a. if Yuma is visited on Wednesday, then San Diego may be visited on Thursday.
  b. if Tucson is visited on Monday, then El Centro may be visited on Wednesday.
  c. if San Diego is visited on Thursday, then Yuma may be visited on Wednesday.
  d. if El Centro is visited on Wednesday, then Tucson may be visited on Monday or Tuesday.
  e. none of the above

11. The U.S. Border Patrol operates more than 10,000 SUVs and pickup trucks, which are known for their effective maneuvering in different types of terrain. These vehicles have individual revolving lights (strobes or LEDs); they may also have light bars and sirens. In a recent year, most of these vehicles were equipped with both revolving lights and sirens. Many that had revolving lights and sirens had strobes, but some had LEDs. Vehicles with light bars and sirens did not have revolving lights.
From the information given here, it can be validly concluded that:
  a. if an SUV had a light bar, it also had a strobe.
  b. if an SUV had an LED, it also had a light bar.
  c. if a pickup truck had a revolving light, it also had a light bar.
  d. if a pickup truck had a light bar and a siren, it did not have a strobe.
  e. none of the above

12. United States Border Patrol Checkpoints are inspection stations located within 100 miles of the Mexican or Canadian national border, or in the Florida Keys. Most checkpoints are located near the Mexican Border, but some are located near the Canadian border. A smaller number are located in the Florida Keys.

From the information given here, it can be validly concluded that:

a. if an inspection station is a Border Patrol Checkpoint, it must be in the Florida Keys or within 100 miles of a national border.
b. if a Border Patrol Checkpoint is in the Florida Keys, it must be within 100 miles of Canada.
c. if an inspection station is a Border Patrol Checkpoint, it must be located near Canada.
d. if an inspection station is a Border Patrol Checkpoint, it must be located near Mexico.
e. if an inspection station is a Border Patrol Checkpoint, it must be located in the Florida Keys.

13. Officer Marks is in line for a promotion. He is eligible to move up from a GS-11 level to a supervisory position at GS-12 if he passes the Border Patrol Career Experience Inventory (CEI), a Managerial Writing Skills Exercise, and a Critical Thinking Skills Exercise. He may also complete an In-Basket Simulation, in which he will review information from voicemail, e-mail messages, and reports that deal with the personnel, operational, budgetary, and administrative issues supervisors and managers handle every day, and then answer questions that show how he would delegate, prioritize, make decisions, and solve the problems presented in the documents.

From the information given here, it CANNOT be validly concluded that:

a. if Officer Marks passes the Critical Thinking Skills Exercise, Border Patrol Career Experience Inventory (CEI), and Managerial Writing Skills Exercise, he will be eligible to move up to a level GS-12.
b. if Officer Marks passes the Critical Thinking Skills Exercise, Border Patrol Career Experience Inventory (CEI), and Managerial Writing Skills Exercise, he will proceed to the In-Basket Simulation.
c. if Officer Marks takes the In-Basket Simulation, he will need to answer questions about decision-making and delegating.
d. if Officer Marks takes the In-Basket Simulation, he will need to take the Critical Thinking Skills Exercise, Border Patrol Career Experience Inventory (CEI), and Managerial Writing Skills Exercises.
e. none of the above

14. Crime scene evidence is divided into two basic classes: physical and biological. *Physical evidence* covers items of nonliving origin, such as fibers, tire marks, fingerprints, footprints, paint, and building materials. *Biological evidence* comes from a living source—generally the victim or perpetrator. It includes DNA extracted from blood or other bodily fluids, such as semen, hair, and saliva. Botanical items, such as pollen and plants, are also considered biological evidence. Fingerprints are often the most valued type of physical evidence because of their ability to identify or eliminate a suspect. However, as DNA analysis technology becomes increasingly automated and rapid, it is likely that forensic investigators will place more emphasis on the collection of biological evidence.

From the information given here, it CANNOT be validly concluded that:

- **a.** if the piece of evidence is paint flakes, then it is considered physical evidence.
- **b.** if the piece of evidence is a flower, then it is considered physical evidence.
- **c.** if the piece of evidence is blood, then it is considered biological evidence.
- **d.** if the piece of evidence is fabric, then it is considered physical evidence.
- **e.** if the piece of evidence is rubber from a tire, then it is considered physical evidence.

15. An individual facing deportation may apply for cancellation of removal to obtain permanent resident status if she meets the following criteria: has maintained continuous physical presence in the United States for at least ten years; has exemplified good moral character during those ten years and has not been convicted of certain crimes; and can prove that removal would result in exceptional hardship to a spouse, parent, or child who is a U.S. citizen or permanent resident. Cancellation of removal may also be granted if she has been battered or subjected to extreme cruelty by a U.S. citizen or permanent resident spouse or parent, or if she is the parent of a child of a U.S. citizen or lawful permanent resident and the child has been battered or subjected to extreme cruelty by a citizen or permanent resident parent.

From the information given here, it can be validly concluded that:

- **a.** if an individual qualifies for cancellation of removal, then she has not been convicted of certain crimes.
- **b.** if an individual has been subjected to extreme cruelty by her spouse, then she is the parent of a U.S. citizen.
- **c.** if an individual has exemplified good moral character, then she can prove that her removal would result in exceptional hardship to her U.S. citizen spouse.
- **d.** if an individual does not qualify for cancellation of removal, then she has not been battered by a U.S. citizen spouse.
- **e.** none of the above

16. In a certain operation, Border Patrol Agents were instructed not to react to illegal entries at the border, but instead to deploy forward to the boundary, detecting attempted entries or deterring crossing at more remote locations. It was believed that using these procedures would make it easier to capture illegal entrants, as they would be concentrated in open areas such as wide expanses of desert instead of escaping into tiny urban alleyways.

From the information given here, it can be validly concluded that:
  a. if an agent is detecting an attempted entry at the border, he is in the open desert.
  b. if an agent is detecting an attempted entry at the boundary, he is in an alleyway.
  c. if an illegal entry is attempted at the border, then agents are instructed to react.
  d. if an agent is deployed to the boundary, then he must react to illegal entries at the border.
  e. none of the above

Spanish Language Proficiency Test

Part I
Read the sentence and then choose the most appropriate synonym for the italicized word or phrase.

1. A muchos turistas les da miedo *perder* el pasaporte cuando viajan al extranjero.
   a. tener
   b. copiar
   c. descuidar
   d. encuentran
   e. robamos

2. *Según* las estadísticas, el 50% de los matrimonios en los Estados Unidos terminan en divorcio.
   a. Al lado de
   b. Alrededor de
   c. Volver
   d. De acuerdo con
   e. Debajo de

3. El agente tuvo que *aclarar* las instrucciones porque el ciudadano no las entendió.
   a. explicar
   b. confundir
   c. mentir
   d. pesar
   e. complicar

4. *Condujimos* seis horas para llegar al hotel antes del anochecer.
   a. Rogamos
   b. Intentamos
   c. Cantamos
   d. Caminamos
   e. Manejamos

5. Estudiamos *aproximadamente* cuatro horas para el examen final.
   a. para
   b. exactamente
   c. tantos
   d. antes de
   e. alrededor de

6. La mamá estaba muy *preocupada* porque su hijo no había llegado de la escuela.
   a. contento
   b. paciente
   c. inquieta
   d. interesado
   e. ocurrir

PRACTICE TEST 1

7. A los alumnos les cae bien su profesora porque es muy *simpática* con ellos.
   a. exigentes
   b. amable
   c. romántico
   d. repugnante
   e. puros

8. El policía *investigó* la evidencia y determinó que le faltaba información clave.
   a. eliminó
   b. enseñó
   c. fue
   d. inspeccionaste
   e. inspeccionó

9. *A pesar de que* tienen mucha evidencia, no logran indicar un sospechoso del crimen.
   a. Aunque
   b. Según
   c. En vez de
   d. Realmente
   e. Desafortunadamente

10. ¿Dónde *encontraste* a mi perro?
   a. compraste
   b. hallar
   c. pintaste
   d. hallaste
   e. perdiste

11. Los precios del seguro del automóvil varían según la región donde *vive* la persona y el tipo de vehículo.
   a. casa
   b. pasa las vacaciones
   c. viaja
   d. habita
   e. hogar

12. Los *incendios* forestales son provocados por la naturaleza y el hombre.
   a. fuegos
   b. encender
   c. fósforos
   d. encendedor
   e. ira

13. Cuando un desastre natural nos *golpea*, siempre habrá pérdidas tanto humanas como económicas.
   a. aprende
   b. sucede
   c. evitan
   d. requiere
   e. administrar

14. Para evitar cualquier accidente automovilístico, es indispensable respetar todas las *normas* de tránsito.
   a. opiniones
   b. creencia
   c. obedecer
   d. reglas
   e. pensar

15. Sólo las personas con una licencia de conducción podrán tener el privilegio de conducir *en el* territorio de los Estados Unidos.
   a. cerca del
   b. lejos del
   c. encima del
   d. al lado del
   e. dentro del

16. Toda persona que quiera pertenecer al ejército deberá *cumplir con* ciertos requisitos.
   a. saber de
   b. conocimiento
   c. satisfacer
   d. logrará
   e. logros

PRACTICE TEST 1

17. Es bueno considerar *los sentimientos* del artista cuando uno ve su obra de arte.
   a. las pasiones
   b. la familia
   c. llorar
   d. llorando
   e. los hechos

18. La educación es necesaria para *la evolución* de cada profesional.
   a. el dinero
   b. el fracaso
   c. el desarrollo
   d. los jefes
   e. aprender

19. Los niños aprendieron a utilizar las vías de evacuación que salen *a través del* campo verde detrás de la escuela.
   a. encima del
   b. debajo del
   c. lejos del
   d. por el
   e. enfrente del

20. Es importante poder reconocer las *señales* de una persona que está nerviosa.
   a. ropa
   b. papeles
   c. indicaciones
   d. documentación
   e. reglas

Part II, Section I
Read each sentence carefully. Select the appropriate word or phrase to fill each blank space.

21. Ella _____ leyendo el periódico cuando el vecino _____ la puerta.
   a. era, empujaba
   b. está, tocaba
   c. estaba, tocó
   d. estuviste, supo
   e. estaban, toco

22. La policía _____ las oficinas _____ del abogado por sospecha de un crimen.
   a. prometen, vieja
   b. invadió, nuevas
   c. pinta, blancas
   d. preguntó, viejos
   e. invadieron, nuevos

23. Aunque mi amiga no me _____ sus notas para estudiar, no _____ trampa para sacar buena nota en el examen de ayer.
   a. prestó, hice
   b. dará, hacía
   c. quiera, hará
   d. prestará, haré
   e. estaban prestando, hubo

24. El agente es _____ y cree que el ciudadano tiene _____ falsos.
   a. nueva, papeles
   b. joven, un pasaporte
   c. astuto, documentos
   d. experimentado, una licencia de conducir
   e. astuta, un pasaporte

PRACTICE TEST 1

25. La mamá no _____ qué hacer con su joyería preciosa, entonces _____ a su hija.
    a. pregunta, la dieron
    b. había, nos la presta
    c. tuvo, le la dio
    d. compraba, me lo dará
    e. sabía, se la regaló

26. El jefe le _____ a su empleado _____ usar el nuevo sistema.
    a. enseñó, cómo
    b. aprendimos, qué
    c. haber, como
    d. había, bien
    e. era, enseñamos

27. El gobierno de los Estados Unidos normalmente _____ una visa a los turistas internacionales para entrar _____ país.
    a. me gustaría, sobre
    b. pidió, ella
    c. exige, al
    d. volando, aeropuerto
    e. saque, tu

28. Le pregunté a mi jefe si había _____ una decisión en cuanto a _____ vacaciones.
    a. hubo, tonto
    b. cuento, sobre
    c. hacer, después de
    d. tomaba, los
    e. tomado, mis

29. La reunión de negocios tuvo lugar ayer en un hotel muy _____ situado _____ la playa y las montañas.
    a. al lado de, hermoso
    b. lujoso, entre
    c. electrónica, deber
    d. algunos, debajo de
    e. bonita, alrededor de

30. El _____ fue acusado de sobornar al juez _____ juicio.
    a. vecina, alto
    b. agentes, acabar
    c. niños, encima de
    d. especialista, qué
    e. abogado, antes del

Part II, Section II
Read each sentence carefully. Select the one sentence that is correct.

31. a. José quiere ir a tomarse un café pero no tiene dinero.
    b. Fabián y su mamá tenemos muchos ahorros pero no sabe en qué gastarlos.
    c. Conoco a mucha gente famosa porque mi padre era famosa.
    d. Quiero mucho mis papás.
    e. Tengo muchas amigas pero ninguno quiere salir con mi.

32. a. La muchacha llevaste el niño lastimado al hospital.
    b. Ellos son muy fastidiados porque no fueron invitados a la fiesta.
    c. El pobre hombre quedó ciego después del accidente.
    d. María no está satisfecho porque no paso el examen ayer.
    e. La ambulancia pasé por mi casa todos los días y siempre me despierta.

33. a. Me gustaría que me ayudas con algo.
    b. Me gusto tu ayuda, por favor.
    c. Necesito que me ayudes con algo.
    d. Me gustaría tú ayudar conmigo.
    e. Me guste la ayuda.

34.
a. ¿Fuimos Uds. a ver el partido de fútbol?
b. Mañana vamos a ver el película famoso con un actor colombiano.
c. Me encantan el nuevo programa de televisión.
d. El equipo suramericano ganó el partido y se llevó el trofeo a casa.
e. ¿Cómo te gustaron la película?

35.
a. Llámame con tu nuevo número telefónico cuando llegues a tu casa.
b. ¿En qué aerolínea vamos tu familia?
c. Le lo di el paquete a tu mamá.
d. Su papá no tiene uno sistema avanzada.
e. Tengo hambriente y quiero a agua.

36.
a. El presidente preguntaste a su gabinete cuando deben tomar acción.
b. El presidente no sabían qué decir entonces el gabinete.
c. El presidente no supo responder ante la situación entonces pidió ayuda al gabinete.
d. El gabinete respondemos ante la situación para el presidente.
e. El presidente no me respondía al gabinete cuando deben responder.

37.
a. ¿Cómo encontraste a mi amigo tan rápidamente en un parque tan grande?
b. ¿De quién encontró mi amigo en el parque rápido?
c. ¿Quién está el amiga grande en el parque que camina rápido?
d. ¿Ud. eres tan grande en esta parque por qué?
e. ¿Dónde es las amigas rápido del parque?

38.
a. El instructor fueron sargento antes del accidente terrible que sucedió el año pasado.
b. Después del accidente, el sargento se convirtió en instructor y enseñó a varios reclutas.
c. Las reclutas aprendió tanto cosas del sargento.
d. El accidente causó que el instructor enseña a los reclutas.
e. El sargento y varios reclutas tuvo una accidente.

39.
a. No podemos dejar ellos entran según los oficiales.
b. Los superiores no queremos nadie más entrar.
c. Los superiores no quieren dejar entrar a nadie más.
d. No queremos nadie entrar menos los oficiales.
e. Dejamos entrar que los superiores solamente.

40.
a. Los alumnos no podieron terminar el proyecto debido a un emergencia.
b. Trataron de explicarle a la profesora pero ella no los quiso escuchar.
c. Los alumnos la amenacé y prometieron hablar con las padres.
d. Las padres te acordaron de hacer algo al respecto.
e. En fin, la profesora ceder y se la dar una extensión.

Part II, Section III

Read each sentence carefully. Select the correct word or phrase to replace the italicized portion of the sentence. In those cases in which the sentence needs no correction, select choice e.

41. *La cuenta* de mi abuela fue increíble. Ella sufrió mucho durante la guerra.
    a. Las camas
    b. Explicar
    c. La mesa
    d. El cuento
    e. No es necesario hacer ninguna corrección.

42. Ellos *pintó* por toda Latinoamérica en once meses.
    a. lloramos
    b. enseñaste
    c. viajaron
    d. creció
    e. No es necesario hacer ninguna corrección.

43. La profesora aclaró *las dudas* de sus alumnos.
    a. las mesas
    b. sus sillas
    c. preguntar
    d. estresada
    e. No es necesario hacer ninguna corrección.

44. Estoy muy *embarazada* porque me caí enfrente de todos en la tienda.
    a. felices
    b. sonriendo
    c. avergonzada
    d. tristemente
    e. No es necesario hacer ninguna corrección.

45. Alex le pidió a su mamá que le *ayudara* con un proyecto para su clase de español.
    a. ayudas
    b. hagan
    c. ayudar
    d. leo
    e. No es necesario hacer ninguna corrección.

46. Sólo el personal autorizado *pueden* entrar al evento organizado por las fuerzas militares.
    a. podrá
    b. entraría
    c. pudimos
    d. no
    e. No es necesario hacer ninguna corrección.

47. La Cruz Roja Internacional está capacitada para *algunos* desastre natural a nivel mundial.
    a. ninguna
    b. cualquier
    c. tantos
    d. alguna
    e. No es necesario hacer ninguna corrección.

48. ¿Cuáles son los familiares que *viajé* con Ud. y hacia qué parte se dirigen?
    a. viajan
    b. dormimos
    c. viajara
    d. hubiera viajado
    e. No es necesario hacer ninguna corrección.

49. Las leyes de los Estados Unidos varían según el estado donde la persona *cometieron* el delito.
    a. hago
    b. cometen
    c. hagamos
    d. cometa
    e. No es necesario hacer ninguna corrección.

50. Si hubiera sabido que iba a llover, habría *traído* mis botas y la chaqueta.
- a. traen
- b. trayendo
- c. trajo
- d. traje
- e. No es necesario hacer ninguna corrección.

Answers

Logical Reasoning

1. **c.** Choice **c** is correct, because the paragraph provides information on only one year for Japan, so it cannot be concluded that more refugees receive asylum each year from Canada than from Japan. Choice **a** is incorrect, because the first paragraph explains the two ways in which refugees can receive legal admission to a country. It is stated in the paragraph that 30,000 refugees were accepted per year in the U.K. and 25,000 were accepted in Canada; therefore choice **b** is incorrect. Choice **d** is incorrect because it restates the first line of the paragraph. Choice **e** is incorrect because the correct answer is found in choice **c**.

2. **e.** Choice **e** is correct because it restates the third sentence in terms of the overlap between immigrants and accountants in the country mentioned within the paragraph. Choice **a** says that most immigrants were accountants or social workers; these are professional occupations, but the second sentence says that most immigrants were not employed in professional occupations, so choice **a** is incorrect. Choice **b** is incorrect because it contradicts information given in the paragraph, which states that some of these immigrants were accountants. Choice **c** is incorrect because it denies that there is overlap between immigrants and social workers, even though this overlap is clear from the third sentence. Because the paragraph does not provide complete information about the non-professionals (immigrant and non-immigrant), choice **d** is incorrect.

3. d. Choice **d** states that the fence will not be constructed due to opposition, but the paragraph only presents the reasons given by the opponents—it does not state the result of the opposition. This information cannot be validly concluded from the paragraph, and choice **d** is therefore the correct response. Choices **a**, **b**, **c**, and **e** restate objections the various groups offer from within the paragraph, so none of these is the correct answer.

4. b. Even though the paragraph states that there is a group of text messages that are requested in investigations and that there is a group of messages that contain information that would not be said face-to-face, there is nothing in the paragraph that says that these groups overlap. Choice **b** is therefore not supported by the paragraph, and is the correct answer. Choices **a** and **e** restate information that is provided in the last sentence of the paragraph, so these answers are not correct. Choices **c** and **d** also restate information found within the paragraph, so these are not the correct answers.

5. c. Choice **c** takes into account all the information provided in the paragraph with no contradictions or omissions, so it is the correct answer. Choice **a** is incorrect because the paragraph does not state that Guard Y can cover the north side. Choice **b** is incorrect because the paragraph does not state that Guard Y can cover the south side. Choice **d** is incorrect because the paragraph does not state that Guard Z can cover the west side. Choice **e** is incorrect because the correct response is found within the answers.

6. c. Choice **c** explains why the age limit was changed—to allow experienced veterans to apply for application into the Border Patrol—based on information found in the paragraph, and is therefore the correct answer. Choice **a** contradicts information given in the first sentence of the paragraph, and is an incorrect answer. Choices **b** and **d** make false assumptions based on information in the paragraph, and are incorrect answers. Choice **e** is also a false assumption. Even though the Border Patrol may want veterans with 20 years of military training and experience, the policy change does not mean that many veterans actually retire at age 37.

7. a. Choice **a** is correct, because it uses the information in the paragraph to explain why alarm systems would make businesses safer, even though businesses with such alarms are broken into more often than those without such alarms. Choices **b**, **c**, and **d** all explain why the alarms might not be effective, but fail to explain why the break-in rate for such businesses would be higher than the break-in rate for businesses without alarms. Choice **e** is incorrect because the business owners' feelings have no bearing on the burglary rates.

8. e. Choice **e** restates the information in the second sentence of the paragraph, and is therefore the correct response. Choices **a** and **b** are incorrect because the paragraph states that agents may also use other forms of transportation. Choices **c** and **d** cannot be concluded from the information provided in the paragraph, and are therefore incorrect.

9. b. If only the four computers that are five years old are updated this year, the twelve that are four years old will need to be updated next year, which will result in a budget increase according to the paragraph, so choice **b** is correct. The four- and five-year-old computers must be updated in the next two years, but the rest will not need to be updated in the third year, so choice **a** is incorrect. If only five computers are updated this year, then next year the eleven remaining four-year-old computers will need to be updated, which necessitates a budget increase—so choice **c** is incorrect. If ten computers (the four five-year-old computers and six of the four-year-old computers) are updated this year, six will need to be updated next year, so choice **d** is incorrect. Choice **e** is incorrect because the correct response is found within the answers.

10. e. According to the requirements, Tucson must be visited first and San Diego must be visited last. El Centro and Yuma can each be visited either second or third. Choices **a**, **b**, **c**, and **d** are all plausible based on the information given and are all therefore valid conclusions drawn from the paragraph, so choice **e** is the correct answer.

11. d. Choice **d** restates information given in the second and last sentences of the paragraph, so it is correct. Choice **a** is incorrect because the last sentence states that a vehicle with a light bar did not have a revolving light, which includes a strobe. Choice **b** is incorrect because an LED is a type of revolving light, and the last sentence states that vehicles with a light bar did not have revolving lights. Choice **c** is incorrect because a vehicle with a revolving light cannot have a light bar. Choice **e** is incorrect because the correct response is found within the answers.

12. a. Choice **a** restates information found within the paragraph, so it is the correct answer. Choice **b** is a false assumption that could not have been concluded from the information in the paragraph, so it is incorrect. Choices **c**, **d**, and **e** contradict information in the first sentence of the paragraph, so they are incorrect answers.

13. b. Since the In-Basket Simulation is optional, it cannot be validly concluded that Officer Marks will proceed to it, so choice **b** is the correct answer. Choices **a**, **c**, and **d** all restate information found in the paragraph, so they are incorrect. Because the correct response is found within the answers, choice **e** is incorrect.

14. b. Choice **b** confuses information found in the fifth sentence, so it cannot be validly concluded from the paragraph and is the correct answer. Choices **a**, **c**, **d**, and **e** all restate information found in the paragraph, so they are incorrect.

15. a. Choice **a** restates information found in the first sentence of the paragraph, so it is the correct answer. Choices **b**, **c**, and **d** contain faulty assumptions that are not supported by the paragraph, so they are incorrect answers. Because the correct response is found in the answers, choice **e** is incorrect.

16. e. Choices **a**, **b**, **c**, and **d** make false assumptions that are not based on the information given, so choice **e** is the correct answer.

PRACTICE TEST 1

Spanish Language

1. **c.** The verb needs to be in the infinitive form, and choices **d** (*encuentran: they find*) and **e** (*robamos: we steal*) are conjugated and are not synonyms of *perder* (*to lose*), so they are not possible answers. Choice **a** (*tener: to have*) does not have the same meaning, nor does choice **b** (*copiar: to copy*). The only possible answer is choice **c**. *Descuidar* means *to neglect* or *to be negligent*.

2. **d.** *Según* means *according to*, and the only possible answer is choice **d** (*De acuerdo con: In agreement with*). Choices **a** (*Al lado de: Next to*), **b** (*Alrededor de: Around*), and **e** (*Debajo de: Under*) do not have the same meaning as *Según*, and do not make any logical sense when inserted into the sentence. Choice **c** is a verb in its infinitive form (*Volver*), which does not have the same meaning or part of speech as *Según*, nor does it make grammatical sense in the sentence. Therefore, choice **d** is the only synonym of *Según*.

3. **a.** Choices **b** (*confundir: to confuse*) and **e** (*complicar: to complicate*) are antonyms of *aclarar* (*to clarify*) and are therefore not possible choices. Choice **c** (*mentir: to lie*) is not a synonym of *aclarar* either, nor is choice **d** (*pesar: to weigh*). Choice **a** (*explicar: to explain*) is a synonym of *aclarar* and therefore the only correct answer.

4. **e.** *Manejar* and *conducir* are synonyms that both mean *to drive* and here they are conjugated in the same *nosotros* form. Therefore, choice **e** (*Manejamos*) is the correct answer. Although all other choices are also conjugated in the *nosotros* form, their meanings are not the same as the italicized verb *Condujimos*. *Rogamos* in choice **a** means *We begged*, *Intentamos* in choice **b** means *We tried*, *Cantamos* in choice **c** means *We sang*, and *Caminamos* in choice **d** means *We walked*.

5. **e.** *Aproximadamente* is a Spanish-English cognate, meaning the word looks similar in both languages and has the same meaning (*approximately*). Choice **a** is not correct when inserted into the sentence, nor is it a synonym; *para* generally means *for* but *por* must be used before a number or amount. Choice **b** (*exactamente: exactly*) is an antonym of the italicized word. Neither choice **c** (*tantos: so many*) nor **d** (*antes de: before*) work grammatically in the sentence, nor are they synonyms of *aproximadamente*. Choice **e** is the only possible answer; *alrededor de* means *around* or *about*.

6. **c.** Choices **a** (*contento: happy*) and **b** (*paciente: patient*) are antonyms of *preocupada* (*worried*), and choice **a** has a masculine ending when it should be feminine since we are referring to a *mother* (*mamá*). Choice **d** (*interesado: interested*) also has a masculine ending and cannot be considered either because its meaning is different. Choice **e** (*ocurrir: to happen*) is an infinitive verb, which does not work grammatically in the sentence, nor is it a synonym of *preocupada*. The synonym needs to be a feminine adjective. Choice **c** (*inquieta: restless*) is the only correct answer.

7. **b.** Choices **a**, **c**, and **e** must be eliminated because they do not agree with the subject. Choice **a** (*exigentes: strict*) and **e** (*puros: pure*) are plural when the adjective should be singular and feminine to agree with *la profesora*; choice **c** (*romántico: romantic*) is masculine. Choice **d** (*repugnante: repugnant*), which is also an English cognate, is an antonym of the italicized word *simpática* (*nice*). Therefore, choice **b** (*amable: nice*) is the only correct answer.

8. e. Choice **d** (*inspeccionaste: you inspected*) is not possible because the conjugation does not agree with the third person subject *el policía*. Although choices **a**, **b**, and **c** are all conjugated correctly, they do not share the same meaning as *investigó* and are therefore eliminated as possible answers. *Eliminó* in choice **a** means *he eliminated*, *enseñó* in choice **b** means *he taught*, and *fue* in choice **c** means *he went*. *Inspeccionó* in choice **e** is correctly conjugated in the third person simple past and is a synonym of *investigó*; therefore, choice **e** is the correct answer.

9. a. Choices **b**, **c**, **d**, and **e** all give different meanings from *A pesar de que* (*Despite*). The sentence suggests that *despite all the available information, they still cannot find a suspect for the crime*. *Según* in choice **b** means *According to*; *En vez de* in choice **c** means *Instead of*; *Realmente* in choice **d** means *Really/actually*; and *Desafortunadamente* in choice **e** means *Unfortunately*. Choice **a** (*Aunque: Although*) is the only possible answer since *although* (*aunque*) and *despite* (*a pesar de que*) are synonyms.

10. d. Choice **b** should be immediately eliminated because it doesn't use the same verb form as the question. *Hallar* is the infinitive form of *to find*. It is a synonym of the verb *encontraste* but it is not correctly conjugated. Choices **a** (*compraste: you bought*), **c** (*pintaste: you painted*), and **e** (*perdiste: you lost*) all give very different meanings that would change the meaning of the question completely. Choice **d** is a conjugated form of the verb *hallar*, which is a synonym of *encontrar*. Choice **d** (*hallaste*) is the correct answer.

11. d. The answer needs to be a verb to agree with *vive* (the verb *lives*), so choices **a** (*casa: house*) and **e** (*hogar: home*) are incorrect because they are nouns. Choices **b** (*pasa las vacaciones: takes vacation*) and **c** (*viaja: travels*) are incorrect because they refer to where a person goes on vacation, which can be different from where a person lives. Choice **d** (*habita: inhabits/lives*) is the only possible option.

12. a. In order to agree with the rest of the sentence, the synonym of *incendios* needs to be a plural noun. Therefore, we can eliminate choices **b** (*encender: to ignite*), **d** (*encendedor: lighter*), and **e** (*ira: anger*). The meanings of those words do not fit grammatically in the sentence and they are not synonyms of *incendios* (*fires*). Choice **c** (*fósforos: matches*) is a plural noun, but its meaning is not the same. Choice **a** (*fuegos: fires*) is the only possible answer.

13. b. In order to agree with the original verb *golpea* (*cuando un desastre natural nos golpea: when a natural disaster hits us*), the correct answer must be in the third person singular form to agree with the subject *un desastre*. We can immediately eliminate choices **c** (*evitan: they avoid*) and **e** (*administrar: to administer/manage*) because they are not conjugated correctly nor are they synonyms. Choices **a** (*aprende: learns*) and **d** (*requiere: requires*) are in the correct tense yet these verbs are not synonyms of *golpea*. Choice **b** (*sucede: happens*) is the only possible answer.

14. d. Choice **d** (*reglas: rules*) is the only answer that is a synonym of *normas* (*standards*). Choices **c** (*obedecer: to obey*) and **e** (*pensar: to think*) are verbs and are not the same part of speech as the noun *normas*. Choices **a** (*opiniones: opinions*) and **b** (*creencia: belief*) are nouns, but only choice **a** is plural like *normas* to agree with the preceding article *las* in the sentence. In addition, the meaning of *opiniones* is different from *normas*. Therefore, choice **d** is the only possible answer.

15. e. Choice **e** (*dentro del: within the*) is the only synonym for *en el* (*in the*). All the other choices are also prepositions of location, but their meanings are completely different. *Cerca del* in choice **a** means *close to*, *lejos del* in choice **b** means *far from*, *encima del* in choice **c** means *on top of*, and *al lado del* in choice **d** means *next to*. Choice **e** is the only possible answer.

16. c. *Cumplir con* means *to fulfill*. A verb is needed for this answer, so we can automatically eliminate choices **b** (*conocimiento: knowledge*) and **e** (*logros: achievements*) since they are nouns. The verb also needs to be in its infinitive form, so choice **d** (*logrará: he/she/it will achieve*) can also be eliminated since it is conjugated. The meanings of *cumplir con* and *saber de* (*to know of*) in choice **a** are different so choice **a** is not possible. Therefore, we are left with choice **c** (*satisfacer: to satisfy*), which is a synonym of *cumplir con* in this sentence and is conjugated correctly. Choice **c** is the only possible answer.

17. a. Choices **b** (*la familia: family*) and **e** (*los hechos: the facts*) have the same part of speech as the noun *los sentimientos*, but they are not synonyms. Choices **c** (*llorar: to cry*) and **d** (*llorando: crying*) are not synonyms either, nor are they the same part of speech. Only choice **a** (*las pasiones: the passions*) conveys the same meaning as *los sentimientos*, and it is therefore the only possible answer.

18. c. Although all choices work grammatically in the sentence, only choice **c** (*el desarrollo: the development*) conveys the same idea as *la evolución* (*the evolution*). Therefore, choice **c** is the only correct answer. *El dinero* in choice **a** means *the money*, *el fracaso* in choice **b** means *the failure*, *los jefes* in choice **d** means *the bosses*, and *aprender* in choice **e** means *to learn*. These choices are not synonyms and therefore not possible answers.

19. d. All choices are prepositions of location, but only choice **d** (*por el: through the*) conveys the same idea as *a través del* (*across/through the*). All the other choices give different locations: *encima del* in choice **a** means *on top of*; *debajo del* in choice **b** means *under*; *lejos del* in choice **c** means *far from*; *enfrente del* in choice **e** means *in front of*. Choice **d** is the only possible answer.

20. c. The article *las* that precedes the noun is feminine and plural so our noun must also be feminine and plural to work grammatically in the sentence, and it must be a synonym of *señales* (*signs*). Those criteria eliminate choices **a** (*ropa*: *clothes*), **b** (*papeles*: *papers*) and **d** (*documentación*: *documentation*). None of those three choices is a synonym of the word *señales*. Choice **e** (*reglas*: *rules*) does not share the same meaning as *señales* either. Therefore, choice **c** is the only synonym. *Indicaciones* means *indications*; it is a synonym and is plural and feminine like *señales* to agree with the rest of the sentence.

21. c. Choice **c** uses the imperfect tense *estaba* to describe what the woman *was doing*, and the simple past *tocó* to describe a completed action when the neighbor *knocked* on the door. It is the only option that utilizes *estar* in its correct imperfect tense. Choice **a** is incorrect because *era* cannot be used for the first blank; a form of *estar* is needed with this progressive tense. Both choices **b** and **e** mix both present and imperfect past tenses so they are not correct; the tenses need to be consistent throughout the sentence. Choice **d** is incorrect with the conjugation of *estar*: *estuviste* is in the familiar *tú* form and that does not agree with the subject *ella* in the sentence; also, *supo la puerta* doesn't have any meaning. Choice **c** is the only possible answer.

22. b. The first blank must be a verb in the third person form to agree with the noun *la policía*. Choice **a** uses *prometen* (*they promise*) as its first answer, and choice **e** uses *invadieron* (*they invaded*); these are different verb conjugations that do not agree with *la policía*; therefore, choices **a** and **c** are not possible answers. The second word blank is an adjective that must be plural and feminine to agree with the noun *las oficinas*. With those criteria, choice **d** (*preguntó, viejos*) is not correct since *viejos* is masculine and does not agree in gender with *oficinas*. Choice **c** (*pinta, blancas*) does not make sense as the police would not *paint offices because they suspect a lawyer of a crime*, as the entire sentence reads. Choice **b** (*invadió, nuevas*) makes logical sense and is grammatically correct.

23. a. The time expression *de ayer* at the end of the sentence indicates that the sentence refers to the past. Choice **a** (*prestó, hice*) is correct because it is the only option that uses both the past tense in both answers and the correct subject-verb agreement (*prestó* agrees with *mi amiga*, and *hice* is in the past to refer to *yo*). Choices **b** (*dará, hacía*), **c** (*quiera, hará*), and **d** (*prestará, haré*) all use the future in their conjugated verbs and are therefore not possible answers. Choice **e** (*estaban prestando, hubo*) uses the past but uses *estaban*, which is plural, to refer to the actions of one person (*mi amiga*). Therefore, choice **e** is not correct and choice **a** is the only possible answer.

24. c. The first blank needs to agree with the masculine subject *agente* and the second blank needs to agree with the masculine and plural adjective *falsos*; given these criteria, choice **c** (*astuto, documentos*) is the only correct answer since it uses *astuto* to agree with *agente* and *documentos* to agree with *falsos*. Choice **a** (*nueva, papeles*) uses a feminine adjective *nueva* to describe the masculine subject *agente*; choice **a** is incorrect. Choices **b** (*joven, un pasaporte*) and **d** (*experimentado, una licencia de conducir*) are incorrect answers because their choices for the second blank do not agree with the adjective *falsos*. Choice **e** (*astuta, un pasaporte*) uses the feminine adjective *astuta* to describe *el agente*, and *un pasaporte* is singular when the object must be plural to agree with the adjective *falsos*. Choice **c** is the only possible answer.

25. e. Choice **e** (*sabía, se la regaló*) is the correct answer because *sabía* agrees with the subject *la mamá*, and *se la regaló* correctly combines the indirect object pronoun *se* (to refer to *su hija*) with the direct object pronoun *la* (to refer to *la joyería*) in the second answer. Choice **a** (*pregunta, la dieron*) uses *la dieron* as its second answer when the verb should be in the third person singular form to agree with the subject *la mamá*. *Había* in choice **b** (*había, nos la presta*) is incomplete for the first blank; it also incorrectly incorporates *nos* in its second answer when the object *nosotros* is never implied; the person receiving the action is *la hija*, not *nosotros*. Choice **c** (*tuvo, le la dio*) fails to change *le* to *se* in *le la dio* for its second answer. *Compraba* in choice **d** (*compraba, me lo dará*) does not make sense with the verbs that follow (*compraba qué hacer con su joyería* does not make sense), and it incorporates *me* in its second answer when it should be referring to *la hija* (*se*). Therefore, choice **e** is the only correct answer.

26. a. For their first answer, choices **b** (*aprendimos*), **c** (*haber*), and **d** (*había*) do not use a verb in the correct third person form to agree with the subject *el jefe*. The first blank with choice **e** (*era*) does not form a logical idea when inserted, and the second answer (*enseñamos*) refers to a subject *nosotros* that is never implied. The two answers in choice **a** (*enseñó, cómo*) are correct to form a coherent sentence that translates as: *The boss taught his employee how to use the new system.*

27. c. The verb for the first blank needs to be in the third person form to agree with *el gobierno de los Estados Unidos*. This criterion eliminates choice **a** (*me gustaría: I would like*) and choice **d** (*volando: flying*). Choice **e** is a formal Ud. command (*saque: take out*) that would have to begin an idea; it is incorrect when placed in the middle of a sentence and not a possible answer. Also, the word *normalmente* in the sentence before the first blank implies a recurring action that requires either the present or imperfect tense to show something that happens or often happened. The first answer in choice **b** (*pidió: requested*) therefore does not work because the simple past implies a one-time occurrence; also, *ella* for the second blank cannot go between *entrar* and *país*. Choice **c** (*exige, al*) is the only possible answer since it uses a logical verb in the third person form for the first blank (*exige: demands*) and *al* for the second blank to complete the idea *entrar al país*.

28. e. The first blank needs to be a verb in its past participle form to complete the past perfect tense (*. . . if he had _____ a decision*). The second blank needs to be an article to go before the feminine and plural noun *vacaciones*. Based on the criteria for the first blank, choice **a** (*hubo: there was/there were*), choice **b** (*cuento: story*), choice **c** (*hacer: to do*), and choice **d** (*tomaba: he was taking/he took*) are not possible answers to complete the action. In choice **e**, *tomado* correctly finishes the verb form *había tomado* for the first blank. The second blank needs to be an article. *Mis* as the second answer in choice **e** is the only possible option to go before *vacaciones* and finish the idea: *I asked my boss if he had made a decision in regard to my vacation.*

29. b. The first blank requires a masculine singular adjective to agree with the noun *hotel*. *Al lado de* in choice **a** is a preposition, not an adjective; *electrónica* in choice **c** is feminine; *algunos* in choice **d** is masculine and plural; *bonita* in choice **e** is feminine. They are not valid choices. The second blank should be a preposition showing where the hotel is situated. Choice **b** (*lujoso: luxurious, entre: between*) is the only answer with a masculine adjective and a logical preposition.

30. e. Choices **a**, **b**, and **c** can automatically be eliminated because their first answers do not agree with the singular masculine article *el* before the blank. *Vecina* in choice **a** is feminine, *agentes* in choice **b** is plural, and *niños* in choice **c** is plural. For choice **d**, its second answer *qué* does not make a grammatically correct idea when inserted. Choice **e** is the only possible answer; it correctly uses a singular masculine noun *abogado* to agree with *el*, and its preposition *antes del* forms a logical idea when placed before *juicio* to express the idea *before the trial* (*antes del juicio*).

31. a. In choice **b**, the *ellos* form of *tener* should be used (*tienen*), not *tenemos*, since the sentence refers to *Fabián and his mom*. In choice **c**, *conocer* is an irregular verb and is not conjugated properly (*conozco*, not *conoco*). In choice **d**, the personal *a* is missing after the verb *quiero*, which is necessary when referring to people (correction: *quiero mucho a mis papás*). In choice **e**, *ninguno* does not agree in gender with the object *amigas* (it should be *ninguna* to refer to a female friend), and the last two words should be combined to read *conmigo*. Choice **a** is the only grammatically correct sentence.

32. c. In choice **a**, the verb *llevaste* does not agree with the subject *la muchacha*. It should be *llevó*. In choice **b**, the sentence incorrectly uses *son* to describe an emotion or condition where it should use the correct form of *estar* (*están*). In choice **d**, *María* is a woman and *satisfecho* should be feminine; also, *paso* is not correctly accented to indicate the past; it should be *pasó*. In choice **e**, the verb *pasar* is not correctly conjugated to refer to *la ambulancia*; it is incorrectly conjugated in the first person *yo* form and should read *pasó*. Choice **c** is the only correct sentence.

33. c. Choice **c** is the correct answer because it appropriately employs the subjunctive with *ayudes*, which is necessary when one person is asking another person to do something. Choice **a** does not use the subjunctive at all for the verb *ayudar*; it should read *ayudes*. Choice **b** doesn't use the correct form of *gustar* for the sentence to make sense; it should read *me gustaría* since it is a request with *por favor* at the end. In choice **d**, instead of using the subjunctive with the second verb, it uses the infinitive form of the verb (*ayudar*), which is incorrect. Choice **e** does not properly conjugate *gustar*; it should be in the third person form to refer to *la ayuda* (*the help*) as *gusta* or *gustó* if it is in the past.

34. d. Choice **a** uses an incorrect verb form *fuimos* to refer to *Uds.*; it should read *fueron*. Choice **b** has the incorrect article in front of *película* and the adjective *famoso* needs to be feminine; it should read *la película famosa*. Choice **c** does not conjugate the verb properly; *me encantan* should be *me encanta* since it refers to only one *new television program*. Choice **e** uses incorrect conjugation also; *gustaron* should be *gustó* since it refers to only one movie. Choice **d** is the only grammatically correct sentence.

35. a. The verb in choice **b** does not agree with the subject (*vamos* and *tu familia* do not match). Choice **c** does not correctly combine the indirect object pronoun with the direct object pronoun (*se lo*, not *le lo*). Choice **d** does not have the correct article or the correct form of the adjective for the noun *sistema*: it should read *un sistema avanzado* since *sistema* is masculine. Choice **e** should not use the personal *a* after *quiero* since *agua* is an object, not a person; also, *hambriente* is not correct in this context; *hambre* is the correct word. Choice **a** is the only grammatically correct sentence.

36. c. Choices **a**, **b**, and **d** do not have the correct verb form to match the subject. The verb *preguntaste* in choice **a** should be *preguntó* since *el presidente* is the subject. *Sabían* in choice **b** should be *sabía* to refer to the subject *el presidente*. *Respondemos* in choice **d** should be *respondió* to agree with the subject *el gabinete*. Choice **e** does not use the correct indirect object pronoun before the verb *respondía* to refer to *el gabinete* (*le*, not *me*); it also incorrectly uses *deben* when it should use *debe* to agree with the subject *el presidente*. Choice **c** is the only correct sentence.

37. a. Choice **b** does not make any sense because *de quién* is used to mean *whose* or signify ownership; the insertion of *de* is incorrect and changes the idea of the sentence. Choice **c** uses a form of *estar* when it should use a form of *ser* to refer to the identity of a person; also, the feminine noun *amiga* needs the article *la* before it, not *el*. Choice **d** does not properly conjugate the form of *ser* to agree with *Ud.*, and *parque* needs the masculine adjective *este* before it, not *esta*; also, in choice **d** the syntax is incorrect and the question word *por qué* should be placed at the beginning of the question, not the end. Choice **e** needs the correct form of *estar*, not *ser*, to refer to the location of *las amigas*; also, the adjective *rápido* needs to be both plural and feminine to agree with its subject *las amigas*. Choice **a** is the only correct sentence.

38. b. In order for choice **a** to be correct, the verb *fueron* needs to change to agree with its subject *el instructor*. The verb *aprendió* in choice **c** needs to change to *aprendieron* to agree with the subject *las reclutas*, and the adjective *tanto* needs to be modified to agree with the plural and feminine noun *cosas*. Choice **d** does not correctly use the subjunctive with the second verb *enseñar*; the first verb *causó que* requires the use of the subjunctive. The verb *tuvo* in choice **e** does not agree with the subject *el sargento y varios reclutas*, and the article *una* does not agree with the noun *accidente*. Choice **b** is the only correct sentence.

39. c. Choice **a** is incorrect because it does not use the subjunctive form for the second verb *entrar* and it is missing the linking word *que* between the two sets of subjects and verbs. The first verb *queremos* in choice **b** is incorrectly conjugated to agree with the noun *los superiores*, and it is also missing the subjunctive form in the second verb and the linking *que*. The same problem occurs in choice **d** with the missing subjunctive form for the verb *entrar* and the missing *que*. The insertion of *que* is incorrect in choice **e** and should be replaced by the personal *a*. Choice **c** is the only correct sentence; in choice **c**, the subjunctive is not necessary.

40. b. Choice **a** is incorrect because *poder* is not correctly conjugated (*podieron* should be *pudieron*) and *emergencia* does not have the correct article (*una*) in front of it. The verb *amenacé* in choice **c** does not agree with its subject *los alumnos*, and the masculine noun *padres* does not have the right masculine article before it. An incorrect article is also used in choice **d** before *padres* and the reflexive verb is not correctly conjugated to refer to its subject (*se*, not *te*). The verbs in choice **e** are not conjugated at all to agree with their subject. Choice **b** is the only correct sentence.

41. d. Choices **a** (*Las camas: The beds*), **c** (*La mesa: The table*), and **e** (*La cuenta: The bill*) do not make any sense when put into the context of the sentence, although they are the correct forms of speech (noun) that the sentence requires. Choice **b** (*Explicar: To explain*) is a verb and is not grammatically correct in the sentence. *El cuento* in choice **d** (*the story*) is the only grammatically correct option that makes sense.

42. c. Choices **a** (*lloramos: we cry*), **b** (*enseñaste: you taught*), **d** (*creció: he/she/it grew*), and **e** (*pintó: he/she/it painted*) do not work because the verb forms do not agree with the subject *ellos*. Choice **c** (*viajaron: they traveled*) is the only option that is correctly conjugated and forms a cohesive sentence.

43. e. Choices **c** (*preguntar: to ask*) and **d** (*estresada: stressed*) can be immediately eliminated because the sentence requires an object, and **c** and **d** are not the correct forms of speech since choice **c** is a verb and **d** is an adjective. A noun is needed for the word in question. Choices **a** (*las mesas: the tables*) and **b** (*sus sillas: their chairs*), while they are the correct forms of speech (nouns), do not make sense in the sentence. Choice **e** (*las dudas: the doubts/questions*) is the only possible answer.

44. c. Although *embarazada* sounds like the word *embarrassed* in English, it is a false cognate. *Embarazada* means *pregnant*. Therefore, choice **e** is incorrect. Choice **c** (*avergonzada*) is the correct option to mean *embarrassed*. Choice **a** (*felices: happy*) is plural and doesn't fit in the sentence since the subject *yo* is singular. Choices **b** (*sonriendo: smiling*) and **d** (*tristemente: sadly*) are the wrong forms of speech and don't make sense when inserted into the sentence. Choice **c** (*avergonzada: embarrassed*) is the only possible answer.

45. e. The sentence is correct as is (choice **e**). No other option uses the correct verb form. Furthermore, the other choices are not in the subjunctive form, which is necessary for this sentence since Alex (the subject) is asking *his mom* to do something. Requests require a subjunctive form. Choice **a** (*ayudas*) refers to *tú*, choice **b** (*hagan*) to *ellos*, choice **c** (*ayudar*) is the infinitive, and choice **d** (*leo*) refers to *yo*. Choice **e** is the only possible form that uses the imperfect subjunctive form *ayudara* that is conjugated in the third person to agree with *su mamá*.

46. a. Due to subject verb/agreement, choices **c** (*pudimos: we could*), **d** (*no* would make the primary verb *entrar* and that is not conjugated in the sentence), and **e** (*pueden: they can*) are not valid since they don't agree with the subject *el personal*. Choice **b** (*entraría*) is the conditional form of the same verb *entrar* that would follow it in the sentence, so that would not make sense (*entraría entrar al evento organizado por . . . : would enter enter the event organized by . . .*). Therefore, choice **a** (*podrá: will be able to*) is the only correct answer; it agrees with the subject *el personal* and makes logical sense when inserted.

47. b. The noun *desastre* following the adjective in question is masculine and singular, so choices **a**, **c**, **d**, and **e** are not possible answers: *ninguna* in choice **a** is feminine; *tantos* in choice **c** is plural; *alguna* in choice **d** is feminine; and *algunos* in choice **e** is plural. Choice **b** (*cualquier: any*) is correct since it agrees with the gender and singularity of the noun *desastre*.

48. a. The correct verb needs to be in plural *ellos* form as it refers to *los familiares*. All the other verb forms presented are either singular (*viajara* in choice **c**, *hubiera viajado* in choice **d**, and *viajé* in choice **e**) or in the *nosotros* form (*dormimos* in choice **b**), which are incorrect. Additionally, choices **c** and **d** utilize the subjunctive form and this structure is not correct for a direct question. Choice **a** (*viajan*) is the only possible answer.

49. d. The verb needs to be conjugated in the third person to correctly refer to the subject *la persona*. Choice **a** is in the first person (*hago: I do*). Choice **b** (*cometen: they commit*) is in the plural form. Choice **c** (*hagamos: we do*) is conjugated in the *nosotros* form, and choice **e** (*cometieron: they committed*) is in the plural past form. The only possible answer is choice **d** (*cometa*), conjugated in the third person to agree with the subject *la persona* and in the subjunctive form because the sentence refers to a possible scenario.

50. e. This sentence is a classic conditional sentence. The correct verb form for the second part of the sentence is the conditional perfect, so the italicized verb needs to be in the past participle form. If you combine the previous word *habría* with choice **a** (*habría traen: I would have they bring*), **b** (*habría trayendo: I would have bringing*), **c** (*habría trajo: I would have he brought*), or **d** (*habría traje: I would have I brought*), the idea would not make any sense. Only choice **e** is correct since it correctly uses the past participle form (*habría traído: I would have brought*).

Practice Test 1: Scoring and Diagnostic Chart

To evaluate how you did on this practice exam, start by totaling the number of correct responses on the two sections of this practice exam. First, find the number of questions you got right in each part. Questions you skipped or got wrong don't count; just add up the number of correct answers.

If at least 70% of your responses on the two parts are correct (47 correct), you are most likely prepared to pass the Border Patrol Exam. However, because the entrance process is competitive, you may need a higher score on the official exam to get accepted into the Border Patrol Academy.

In addition to seeing how you performed overall, you can use the following scoring chart to help diagnose your strengths and weaknesses in the different skills assessed on the exam, to better focus your study preparation.

LOGICAL REASONING SECTION	
SKILL	QUESTION
Reasoning about Groups and Categories	1–8
Reasoning about Events or Situations	9–16

SPANISH LANGUAGE SECTION	
SKILL	QUESTION
Part I	1, 2, 3, 4, 5, 6, 7, 8, 9, 10, 11, 12, 13, 14, 15, 16, 17, 18, 19, 20
Part II, Section I	21, 22, 23, 24, 25, 26, 27, 28, 29, 30
Part II, Section II	31, 32, 33, 34, 35, 36, 37, 38, 39, 40
Part II, Section III	41, 42, 43, 44, 45, 46, 47, 48, 49, 50

CHAPTER 4 ▶ PRACTICE TEST 2

Similar to the first practice test, this second practice test contains questions to challenge your logical reasoning and Spanish-language abilities. Again, you should simulate the actual test-taking experience as closely as you can, including giving yourself about four and a half hours to complete the test.

LEARNINGEXPRESS ANSWER SHEET

1. ⓐ ⓑ ⓒ ⓓ ⓔ
2. ⓐ ⓑ ⓒ ⓓ ⓔ
3. ⓐ ⓑ ⓒ ⓓ ⓔ
4. ⓐ ⓑ ⓒ ⓓ ⓔ
5. ⓐ ⓑ ⓒ ⓓ ⓔ
6. ⓐ ⓑ ⓒ ⓓ ⓔ
7. ⓐ ⓑ ⓒ ⓓ ⓔ
8. ⓐ ⓑ ⓒ ⓓ ⓔ
9. ⓐ ⓑ ⓒ ⓓ ⓔ
10. ⓐ ⓑ ⓒ ⓓ ⓔ
11. ⓐ ⓑ ⓒ ⓓ ⓔ
12. ⓐ ⓑ ⓒ ⓓ ⓔ
13. ⓐ ⓑ ⓒ ⓓ ⓔ
14. ⓐ ⓑ ⓒ ⓓ ⓔ
15. ⓐ ⓑ ⓒ ⓓ ⓔ
16. ⓐ ⓑ ⓒ ⓓ ⓔ

1. ⓐ ⓑ ⓒ ⓓ ⓔ
2. ⓐ ⓑ ⓒ ⓓ ⓔ
3. ⓐ ⓑ ⓒ ⓓ ⓔ
4. ⓐ ⓑ ⓒ ⓓ ⓔ
5. ⓐ ⓑ ⓒ ⓓ ⓔ
6. ⓐ ⓑ ⓒ ⓓ ⓔ
7. ⓐ ⓑ ⓒ ⓓ ⓔ
8. ⓐ ⓑ ⓒ ⓓ ⓔ
9. ⓐ ⓑ ⓒ ⓓ ⓔ
10. ⓐ ⓑ ⓒ ⓓ ⓔ
11. ⓐ ⓑ ⓒ ⓓ ⓔ
12. ⓐ ⓑ ⓒ ⓓ ⓔ
13. ⓐ ⓑ ⓒ ⓓ ⓔ
14. ⓐ ⓑ ⓒ ⓓ ⓔ
15. ⓐ ⓑ ⓒ ⓓ ⓔ
16. ⓐ ⓑ ⓒ ⓓ ⓔ
17. ⓐ ⓑ ⓒ ⓓ ⓔ
18. ⓐ ⓑ ⓒ ⓓ ⓔ
19. ⓐ ⓑ ⓒ ⓓ ⓔ
20. ⓐ ⓑ ⓒ ⓓ ⓔ
21. ⓐ ⓑ ⓒ ⓓ ⓔ
22. ⓐ ⓑ ⓒ ⓓ ⓔ
23. ⓐ ⓑ ⓒ ⓓ ⓔ
24. ⓐ ⓑ ⓒ ⓓ ⓔ
25. ⓐ ⓑ ⓒ ⓓ ⓔ
26. ⓐ ⓑ ⓒ ⓓ ⓔ
27. ⓐ ⓑ ⓒ ⓓ ⓔ
28. ⓐ ⓑ ⓒ ⓓ ⓔ
29. ⓐ ⓑ ⓒ ⓓ ⓔ
30. ⓐ ⓑ ⓒ ⓓ ⓔ
31. ⓐ ⓑ ⓒ ⓓ ⓔ
32. ⓐ ⓑ ⓒ ⓓ ⓔ
33. ⓐ ⓑ ⓒ ⓓ ⓔ
34. ⓐ ⓑ ⓒ ⓓ ⓔ
35. ⓐ ⓑ ⓒ ⓓ ⓔ
36. ⓐ ⓑ ⓒ ⓓ ⓔ
37. ⓐ ⓑ ⓒ ⓓ ⓔ
38. ⓐ ⓑ ⓒ ⓓ ⓔ
39. ⓐ ⓑ ⓒ ⓓ ⓔ
40. ⓐ ⓑ ⓒ ⓓ ⓔ
41. ⓐ ⓑ ⓒ ⓓ ⓔ
42. ⓐ ⓑ ⓒ ⓓ ⓔ
43. ⓐ ⓑ ⓒ ⓓ ⓔ
44. ⓐ ⓑ ⓒ ⓓ ⓔ
45. ⓐ ⓑ ⓒ ⓓ ⓔ
46. ⓐ ⓑ ⓒ ⓓ ⓔ
47. ⓐ ⓑ ⓒ ⓓ ⓔ
48. ⓐ ⓑ ⓒ ⓓ ⓔ
49. ⓐ ⓑ ⓒ ⓓ ⓔ
50. ⓐ ⓑ ⓒ ⓓ ⓔ

Logical Reasoning Test

1. Cancellation of removal is a proceeding set in front of an immigration judge that is available to certain long-term residents of the United States. This proceeding allows an individual being faced with removal to obtain permanent resident status if he or she meets certain criteria: for example, has maintained continuous physical presence in the United States for at least ten years; has exemplified good moral character during those ten years and has not been convicted of certain crimes; and can prove that removal would result in exceptional hardship to a spouse, parent, or child who is a U.S. citizen or permanent resident. Cancellation of removal may also be granted if the applicant has been battered or subjected to extreme cruelty by a U.S. citizen or permanent resident spouse or parent, or if he or she is the parent of a child of a U.S. citizen or lawful permanent resident and the child has been battered or subjected to extreme cruelty by a citizen or permanent resident parent.

From the information given here, it can be validly concluded that:

a. a person who is facing removal can choose from one of three criteria to apply for cancellation.
b. a person who has been subjected to extreme cruelty need not have maintained continuous physical presence in the United States to apply for cancellation of removal.
c. a person may face removal if it cannot be proved that he or she has committed a crime.
d. a permanent resident cannot apply for cancellation of removal.
e. a long-term resident may be eligible for cancellation of removal if he or she meets specific criteria.

2. Zachary is a former agent who was disabled due to an injury he sustained while performing the duties of his job. He is entitled to compensation according to the Federal Employee Compensation Act according to these conditions: If the beneficiary is married and/or has dependents, benefits are paid at the rate of three-quarters of the person's salary at the time of the job-related injury; otherwise, benefits are paid at the rate of one-half of the person's salary. Zachary receives one-half of his salary at the time of injury.

From the information given here, it can be validly concluded that Zachary:

a. has never been married.
b. is not married and has no dependents.
c. is not married but has dependents.
d. is married and has dependents.
e. is married but has no dependents.

3. A United States Permanent Resident Card, or "green card," serves as authorization for legal employment in this country. This card must be renewed every ten years. Green card holders may apply for renewal beginning six months in advance of the card's expiration date. To do so, the applicant is required to appear in person with his or her current green card, application, renewal fee, and current photos. It may take up to one year for the applicant to receive the new green card; temporary documents are provided in the interim.
From the information given here, it can be validly concluded that:
   a. some green card renewals are provided more than one year after application for renewal.
   b. some green cards have no expiration date.
   c. green card holders may apply for renewal four months before the current green card expires.
   d. green cards are the only work authorization documents that expire after ten years.
   e. a passport can serve in place of a current green card for renewal purposes.

4. In virtually every law enforcement agency in the United States, the lethal force policy is the same: If under threat of serious injury or death, lethal force may be used. In attempting to apprehend drug traffickers in a particular state, some agents shot nonlethal beanbag rounds. The drug traffickers returned fire with real bullets, and the agents then fired live ammunition.
From the information given here, it can be validly concluded that:
   a. beanbag rounds are seldom effective.
   b. the agents acted in accordance with the lethal force policy.
   c. agents generally carry more live rounds than nonlethal rounds.
   d. agents generally carry fewer live rounds than nonlethal rounds.
   e. none of the above

5. There are two primary sources of citizenship in the United States: birthright citizenship, in which a person receives citizenship by virtue of being born in the United States or its territories (for example, the U.S. Virgin Islands or Guam), and naturalization, in which a person receives citizenship through application for and approval of citizenship. In a certain workplace, some employees hold birthright citizenship and some were naturalized. Some employees who were born in Guam are citizens, some female employees are citizens, and none of the male employees have been naturalized.
From the information given here, it can be validly concluded that:
   a. no female employees were born in Guam.
   b. no male employees were born in Guam.
   c. there are more male than female employees in the workplace.
   d. there are more female than male employees in the workplace.
   e. none of the above

6. Agents uncovered evidence that indicated that dealings in illegal handguns were being conducted at a local shooting range. On further investigation, the agents discovered that all the handguns being sold illegally were made by Quality Firearms, but some of the Quality Firearms brand handguns they found at the range were legally owned and were not being sold.
From the information given here, it CANNOT be validly concluded that:
   a. some handguns available at the shooting range were not made by Quality Firearms.
   b. some Quality Firearms handguns are legally owned.
   c. some Quality Firearms handguns are illegally being sold.
   d. some handguns made by a manufacturer other than Quality Firearms are illegally being sold.
   e. none of the above

7. Crimes may be characterized according to two types: *malum in se* (evil in and of itself) or *malum prohibitum* (wrong due to prohibition by law). Theft is an example of a *malum in se* crime, since it is generally perceived to be wrong whether there are laws prohibiting theft or not. Gambling is an example of a *malum prohibitum* crime, since it is prohibited in certain jurisdictions but allowed in others. Some areas do not distinguish between crimes *malum in se* and *malum prohibitum*, but many do.
From the information given here, it can be validly concluded that:
   a. sometimes failing to file a tax return is characterized as *malum in se*.
   b. some crimes characterized as *malum prohibitum* are not declared by a particular jurisdiction to be an offense.
   c. some crimes characterized as *malum in se* are not evil in and of themselves.
   d. some areas distinguish between *malum in se* and *malum prohibitum* crimes.
   e. most areas do not distinguish between *malum in se* and *malum prohibitum* crimes.

8. Approximately 40,000 immigrants are currently living in a certain county. While most of these immigrants are living in the county illegally, many of them are not. Many of the legal immigrants are from El Salvador and many are from Nicaragua. A smaller number of the legal immigrants are from Guatemala.

From the information given here, it can be validly concluded that:
- a. most of the immigrants are either from El Salvador or Nicaragua.
- b. it is not the case that some of those from Nicaragua are illegal immigrants.
- c. none of those from El Salvador are illegal immigrants.
- d. most of the immigrants are living in the county legally.
- e. some of those from El Salvador are living in the county legally.

9. Gun safety training instills proper handling techniques through a set of specific rules. Gun handlers are expected to treat firearms with care, as they are considered inherently dangerous. Although there are several sets of rules for gun safety, some basic tenets include assuming that the firearm is always loaded, never pointing the firearm at anything unless the intention is to destroy it, and never touching the trigger until the sight is on the target.

From the information given here, it CANNOT be validly concluded that:
- a. if a firearm is pointed at a target, then the handler intends to destroy it.
- b. if a handler is holding a firearm, then he assumes it is loaded.
- c. if the trigger is being touched, then the sight is on a target.
- d. if a handler's sight is not on the target, then he is not touching the trigger.
- e. if a handler's sight is on a target, then the trigger is being touched.

10. The Rio Grande Valley Sector Canine Unit has four canine teams available to patrol the northern, southern, western, and eastern checkpoints. Canine Team 1 is not on the north or west side. Canine Team 2 is either on the north or south side. Canine Team 3 is not on the north or west side. Canine Team 4 is directly opposite Canine Team 1, and Canine Team 3 is directly opposite Canine Team 2.

From the information given here, it can be validly concluded that:

a. if Canine Team 2 is on the north side, then Canine Team 3 is on the west side.
b. if Canine Team 1 is on the south side, then Canine Team 4 is on the west side.
c. if Canine Team 2 is on the north side, then Canine Team 3 is on the south side.
d. if Canine Team 1 is on the east side, then Canine Team 4 is on the north side.
e. if Canine Team 2 is on the south side, then Canine Team 3 is on the north side.

11. A lawful permanent resident is a foreign national who has been granted the privilege of permanently living and working in the United States as a green card holder. One of the requirements of applying for U.S. citizenship is to be a permanent resident for a continuous five years. To become a lawful permanent resident based on having a relative who is a citizen of the U.S. or who is a lawful permanent resident, one must go through a multi-step process.

From the information given here, it CANNOT be validly concluded that:

a. if an individual has a relative who is a U.S. citizen, then he or she may apply to be a permanent resident.
b. if an individual is a permanent resident, then he or she is not a U.S. citizen.
c. if an individual is a permanent resident based on having a relative who is a U.S. citizen, then he or she has passed through a multi-step process.
d. if an individual has a relative who is a U.S. citizen, then he or she is automatically a permanent resident.
e. none of the above

12. Physical fitness training is an essential component in becoming a Border Patrol Agent. This training has several benefits: to condition an agent physically so she can react in a way that minimizes injury to herself and to others in physically dangerous situations; to condition her psychologically so she is confident in her own physical ability (which in turn enables her to react positively to physically strenuous or dangerous situations); and to ensure that she understands and remains aware of her own physical limitations.
From the information given here, it can be validly concluded that:
- **a.** if an agent is in a dangerous situation, then she has been conditioned physically.
- **b.** if an agent is not physically fit, then she is not aware of her own physical limitations.
- **c.** if an agent is conditioned physically, she can minimize injury in dangerous situations.
- **d.** if an agent is not physically fit, then she can react positively to strenuous situations.
- **e.** none of the above

13. Specific procedures have been created for apprehending suspects. These procedures may vary, but in general, certain aspects hold true: one must not assume that a suspect is in a particular location without solid facts to back it up; doing so will increase the likelihood that the suspect will be lost, since suspects have many tactics to avoid apprehension. One must also establish a perimeter containment that cuts off the suspect's route of travel.
From the information given here, it can be validly concluded that:
- **a.** if the proper procedures are followed, then a suspect will not be apprehended.
- **b.** if a suspect is lost, then proper procedures have not been followed.
- **c.** if a suspect's route of travel has been cut off, then the perimeter containment has been established.
- **d.** if a suspect is assumed to be in a particular location, then solid facts will not assist in apprehension.
- **e.** none of the above

14. Training at the Border Patrol Academy is often viewed as one of the most difficult in federal law enforcement. Trainees are required to continually maintain a passing score in all the courses of instruction. These include courses in Border Patrol operations, law, Spanish language training, physical training, driver training, and training in the use of firearms. After graduating from the Academy, individuals are required to continue to take operations, law, and Spanish classes at the headquarters of the Border Patrol Sector to which he or she is assigned, as well as to pass two sets of probationary exams.

From the information given here, it can be validly concluded that:

a. if an individual is sitting for the first probationary exam, then he or she has not graduated from the Academy.
b. if an individual is taking classes at the headquarters of the Border Patrol Sector to which he or she is assigned, then he or she has graduated from the Academy.
c. if a trainee does not pass one of the Academy courses, then he or she will be required to pass two sets of probationary exams.
d. if an individual is training in the use of firearms, then he or she is taking classes at the headquarters of the Border Patrol Sector to which he or she is assigned.
e. if an individual is taking classes in law, then he or she has not graduated from the Academy.

15. A military veteran can benefit from transitioning to the Border Patrol because he can apply his time served in the military to his federal retirement plan. To do so, he must buy back his time, either by making a lump-sum payment or by having small increments deducted from his Border Patrol paychecks. For example, an agent with 15 years in the Army can apply this to time spent with the Border Patrol, and when he retires with 20 years in the Border Patrol, he will receive retirement pay for 35 years of service.

From the information given here, it CANNOT be validly concluded that:

a. if a veteran wishes to buy back his time served in the military, then he can choose for deductions to be made from his Border Patrol paychecks.
b. if an agent transitions to the Border Patrol from the military, then he may choose to combine his time from the military to apply to his retirement.
c. if a veteran wishes to buy back his time served in the military, then he can make a lump-sum payment.
d. if a veteran applies his military time spent to his time with the Border Patrol, then he can receive retirement pay for combined years of service.
e. none of the above

PRACTICE TEST 2

16. A permanent resident of the United States who holds a green card (Permanent Resident Card, Form I-551) may travel freely outside of the United States. A passport from the country of citizenship is generally all that is needed. To re-enter the United States, however, a permanent resident must present Form I-551 for readmission. A re-entry permit is needed to return to the United States from trips greater than one year but less than two years in duration.

From the information given here, it can be validly concluded that:

a. if an individual travels outside of the United States with a passport from his or her country of citizenship, then he or she is a permanent resident.
b. if a permanent resident presents Form I-551 for readmission, then he or she is returning from a trip outside of the United States that was greater than two years in duration.
c. if a permanent resident presents Form I-551 for readmission, then he or she is returning from a trip outside of the United States.
d. if an individual is a permanent resident, then he or she may not travel outside of the United States.
e. none of the above

Spanish Language Proficiency Test

Part I
Read the sentence and then choose the most appropriate synonym for the italicized word or phrase.

1. El incumplimiento es causa inmediata para cualquier despido *laboral*.
   a. apropiado
   b. recreativo
   c. relevante
   d. importante
   e. de trabajo

2. María no lavó ni cocinó bien los ingredientes de la sopa; *por lo tanto*, se enfermó muy gravemente.
   a. además
   b. sin embargo
   c. consecuentemente
   d. pero
   e. cómo

3. Muchos inmigrantes luchan por tener los mismos derechos civiles que tienen los ciudadanos; *sin embargo*, el proceso es largo y difícil.
   a. usualmente
   b. felizmente
   c. afortunadamente
   d. y
   e. no obstante

4. Cuando Alejandra *alistó* la maleta el viernes para ir a visitar a su mamá, nunca se imaginó que la frontera iba a estar tan congestionada.
   a. empacó
   b. llamó
   c. llevó
   d. encendió
   e. fue

PRACTICE TEST 2

5. En los últimos cinco años el índice criminal ha *disminuido* gracias al aumento y los esfuerzos de la policía.
   a. expandido
   b. crecido
   c. reducido
   d. juzgado
   e. aumentado

6. Los ganadores del sorteo tendrán treinta días hábiles para *reclamar* su premio.
   a. comprar
   b. pedir
   c. rechazar
   d. regalar
   e. deber

7. Al llegar a la cárcel, el detenido pidió un abogado para explicar los *sucesos* de la noche.
   a. eventos
   b. charcos
   c. vasos
   d. estrellas
   e. robos

8. En 1968, los Juegos Olímpicos en México fueron los primeros en ser *celebrados* en un país en vía de desarrollo.
   a. suspendidos
   b. conmemorados
   c. despreciados
   d. cancelados
   e. descubiertos

9. Los agentes aduaneros de los aeropuertos buscan personas que cumplan con *el perfil* de un terrorista.
   a. mi trabajo
   b. tu palabra
   c. los rasgos
   d. los ojos
   e. los ciudadanos

10. El buen entrenamiento del personal y el adiestramiento canino son *imprescindibles* para la seguridad fronteriza del país.
   a. débiles
   b. innecesarios
   c. indispensables
   d. agresivos
   e. una opción

11. Los deportistas estarán sometidos a una fuerte *capacitación* antes del inicio de la temporada.
   a. vacaciones
   b. botella de agua
   c. formación
   d. descanso
   e. viaje

12. El presidente del país está *custodiado* por fuertes organismos de seguridad.
   a. autorizado
   b. enseñado
   c. alimentado
   d. libre
   e. protegido

13. El sindicato de la empresa entró en huelga y exigió un aumento de *sueldo*.
   a. salario
   b. derechos civiles
   c. días de vacaciones
   d. café
   e. tiempo libre

14. El alto oleaje de las playas *provocó* el cierre temporal para los bañistas.
   a. causó
   b. abrió
   c. ladró
   d. cerró
   e. impidió

15. Los menores de edad podrán *salir* del país sólo con la autorización de sus padres.
  a. descubrir
  b. disfrutar
  c. entrar
  d. ingresar
  e. irse

16. A pesar de su *enfermedad*, el artista había firmado un contrato y no podía posponer la fecha de entrega de su obra maestra.
  a. mudanza
  b. malestar
  c. vacaciones
  d. experiencia
  e. certificado

17. Muchos activistas *manifestaron* su oposición al tratamiento de los animales salvajes enfrente del zoológico.
  a. declararon
  b. demandaron
  c. mintieron
  d. volvieron
  e. enviaron

18. La tormenta eléctrica causó mucha *inquietud* entre los animales del parque zoológico.
  a. felicidad
  b. nervosidad
  c. alegría
  d. ira
  e. autoridad

19. Después de que varias personas *se quejaron* de la higiene del restaurante, llegaron las autoridades y lo multaron.
  a. se reían
  b. protestaron
  c. se sentaron
  d. se fueron
  e. se sonreían

20. Ella *logró* su sueño de ser una cantante famosa.
  a. renunció a
  b. se rindió a
  c. realizó
  d. abandonó
  e. intentó

Part II, Section I
Read each sentence carefully. Select the appropriate word or phrase to fill each blank space.

21. Para _____ a cualquier establecimiento gubernamental, hay que cumplir con _____ normas de seguridad.
  a. entrando, un
  b. ingresar, ciertas
  c. mira, alguna
  d. ingresando, algunas
  e. entrar, ciertos

22. Muchas tiendas comerciales _____ descuentos a los miembros _____ de las fuerzas militares.
  a. brindan, activos
  b. proveer, jubilados
  c. ofrecen, jubilado
  d. otorgo, activas
  e. provee, contento

23. La ciudad _____ el restaurante la semana pasada porque no cumplía con los _____ estatales de higiene.
  a. abrió, normas
  b. cierra, requisitos
  c. despidieron, normas
  d. cerró, requisitos
  e. cerrará, estándares

24. _____ mexicanos disfrutan de una _____ ciudadanía que les permite ser ciudadanos de México y de los Estados Unidos.
   a. Algunas, dobles
   b. Dichosos, único
   c. Viejas, excelente
   d. Ud., mexicano
   e. Algunos, doble

25. _____ entregué a su hermano _____ no confío en usted.
   a. Te lo, quien
   b. Se lo, porque
   c. Lo se, cómo
   d. Le lo, por qué
   e. Se lo, qué

26. Debí _____ dicho la verdad, pero _____ miedo de las consecuencias.
   a. decir, tengo
   b. he, tendré
   c. haber, tenía
   d. habrá, tendrá
   e. estar, estaba

27. La mayoría de personas argumenta que la tecnología nos _____ mejorado la vida, mientras otros dicen que los cambios han _____ las cosas más complicadas que antes.
   a. ha, vuelto
   b. han, volvido
   c. habían, volver
   d. ha, vueltos
   e. ayuda, vuelve

28. A pesar de que el bombero tenía el día libre, _____ obligado a luchar contra el incendio más grande que cualquier persona _____ visto.
   a. fuiste, ha
   b. se siente, haber
   c. está, tener
   d. se sintió, había
   e. se estuvo, habrá

29. Cuando Juliana fue a _____ su mamá en el hospital, no _____ pudo ver debido a una contaminación radioactiva en el edificio.
   a. vio a, lo
   b. visitar a, la
   c. hablara con, le
   d. viera, se
   e. visitar, lo

30. Cada viajero turista _____ tener su visa correspondiente _____ su destino.
   a. debe, según
   b. debo, sobre
   c. deber, de acuerdo con
   d. puede, debajo de
   e. deben, antes

Part II, Section II

Read each sentence carefully. Select the one sentence that is correct.

31.
a. Los hospitales en las personas necesita una agenda para asistir a la clínica.
b. Cada hospital o clínica tiene su respectivo horario de visitas para los pacientes.
c. El paciente internada fue enfermo entonces salen del hospital.
d. El respectivo horario de la clínica fueron cambiadas por las visitas familiares.
e. El hospital y la clínica recibo visitas después de las personas pacientes.

32.
a. Los atletas que participan en deportes extremos son más propensos a tener accidentes fatales.
b. Los atletas de deportes extremos tener accidentes.
c. Los deportes propensas tienen accidentes debido a los atletas extremas.
d. Los atletas extremos estaban más propensos hoy en día a tener un accidente.
e. Los atletas que participar en deportes extremos ser más propensos a tener accidentes fatales.

33.
a. La hotelería de la ciudad te preparaste para el aumento de turistas este verano.
b. La hotelería de la ciudad se prepara para el aumento de turistas este verano.
c. La hotelería de la ciudad le lo prepararon para el aumento de turistas el verano pasado.
d. La hotelería de la ciudad se los prepararé para el aumento de turistas el verano pasado.
e. La hotelería de la ciudad seré preparada este verano con muchos turistas.

34.
a. Las directivas de la compañía realizó una cena para el personal administrativo el próximo año.
b. El personal administrativo seré invitada a una cena gracias a los directivas de la compañía.
c. El personal de la compañía no aceptarás una cena realizada por las directivas administrativas.
d. Las directivas de la compañía realizarán una cena para el personal administrativo el día festivo.
e. Gracias a las directivas de la compañía, el personal administrativo no comeremos el día festivo pasado.

35.
a. Los juegos pirotécnicos tendrá personal supervisando la seguridad.
b. La exhibición de los juegos pirotécnicos se dará con la supervisión del personal de seguridad.
c. El personal supervisar la seguridad asegura el bueno exhibición de los juegos pirotécnicos.
d. El juego de seguridad tendrá la supervisión de los personal pirotécnicos.
e. La exhibición pirotécnico se dará con el personal pirotécnica.

36.
a. Para la determinación del perfil de cada migrante o turista, hay que tener en cuenta la nacionalidad o cultura del individuo.
b. Cuando determinando cada migrante o turista perfil, tener en cuenta tu cultura o nacionalidad.
c. Para determinar el perfil de cada migrante o turista, recordar en cuenta la nacionalidad son muy importantes.
d. Es importante darse cuenta del cultura de alguien determinar el perfil.
e. Recuerde la cultura y nacionalidad cuando determinando cada migrante o turista perfil por favor.

PRACTICE TEST 2

37. a. Gracias al ciencia forense, delincuentes son capturado y casos son cerrado.
b. Los delincuentes y casos no dura mucho gracias al ciencia forense que ayudan mucho.
c. La ciencia forense es muy útil capturar a los delincuentes.
d. Los casos criminales son capturado gracias a la ciencia forense.
e. La ciencia forense ayuda a capturar a delincuentes y cerrar casos a nivel mundial.

38. a. El odontólogo recomendó que el paciente ve a un especialista.
b. El odontólogo recomendó que el paciente viera a un especialista.
c. El odontólogo recomienda que el paciente ve a un especialista.
d. El odontólogo hubiera recomendado que el paciente ve a un especialista.
e. El odontólogo recomendaría que el paciente vería a un especialista.

39. a. Necesitamos hablar con el abogado en cuanto llegue a la oficina.
b. Quisiéramos que el doctor nos llama cuando llegue.
c. Necesitamos que el abogado nos llama cuando llega a la oficina.
d. Si el abogado llega temprano, por favor dilo que me llama.
e. Necesitamos hablar con el abogado tan pronto llega a la oficina.

40. a. Les pagamos cincuenta dólares a la niñera por cuidar a los tres niños por cuatro horas.
b. La pagamos cincuenta dólares a la niñera por cuidar a los tres niños por cuatro horas.
c. Le pagamos cincuenta dólares a la niñera por cuidar a los tres niños por cuatro horas.
d. Te pagamos cincuenta dólares a la niñera por cuidar a los tres niños por cuatro horas.
e. Las pagamos cincuenta dólares a la niñera por cuidar a los tres niños por cuatro horas.

Part II, Section III

Read each sentence carefully. Select the correct word or phrase to replace the italicized portion of the sentence. In those cases in which the sentence needs no correction, select choice e.

41. México exigió a los deportistas colombianos que *tuvieran* sus visas al día para poder jugar futbol en su país.
a. tuvieron
b. tienen
c. tener
d. habrían tenido
e. No es necesario hacer ninguna corrección.

42. Ya que el personal de limpieza sólo tiene acceso al edificio durante la mañana, todos fueron *eliminada* como posibles sospechosos.
a. incluyeron
b. descartados
c. eliminado
d. eliminaban
e. No es necesario hacer ninguna corrección.

43. Las buenas condiciones del clima favorecen el buen *operación* de los aeropuertos a nivel mundial.
a. marchas
b. actividad
c. movimientos
d. funcionamiento
e. No es necesario hacer ninguna corrección.

44. Estaba *mucho* distraído por el libro que se me pasó el tiempo y llegué tarde a la reunión.
a. tan
b. tanto
c. media
d. muchísima
e. No es necesario hacer ninguna corrección.

45. El concierto a beneficio de las víctimas del terremoto se *realizaran* pronto y todos los fondos se dirigirán a la Cruz Roja.
   a. realizará
   b. realizarán
   c. hubiera realizado
   d. realizó
   e. No es necesario hacer ninguna corrección.

46. Si *hubiéramos* sabido sobre los efectos dañinos del cigarrillo, habríamos dejado de fumar hace años.
   a. hemos
   b. habíamos
   c. ha
   d. hayamos
   e. No es necesario hacer ninguna corrección.

47. *Había* ido a la despedida de Juliana si hubiera sabido que ella jamás volvería al país.
   a. Habría
   b. He
   c. Haber
   d. Habrás
   e. No es necesario hacer ninguna corrección.

48. Solo el personal *administración* del restaurante está autorizado para realizar descuentos.
   a. subordinada
   b. administrativo
   c. gerencia
   d. jefa
   e. No es necesario hacer ninguna corrección.

49. La agencia requiere que todos sus agentes *hable* español.
   a. hablan
   b. hablarán
   c. se habla
   d. hablen
   e. No es necesario hacer ninguna corrección.

50. El gerente es autónomo de *toma* sus propias decisiones para el aumento de ventas y de ofertas en la compañía.
   a. tomando
   b. tomar
   c. haya tomado
   d. tomara
   e. No es necesario hacer ninguna corrección.

Answers

Logical Reasoning

1. **e.** Choice **e** restates information provided by the paragraph, and is therefore the correct answer. Choice **a** states that a person can choose one of three criteria to apply for cancellation; however, the paragraph lists the criteria with "and," not "or," indicating that he or she must meet all the criteria, so this answer is incorrect. The paragraph never states that a person who has been subject to extreme cruelty is exempt from meeting the other criteria, so choice **b** is incorrect. Choice **c** is negated by the information in the paragraph, so this answer is incorrect. Rules governing permanent residents are not discussed in the paragraph, so choice **d** is incorrect.

2. **b.** Choice **b** states that Zachary is not married and has no dependents. This is the only condition for which he would receive benefits at one-half of his salary at the time of injury, so this is the correct answer. Choice **a** lists a condition that is not covered by the information in the paragraph, so it is incorrect. Choices **c**, **d**, and **e** all list conditions for which Zachary would be eligible for the increased (three-quarters) benefit, so they are incorrect answers.

3. **c.** Choice **c** is correct because four months prior to expiration falls within the six-month window for renewal stated within the paragraph. The paragraph states that it may take "up to" one year, not more than a year, for renewals to be provided, so choice **a** is incorrect. Choice **b** is incorrect because it is never stated in the paragraph that some green cards never expire. Since the paragraph does not address other types of work authorization documents, the information in choice **d** is incorrect. Choice **e** is incorrect because a passport is not listed as appropriate documentation in the paragraph.

4. **b.** From the information in the paragraph it can be concluded that the agents acted in accordance with the lethal force policy, so choice **b** is correct. Choice **a** makes the assumption that beanbag rounds are seldom effective, but the paragraph does not provide information on whether they have been effective in other instances, so this answer is incorrect. Choices **c** and **d** make assumptions about how many rounds agents carry, but this information is not found in the paragraph, so these answers are incorrect. Choice **e** is incorrect because the correct choice can be found within the answer choices.

5. **e.** Choice **e**, in which none of the other choices provide a valid conclusion from the information provided in the paragraph, is the correct answer. Choices **a**, **b**, **c**, and **d** all offer information that cannot be supported by the information provided in the paragraph, so these answers are incorrect.

6. **d.** Choice **d** provides information that cannot be validly concluded from the paragraph, so this answer is correct. Choices **a**, **b**, and **c** provide information that is supported by the paragraph, and are therefore incorrect. Choice **e** is incorrect because the correct response is found within the answers.

7. **d.** Choice **d** restates information found in the paragraph, so it is the correct answer. Choices **a**, **b**, and **c** confuse the two categories of crime as stated in the paragraph, so they are incorrect. Choice **e** contradicts information found in the paragraph, so it is incorrect.

8. **e.** Choice **e** is correct because it stands to reason that if many of the legal immigrants are from El Salvador, then some of the legal immigrants are from El Salvador. Choice **a** is incorrect because although many of the legal immigrants are from El Salvador or Nicaragua, the paragraph does not specify where most of the immigrants are from. Choices **b**, **c**, and **d** are incorrect because this information is not supported by the paragraph.

9. **e.** Although the rule is that the trigger should not be touched until the sight is on the target, the opposite is not necessarily true, so choice **e** cannot be validly concluded, and it is the correct answer. Choices **a**, **b**, **c**, and **d** restate information found in the paragraph, so they are incorrect answers.

10. **c.** Choice **c** aligns with information found in the third, fourth, and fifth sentences, so it is the correct response. Choice **a** is incorrect because Canine Team 3 cannot be on the west side. Choices **b** and **d** are incorrect because Canine Team 1 must be directly opposite Canine Team 4. Choice **e** is incorrect because Canine Team 3 cannot be on the north side.

11. **d.** Choice **d** contradicts information found in the third sentence of the paragraph, so it is the correct answer. Choices **a**, **b**, and **c** restate information found in the paragraph, so they are not correct answers. Because the correct response is found in the answers, choice **e** is incorrect.

12. **c.** Choice **c** restates information provided in the second sentence in the paragraph, so it is the correct answer. Choices **a**, **b**, and **d** present faulty assumptions that could not have been concluded from the information in the paragraph, so they are incorrect answers. Because the correct response is found within the answers, choice **e** is incorrect.

13. **c.** Choice **c** restates information provided in the last sentence in the paragraph, so it is the correct answer. Choices **a**, **b**, and **d** present faulty assumptions that could not have been concluded from the information in the paragraph, so they are incorrect answers. Because the correct response is found within the answers, choice **e** is incorrect.

14. **b.** Choice **b** restates information found in the fourth sentence of the paragraph, and is therefore the correct answer. Choices **a** and **c** are incorrect because probationary exams occur after graduation. Choice **d** is incorrect because training in the use of firearms takes place before graduation, and courses at the assigned sector are after graduation. Choice **e** is incorrect because individuals take classes in law after graduating.

15. **e.** Because all the choices contain information that has been restated from the paragraph, choice **e** is the correct answer.

16. c. Choice **c** restates information presented in the first and third sentences in the paragraph, so it is the correct answer. Choice **a** is incorrect because the paragraph does not say that only a permanent resident can travel outside of the United States with a passport from his or her own country of citizenship. Choice **b** is incorrect because the trip outside of the United States must be less than two years in duration. Choice **d** is incorrect because the paragraph states the requirements for a permanent resident to travel outside of the United States. Because the correct response is found within the answers, choice **e** is incorrect.

Spanish Language

1. e. Choices **a** (*apropiado: appropriate*) and **c** (*relevante: relevant*) are synonyms of each other but do not represent the same meaning as *laboral* (*work-related*). Choice **b** (*recreativo: recreational*) gives an opposite meaning of the original word, which pertains to work, not recreation. Choice **d** (*importante: important*) is not a synonym either, so choice **e** (*de trabajo: work-related*) is the only possible answer.

2. c. Another transition word is needed and choice **c** (*consecuentemente: consequently*) is the only transition word that conveys the same cause and effect idea as the italicized phrase *por lo tanto*, which means *therefore*. *Además* in choice **a** means *moreover* or *furthermore*, which is used to add an additional idea, not to show a cause and effect relationship. Nor does choice **b** show a cause and effect relationship, since *sin embargo* means *however* and would be used to introduce a contrasting idea. *Pero* in choice **d** means *but* and would introduce a contrasting idea just like *sin embargo*. Choices **b** and **d** can be considered synonyms of each other, but they are not synonyms of *por lo tanto*. Choice **e** (*cómo*) means *how* and does not function in this sentence as a synonym of the transition phrase *por lo tanto*. Choice **c** is the only possible answer.

3. e. Like the previous question, this exercise also requires another transition word that gives the same meaning as *sin embargo*, which means *however*. Choices **b** (*felizmente: happily*) and **c** (*afortunadamente: fortunately*) convey a positive tone that does not agree with the original italicized word nor the sentence, which describes a long and difficult process. Choice **a** (*usualmente: usually*) is a time modifier that does not convey the same idea as *sin embargo*. Choice **d** (*y: and*) is a transition word, but it does not convey the contrasting idea of the original phrase *sin embargo*. Therefore, choice **e** (*no obstante: nevertheless*) is the only possible answer.

4. a. *Alistó* is the conjugated form of *alistar*, which means *to get ready* or *to prepare*. Choice **a** (*empacó: she packed*) is the only verb whose meaning is similar to the italicized word in the given context of preparing a suitcase. All other choices work grammatically in the sentence, but they are not synonyms of *alistó*; *llamó* in choice **b** means *she called*; *llevó* in choice **c** means *she took*; *encendió* in choice **d** means *she lit*; *fue* in choice **e** means *she went*.

5. c. *Disminuido* is the past participle form of the verb *disminuir*, which means *to decrease* or *to diminish*. Although all choices are given in the correct past participle form, choices **a**, **b**, and **e** are antonyms of the italicized verb *disminuido: expandido* in choice **a** means *expanded*; *crecido* in choice **b** means *grown*; *aumentado* in choice **e** means *increased*. Choice **d** (*juzgado: judged*) does not make sense in the context. Choice **c** (*reducido: reduced*) is the only possible synonym.

6. b. *Reclamar* means *to claim*; in this example, it is given in the context of *claiming a prize*. Choices **a**, **c**, and **d** have entirely different meanings from *reclamar*: *comprar* in choice **a** means *to buy*; *rechazar* in choice **c** means *to reject*; *regalar* in choice **d** means *to give (as a gift)*. Choice **e** does not make sense in the context of the sentence as *deber* means *to owe* and that is not a synonym of *reclamar*. Choice **b** (*pedir: to order/request*) is the only synonym of the word *reclamar*.

7. a. Although a synonym is needed, the synonym needs to work grammatically in the sentence as well. Choice **d** (*estrellas: stars*) should automatically be eliminated because it is feminine and does not agree in gender with the rest of the sentence. Furthermore, it is not a synonym of *los sucesos*, which means *the happenings* or *the events*. Choices **b** (*charcos: puddles*), **c** (*vasos: glasses*), and **e** (*robos: robberies*) are not synonyms of the word *sucesos* and therefore are not possible answers. Only *eventos* in choice **a**, which means *events*, is a synonym of *sucesos* and the only possible answer.

8. b. Choices **a** (*suspendidos: suspended*) and **d** (*cancelados: canceled*) are synonyms of each other, but not of the word *celebrados*, which means *celebrated* or *performed* in this context. Choice **c** (*despreciados: despised* or *scorned*) is an antonym of the word *celebrados*. Choice **e** (*descubiertos: discovered*) conveys a completely different idea that does not work in the context since the Olympics are not *discovered*. Choice **b** (*conmemorados: commemorated*) is the only synonym and possible answer.

9. c. *El perfil* means *the profile*, which in this sentence refers to *the profile of a terrorist*. Choices **a** (*mi trabajo: my work*) and **b** (*tu palabra: your word*) are not synonyms of *el perfil*. Choices **d** (*los ojos: the eyes*) and **e** (*los ciudadanos: the citizens*) are not synonyms of *el perfil* either. *Los rasgos* in choice **c**, which means *the traits* or *the characteristics*, is the only possible answer.

10. c. *Imprescindibles* means *essential* or *indispensable*. *Innecesarios* in choice **b**, meaning *unnecessary*, and *una opción* in choice **e**, meaning *an option*, are antonyms of the word *imprescindibles* since they convey the idea of something being *needless* or *unessential*. Choices **a** (*débiles: weak*) and **d** (*agresivos: aggressive*) are not synonyms. *Indispensables* in choice **c** is an English cognate meaning *indispensable* in English; it is the only synonym of *imprescindible*. Choice **c** is the only possible answer.

11. c. *Capacitación* means *training*, as in the training that athletes must go through before they begin the sports season. Choice **c** (*formación: training*) is the only synonym for *capacitación* and the only possible answer. Choices **a** (*vacaciones: vacation*), **d** (*descanso: rest*), and **e** (*viaje: trip*) give an entirely different meaning related to taking time off. Choice **b** (*botella de agua: bottle of water*) doesn't make sense in the context of the sentence. Choice **c** is the only synonym and possible answer.

12. e. The word in question *custodiado* means *guarded* or *watched over* and a synonym can be found by looking for an English cognate among the choices. *Protegido* in choice **e** means *protected* and is the word closest in meaning to *custodiado* and therefore the correct answer. *Autorizado* in choice **a** means *authorized*; *enseñado* in choice **b** means *taught*; *alimentado* in choice **c** means *fed*; and *libre* in choice **d** means *free*. None of the words in choices **a**, **b**, **c**, or **d** are synonyms of *custodiado*. Choice **e** is the only possible answer.

13. a. The word *sueldo* refers to *salary*. Choice **a** (*salario*) is the only option that is a synonym of *sueldo*; it is also an English cognate and easier to recognize among the choices. All other choices convey a different meaning and are therefore incorrect. *Derechos civiles* in choice **b** means *civil rights*; *días de vacaciones* in choice **c** means *vacation days*; *café* in choice **d** means *coffee*; and *tiempo libre* in choice **e** means *free time*.

14. a. Choice **a** (*causó: caused*) is the only word that is a synonym of *provocó* (*incited* or *provoked*). Choice **b** (*abrió: opened*) and **e** (*impidió: impeded* or *deterred*) give a different meaning; choice **c** (*ladró: barked*) does not make logical sense in the sentence; and choice **d** (*cerró: closed*) does not make sense when you insert the word into the sentence (*cerró el cierre* [*closed the closure*] is redundant and sounds strange). Furthermore, *cerró* is not a synonym of *provocó*. Choice **a** is the only possible synonym.

15. e. *Salir* means *to leave*. Choices **a** (*descubrir: to discover*), **b** (*disfrutar: to enjoy*), **c** (*entrar: to enter*), and **d** (*ingresar: to enter* or *to come in*) all give a different meaning from the italicized word *salir*. Choice **e** (*irse: to leave* or *to go*) is the only synonym of the word and therefore the only possible answer.

16. b. *Enfermedad* means *sickness* or *illness*. The meaning of choice **a** (*mudanza: move*) is completely different from *enfermedad*. Choice **c** (*vacaciones: vacation*) is not a synonym of *enfermedad*, and it is plural and would be grammatically incorrect if inserted into the sentence (*su vacaciones* is not grammatically correct; it would be *sus vacaciones*). The meanings of choices **d** (*experiencia: experience*) and **e** (*certificado: certificate*) are not synonyms of *enfermedad*. Choice **b** (*malestar: physical discomfort*) is the only synonym of *enfermedad* and therefore the only possible answer.

17. a. *Manifestaron* comes from the verb *manifestar*, which means *to show* or *to declare*. *Declararon* in choice **a** is an English cognate and means *they declared* or *they made known* in its conjugated form; it is a synonym and therefore the correct answer. Choice **b** (*demandaron*) is a false cognate and does not mean the same in Spanish as the word *demand* does in English. *Demandaron* means *they sued* in its most common usage; it can also mean *they requested*. Choices **c** (*mintieron: they lied*), **d** (*volvieron: they returned*), and **e** (*enviaron: they sent*) are not synonyms of the word *manifestaron*, either. Choice **a** is the only possible answer.

18. b. *Inquietud* means *restlessness* in English. Choices **a** (*felicidad: happiness*) and **c** (*alegría: happiness*) are both antonyms of the word *inquietud*. Choice **d** (*ira: anger*) gives a negative connotation, but the meaning is much stronger than what is being expressed with *inquietud*. Choice **e** (*autoridad: authority*) does not convey the same meaning either. *Nervosidad* in choice **b** means *nervousness* and is the word closest in meaning to *inquietud* and therefore the correct answer.

19. b. *Protestaron* in choice **b** comes from the verb *protestar*, which can mean *to express a complaint*. It is the only synonym of the verb *se quejaron* (*they complained*). *Se reían* in choice **a** means *they laughed*; *se sentaron* in choice **c** means *they sat*; *se fueron* in choice **d** means *they left*; *se sonreían* in choice **e** means *they smiled*. These choices do not convey the same idea; choice **b** is the only possible answer.

20. c. *Logró* means *she achieved*. Choices **a**, **b**, and **d** are antonyms of the verb *lograr*. *Renunció a* in choice **a** means *she quit*; *se rindió a* in choice **b** means *she gave up on*; *abandonó* in choice **d** means *she abandoned*. Choice **e** (*intentó: she tried*) is not a synonym either. Choice **c** (*realizó: she accomplished*) is the only possible answer.

21. b. Whenever a verb immediately follows *para*, it needs to be in its infinitive form. That criterion alone eliminates choices **a**, **c**, and **d** because their first answers are conjugated: choice **a** suggests *entrando*, which is in the gerund form; choice **c** suggests *mira*, which is conjugated in the third person present form; and choice **d** suggests *ingresando*, which is also in the gerund form. Therefore, none of the choices **a**, **c**, or **d** will work grammatically in the sentence. In the second blank, in order to agree with *normas*, the adjective needs to be plural and feminine. Therefore, choice **e** (*entrar, ciertos*) is eliminated because its second answer *ciertos* is masculine. Choice **b** (*ingresar, ciertas*) is the correct answer because the first verb is in its infinitive form, and the second adjective is both plural and feminine to agree with *normas de seguridad*.

PRACTICE TEST 2

22. a. The verb for the first blank must be conjugated in the third person plural form to agree with its subject *tiendas*. As a result, choice **b** (*proveer, jubilados*) can be eliminated because its first answer is in the infinitive form. Choice **d** (*otorgo, activas*) can also be eliminated because *otorgo* is conjugated in the first person *yo* form. Choice **e** (*provee, contento*) is also eliminated because provee is conjugated in the third person singular *él/ella* form, which doesn't agree with the subject *tiendas*. Choices **a** and **c** are left. The second blank in the sentence refers to an adjective for *miembros* so it must be plural and masculine. Choice **c** (*ofrecen, jubilado*) has its second answer *jubilado* as singular. Choice **a** (*brindan, activos*) is the only answer that correctly satisfies the criteria to complete the sentence: the first answer *brindan* agrees with *tiendas*, and *activos* is the correct adjective to agree with *miembros*.

23. d. A time reference of *last week* (*la semana pasada*) is made in the sentence so the verb in the first blank must be in the past tense. As a result, choice **b** (*cierra, requisitos*) can be eliminated because its first answer *cierra* is in the present tense. Also, choice **e** (*cerrará, estándares*) can be eliminated because its first answer *cerrará* is in the future tense. The subject is *the city* (*la ciudad*) so the verb must also be in the third person singular form. This criterion eliminates choice **c** (*despidieron, normas*) because the first verb *despidieron* (*they fired*) is in the *ellos* form. Choice **a** (*abrió, normas*) uses a verb in the correct form for the first answer, but the verb choice (*abrió: it opened*) doesn't make sense because a city would not *open a restaurant because it didn't comply with hygiene standards*. Furthermore, its second answer *normas* does not agree with the article *los* before it; *normas* is feminine and needs the article *las*. Choice **d** (*cerró, requisitos*) is the only correct answer because its first answer is correctly conjugated, and the second answer (*requisitos: requisites*) is masculine and plural to agree with the article *los* before it.

24. e. In order to agree with the noun *mexicanos*, the first word must be plural and masculine. This criterion eliminates choice **a** (*Algunas: Some*) and **c** (*Viejas: Old*) as first answers because they are feminine adjectives and must precede a feminine noun. Choice **d** (*Ud., mexicano*) is also incorrect because *Ud.* refers to one person (the formal *you*) and cannot go before *mexicanos*. Choices **b** and **e** are left. The word for the second blank must be feminine and singular to agree with *ciudadanía*. The second answer in choice **b** (*único: unique/only*) is masculine and does not agree with *ciudadanía*. As a result, choice **e** (*Algunos, doble*) is the only valid answer since *Algunos* agrees with *mexicanos* and *doble* agrees with *ciudadanía*.

25. b. In this sentence, something is being delivered to someone's *brother* (*a su hermano*) so the indirect object is a third person. The first answer for choice **a** (*Te lo*) is incorrect because the indirect object pronoun is *te*. The first answer for choice **c** (*Lo se*) is also incorrect because the indirect object pronoun should go before the direct object pronoun (*Se lo*, not *Lo se*). The first answer in choice **d** (*Le lo*) is incorrect because when an indirect and direct object pronoun are combined and both begin with *l* such as *le lo* or *les lo*, the first *le* or *les* needs to change to *se* so it reads *se lo*. The only choices that correctly combine the correct indirect object pronoun with a direct object pronoun for this sentence are choices **b** (*Se lo, porque*) and **e** (*Se lo, qué*). The second answer in choice **e** does not fit grammatically in the sentence because *qué* means *what* and the sentence does not read logically. The only correct answer is choice **b** (*Se lo, porque*) to complete the sentence: *I delivered it to your brother because I don't trust you.*

26. c. *Haber* in choice **c** is the only correct option for the first blank to express the thought *I should have said* since *debí* is already conjugated and the past participle *dicho* follows the blank. An infinitive form of the verb *haber* is needed between those two words. Choice **a** uses the verb *decir*; choice **b** conjugates *haber* as *he*; choice **d** conjugates *haber* as *habrá*; choice **e** uses *estar*, which does not work in this grammatical structure to express a past regret. These answers do not make a grammatically correct sentence. Choice **c** (*haber, tenía*) is the only possible answer: it correctly uses *haber* in the first blank and the imperfect tense *tenía* in the second blank to describe the idea: *I should have told the truth but I was scared of the consequences.*

27. a. The answers for both blanks should complete the present perfect tense. The first blank should be the correct conjugation of *haber* before the past participle *mejorado*. In the second blank, the past participle is needed to complete the idea where the auxiliary *han* is given. Choice **e** (*ayuda, vuelve*) is not a possible answer because neither answer correctly completes the verb tenses. For the first blank, the subject *la tecnología* is singular so we can eliminate choices **b** (*han, volvido*) and **c** (*habían, volver*) because their form of *haber* is conjugated in the plural *ellos* form. If we look at the second answers in choices **a** and **d**, the only difference is that **d** uses *vueltos* with an *s* versus *vuelto* in choice **a**. In the present perfect tense, the past participle will never become plural so we know that choice **a** (*ha, vuelto*) is the only correct answer.

28. d. The first verb *tenía* in the sentence indicates that the sentence refers to an event in the past. Therefore, only the verbs in the past tense will work, so choices **b** (*se siente, haber*) and **c** (*está, tener*) can be eliminated because their first answers are in the present tense. Choice **a** (*fuiste, ha*) is incorrect because *fuiste* refers to the informal *tú*, which does not agree with the subject *el bombero*. Choice **e** (*se estuvo, habrá*) is incorrect because *se* doesn't belong with *estuvo* in this context, and the future *habrá* is incorrect in this sentence, referring to the past. Choice **d** (*se sintió, había*) is the only possible answer; *se sintió* correctly refers to the subject *el bombero* and *había* completes the past perfect tense to express the idea *had seen*. The entire sentence reads: *Despite the firefighter having the day off, he felt obligated to fight the biggest fire anyone had seen.*

29. b. Because the first blank follows *fue a*, a verb in its infinitive form is needed afterward since Spanish does not allow for two conjugated verbs next to each other. That criterion eliminates choices **a** (*vio a, lo*), **c** (*hablara con, le*), and **d** (*viera, se*) since the first answers are conjugated verbs, not infinitives. The personal *a* is needed between a verb and a person (in this case, *su mamá*) so we must choose choice **b** (*visitar a, la*) versus choice **e** (*visitar, lo*). Furthermore, only *la* is correct for the second blank since a direct object pronoun is needed to refer to *mamá*, and *mamá* is feminine. Choice **b** is the only possible answer.

30. a. The first verb must be conjugated in the third person to agree with the subject *viajero turista*. Only choices **a** (*debe, según*) and **d** (*puede, debajo de*) have their first verbs in the third-person singular form. Choices **b**, **c**, and **e** are automatically eliminated as possibilities: choice **b** (*debo, sobre*) has its first verb in the *yo* form; choice **c** (*deber, de acuerdo con*) has its first verb in the infinitive form; choice **e** (*deben, antes*) has its first verb in the plural *ellos* form. Choices **a** and **d** are left. With choice **d** (*puede, debajo de*), however, the second answer does not make any logical sense since *a visa can't be obtained under the destination*. Therefore, choice **a** (*debe, según*) is the only correct answer since *según* means *according to* and makes sense in the context.

31. b. The subject *necesita* in choice **a** does not agree with the subject *los hospitales*, so the sentence is grammatically incorrect. Furthermore, the sentence is illogical since it translates as *the hospitals in the people needs an agenda to attend the clinic*. In choice **c**, instead of the verb *fue* to refer to a person's health, the verb *estar* should be used and appropriately conjugated; furthermore, the second verb *salen* does not agree with the subject *el paciente*. In choice **d**, the verb and adjective *fueron cambiados* do not agree with the noun *el horario* because *el horario* is singular. Choice **e** also employs incorrect subject-verb agreement with the plural subject *el hospital y la clínica* and the singular first-person verb *recibo*. Choice **b** is the only sentence with correct subject-verb agreement.

32. a. Choice **a** is the only correctly conjugated sentence that makes logical sense. The verb *tener* in choice **b** is not conjugated to agree with its subject *los atletas*. The feminine adjective *propensas* in choice **c** does not agree in gender with the masculine noun *deportes*, nor does the adjective *extremas* agree with its noun *los atletas*. Furthermore, *propensas* does not make sense to describe *deportes*. Choice **d** refers to the present with *hoy en día* but its verb *estaban* is in the past. Therefore, choice **d** is incorrect as well. In choice **e**, the verbs *participar* and *ser* are not conjugated to agree with their subject *los atletas*. Choice **a** is the only correct sentence and possible answer.

33. b. Choice **a** is not possible because it incorrectly conjugates the reflexive verb *prepararse* in the *tú* form, which doesn't agree with the subject *la hotelería*. The verb *prepararon* in choice **c** is not properly conjugated to agree with the subject *la hotelería*, and the combination of the indirect and direct object pronouns (*le lo*) is incorrect. Choice **d** refers to the past (*el verano pasado*) yet has its verb conjugated in the future (*prepararé*); also, the verb conjugation and combination of indirect and direct object pronouns is incorrect. The verb *seré* in choice **e** does not agree with the noun *la hotelería*. Choice **b** is the only possible answer that correctly conjugates the reflexive verb *prepararse* to agree with its subject.

34. d. Choice **a** does not have correct subject-verb agreement with the verb *realizó* and the plural subject *las directivas*; also, the verb is conjugated in the past (*realizó*) when the sentence refers to the future (*el próximo año*). The verb *seré* in choice **b** does not agree with the third-person subject *el personal*; also, *directivas* has an incorrect article, *los*, in front of it. The verb *aceptarás* in choice **c** is incorrectly conjugated to agree with the noun *el personal*. Choice **e** has incorrect conjugation of the verb *comeremos* to agree with its subject *el personal administrativo*; also, the verb is conjugated in the future when the past is indicated (*el día festivo pasado*). Choice **d** is the only sentence with correct subject-verb agreement.

35. b. Choice **a** does not have subject-verb agreement between *tendrá* and the subject *los juegos* and it incorrectly employs the gerund form of *supervisar*. The verb *supervisar* in choice **c** is not conjugated to agree with its subject *el personal*. Choice **d** confuses the nouns with their correct adjectives; also, *personal* has an incorrect article before it (*los*) and its adjective (*pirotécnicos*) should be singular. Choice **e** does not change the adjectives *pirotécnico* and *pirotécnica* to agree in gender with the nouns *la exhibición* and *el personal* that they modify. Choice **b** is the only possible answer due to its correct subject-verb agreement.

36. a. The gerund is improperly used in choices **b** (*cuando determinando*) and **e** (*cuando determinando*) when it should be the simple present; also, in choice **b**, the wrong possessive adjective (*tu*) is used before *cultura* when referring to a migrant or tourist. The verb *tener* in choice **b** needs to be conjugated. In choice **c**, after the comma, *recordar* is incorrectly used as an expression with *en cuenta* (the correct expression is *tener en cuenta*), and the verb *son* does not agree with the subject *recordar*. In choice **d**, the joining word *para* is omitted before *determinar* and therefore makes the sentence incomplete. Choice **a** is the only sentence that is correctly conjugated and makes grammatical sense.

37. e. Choice **a** is incorrect because *ciencia* does not have the correct article before it; also, the adjectives *capturado* and *cerrado* are not plural to agree with their nouns *delincuentes* and *casos*. Choice **b** is incorrect because the verb *dura* does not agree with the plural subject *delincuentes* and *casos*. Choice **c** incorrectly omits *para* between *útil* and *capturar*. Choice **d** does not make sense as it says that *the criminal cases are captured* and the adjective *capturado* is not plural to agree with its subject *los casos*. Choice **e** is the only possible answer that uses a correct grammatical structure.

38. b. The combination *recomendar + que* requires the use of the subjunctive. Choice **b** is the only option that uses the subjunctive with the second verb (*viera*) and is therefore the only possible answer. Choice **a** uses the regular present form *ve* and is incorrect. Both choices **c** and **d** use the same incorrect form *ve* for their second verbs where the subjunctive is required. Choice **e** uses the conditional form for the second verb (*vería*), but in this sentence the verb needs to be in the imperfect subjunctive form.

39. a. All of the choices require the subjunctive mood in their sentences, but only choice **a** utilizes the subjunctive correctly. Choice **a** is the only possible answer. The verb *llama* in choice **b** should be in the subjunctive form since a request is being made. In choice **c**, a subjunctive form of *llamar* is needed as well because it is also a request. In choice **d**, the indirect object pronoun *le* should be used after *di* instead of *lo*; also, the subjunctive form *llame* is needed instead of *llama*. In choice **e**, the expression *tan pronto* requires the use of the subjunctive in the verb that follows it, which means *llega* is incorrect and should be conjugated as *llegue*.

40. c. The only difference between all the choices is the indirect object pronoun used to represent *la niñera*. With the verb *pagar*, whom you pay is the indirect object. In this case, it is *the babysitter*, or *la niñera*. Therefore, choices **b** (*la pagamos*) and **e** (*las pagamos*) are incorrect because they utilize direct object pronouns. Choices **a** (*les pagamos*) and **d** (*te pagamos*) use indirect object pronouns, but they are not the correct pronouns to refer to a third person (*la niñera*). *Le* is the only possible indirect object pronoun to refer to *la niñera*, which makes choice **c** (*le pagamos*) the only possible answer.

41. e. The first verb *exigir* requires the subjunctive form in the verb that follows *que* since it is a request. Since the verb *exigió* is in the past form, the subjunctive form of *tener* should also be in the past. Therefore, the imperfect subjunctive form is needed for *tener*. Choice **e** (*tuvieran*) given in the sentence is in the subjunctive form and the only possible answer. Choice **a** (*tuvieron*) is in the simple past, choice **b** (*tienen*) in the simple present, choice **c** (*tener*) in the infinitive, and choice **d** (*habrían tenido*) is in the conditional perfect.

42. b. The phrase *todos fueron eliminada* is the passive voice, but choice **e** (*eliminada*) is incorrect because it is feminine and singular and doesn't match the plural and masculine subject *todos*. A masculine and plural past participle is needed to correctly complete the phrase in the passive voice. Choices **a** (*incluyeron*) and **d** (*eliminaban*) are verbs in the past that do not fit the criteria. Choice **c** (*eliminado*) is a masculine past participle form, but it is not plural. Therefore, choice **b** (*descartados*) is the only possible answer because it is in the masculine and plural past participle form.

43. d. The article and adjective *el buen* before the word in question indicates the word needs to be masculine and singular. As a result, choice **e** (*operación*) is incorrect because it is feminine. The same criteria can be applied to choice **a** (*marchas*), which is incorrect because it is feminine and plural; choice **b** (*actividad*) is incorrect because it is feminine; and choice **c** (*movimientos*) is incorrect because it is plural. Therefore, choice **d** (*funcionamiento*) is the only possible answer because it is masculine and singular to correctly complete the phrase *el buen funcionamiento*.

44. a. Choice **e** (*mucho*) is an adjective used to describe nouns. The word *distraído* that follows the word in question is an adjective, not a noun. Choice **e** is incorrect. An adverb is needed to describe the adjective *distraído*. Therefore, we can also eliminate choices **b** (*tanto*) and **d** (*muchísima*) since they are both adjectives and are incorrect when placed before an adjective like *distraído* in this sentence. Choice **c** (*media*) is feminine and does not agree with the masculine adjective *distraído*. Therefore, choice **a** (*tan*) is the only possible answer to complete the idea *Estaba tan distraído* (*I was so distracted*).

45. a. The word *pronto* and the future tense of the second verb (*se dirigirán*) indicate the future is the correct tense for the first verb. Therefore, we can eliminate choices **c** (*hubiera realizado*) and **d** (*realizó*), which refer to the past conditional and simple past. Choice **e** (*se realizaran*) is the imperfect subjunctive, and the subjunctive form is incorrect in the sentence; also, choice **e** is plural when the subject *el concierto* is singular. Choice **b** (*realizarán*) is the future, but it is also the incorrect plural *ellos* form for the singular subject *el concierto*. Choice **a** (*realizará*) is singular and in the future; therefore, it is the only correct answer.

46. e. *If we had known about the harmful effects of cigarettes, we would have stopped smoking years ago.* This sentence follows the classic formation of a conditional sentence in Spanish. The imperfect subjunctive form is needed for the first verb since we are referring to a conditional situation in the past (*If we had known about . . .*). Choice **a** (*hemos*) would form the present perfect tense *hemos sabido* (*we have known*), so choice **a** is incorrect. Choice **b** (*habíamos*) would form the past perfect of *we had known*, but it is missing the subjunctive *if* element. Choice **c** (*ha*) forms the present perfect *ha sabido* (*he/she has known*), the same tense as choice **a** yet with a different subject; therefore, choice **c** is also incorrect. Choice **d** (*hayamos*) is the present subjunctive but the sentence refers to the past; choice **d** is incorrect. Choice **e** (*hubiéramos*) is in the imperfect subjunctive to form the idea *if we had known*; choice **e** is the only possible answer.

47. a. This sentence also follows the classic third conditional sentence form like the previous question. In this case, the *if* clause is in the second part of the sentence (notice the absence of the comma to indicate that the *if* clause is last), so the conditional form of *habría ido* must begin the sentence. Choice **a** (*Habría*) is the only possible answer to complete the sentence *I would have gone to Juliana's goodbye party if I had known she would never return to the country*. Choice **b** (*He*) is incorrect since it represents the present perfect form (*He ido: I have gone*). Choice **c** (*Haber*) is in the infinitive form; it is incorrect because the verb needs to be conjugated. Choice **d** (*Habrás*) is incorrect because it refers to the future; also, the change in subject to *tú* (*habrás ido: you will have gone*) does not agree with the rest of the sentence. Choice **e** (*Había*) is the imperfect, which simply describes an action in the past (*Había ido: I had gone*). Choice **a** is the only possible answer.

48. b. In this sentence, the word that follows *personal* must be an adjective to agree with the noun *personal* (*personnel*). The article *el* before *personal* indicates that the adjective needs to be masculine. Choice **a** (*subordinada*) is incorrect because it is a feminine adjective. Choices **c** (*gerencia*), **d** (*jefa*), and **e** (*administración*) are incorrect because they are feminine nouns. Even if we were to use *personal* as an adjective in this sentence, *el* does not agree in gender with all the feminine nouns in choices **c**, **d**, and **e**. Because of *el*, we need a masculine word after *personal*. Therefore, choice **b** (*administrativo*) is the only possible answer.

49. d. The combination of *requerir que* means the subjunctive must be used with *hablar* since it is a request. We are referring to multiple people (*agentes*) so the conjugation must also be plural. Choice **a** (*hablan*) is incorrect because it is in the simple present tense. Choice **b** (*hablarán*) is in the simple future. Choice **c** (*se habla*) is in the simple present as well. Choice **e** (*hable*) is in the subjunctive, but it is singular and doesn't agree with the plural subject *agentes*. Therefore, choice **d** (*hablen*) is the only possible answer because it is in the subjunctive form and is plural to agree with the subject *agentes*.

50. b. In order for this sentence to be grammatically correct, it needs the infinitive form of the verb *tomar*. Whenever a verb follows the preposition *de*, it should be in the infinitive form. Choice **a** (*tomando*) is in the gerund form, choice **c** (*haya tomado*) is in the present perfect subjunctive, choice **d** (*tomara*) is in the imperfect subjunctive, and choice **e** (*toma*) is in the simple present. Therefore, all other choices are incorrect and choice **b** (*tomar*) is the only possible answer.

Practice Test 2: Scoring and Diagnostic Chart

To evaluate how you did on this practice exam, start by totaling the number of correct responses on the two sections of this practice exam. First, find the number of questions you got right in each part. Questions you skipped or got wrong don't count; just add up the number of correct answers.

If at least 70% of your responses on the two parts are correct (47 correct), you are most likely prepared to pass the Border Patrol Exam. However, because the entrance process is competitive, you may need a higher score on the official exam to get accepted into the Border Patrol Academy.

In addition to seeing how you performed overall, you can use the following scoring chart to help diagnose your strengths and weaknesses in the different skills assessed on the exam, to better focus your study preparation.

LOGICAL REASONING SECTION	
SKILL	QUESTION
Reasoning about Groups and Categories	1–8
Reasoning about Events or Situations	9–16

SPANISH LANGUAGE SECTION	
SKILL	QUESTION
Part I	1, 2, 3, 4, 5, 6, 7, 8, 9, 10, 11, 12, 13, 14, 15, 16, 17, 18, 19, 20
Part II, Section I	21, 22, 23, 24, 25, 26, 27, 28, 29, 30
Part II, Section II	31, 32, 33, 34, 35, 36, 37, 38, 39, 40
Part II, Section III	41, 42, 43, 44, 45, 46, 47, 48, 49, 50

CHAPTER 5 ▶ PRACTICE TEST 3

This is the final practice test that contains logical reasoning and Spanish-language questions. (The next three tests will still have logical reasoning questions, but will test your skills with an artificial language.) Again, you should simulate the actual test-taking experience as closely as you can, including giving yourself four and a half hours to complete the test.

LEARNINGEXPRESS ANSWER SHEET

1. ⓐ ⓑ ⓒ ⓓ ⓔ
2. ⓐ ⓑ ⓒ ⓓ ⓔ
3. ⓐ ⓑ ⓒ ⓓ ⓔ
4. ⓐ ⓑ ⓒ ⓓ ⓔ
5. ⓐ ⓑ ⓒ ⓓ ⓔ
6. ⓐ ⓑ ⓒ ⓓ ⓔ
7. ⓐ ⓑ ⓒ ⓓ ⓔ
8. ⓐ ⓑ ⓒ ⓓ ⓔ
9. ⓐ ⓑ ⓒ ⓓ ⓔ
10. ⓐ ⓑ ⓒ ⓓ ⓔ
11. ⓐ ⓑ ⓒ ⓓ ⓔ
12. ⓐ ⓑ ⓒ ⓓ ⓔ
13. ⓐ ⓑ ⓒ ⓓ ⓔ
14. ⓐ ⓑ ⓒ ⓓ ⓔ
15. ⓐ ⓑ ⓒ ⓓ ⓔ
16. ⓐ ⓑ ⓒ ⓓ ⓔ

1. ⓐ ⓑ ⓒ ⓓ ⓔ
2. ⓐ ⓑ ⓒ ⓓ ⓔ
3. ⓐ ⓑ ⓒ ⓓ ⓔ
4. ⓐ ⓑ ⓒ ⓓ ⓔ
5. ⓐ ⓑ ⓒ ⓓ ⓔ
6. ⓐ ⓑ ⓒ ⓓ ⓔ
7. ⓐ ⓑ ⓒ ⓓ ⓔ
8. ⓐ ⓑ ⓒ ⓓ ⓔ
9. ⓐ ⓑ ⓒ ⓓ ⓔ
10. ⓐ ⓑ ⓒ ⓓ ⓔ
11. ⓐ ⓑ ⓒ ⓓ ⓔ
12. ⓐ ⓑ ⓒ ⓓ ⓔ
13. ⓐ ⓑ ⓒ ⓓ ⓔ
14. ⓐ ⓑ ⓒ ⓓ ⓔ
15. ⓐ ⓑ ⓒ ⓓ ⓔ
16. ⓐ ⓑ ⓒ ⓓ ⓔ
17. ⓐ ⓑ ⓒ ⓓ ⓔ
18. ⓐ ⓑ ⓒ ⓓ ⓔ
19. ⓐ ⓑ ⓒ ⓓ ⓔ
20. ⓐ ⓑ ⓒ ⓓ ⓔ
21. ⓐ ⓑ ⓒ ⓓ ⓔ
22. ⓐ ⓑ ⓒ ⓓ ⓔ
23. ⓐ ⓑ ⓒ ⓓ ⓔ
24. ⓐ ⓑ ⓒ ⓓ ⓔ
25. ⓐ ⓑ ⓒ ⓓ ⓔ
26. ⓐ ⓑ ⓒ ⓓ ⓔ
27. ⓐ ⓑ ⓒ ⓓ ⓔ
28. ⓐ ⓑ ⓒ ⓓ ⓔ
29. ⓐ ⓑ ⓒ ⓓ ⓔ
30. ⓐ ⓑ ⓒ ⓓ ⓔ
31. ⓐ ⓑ ⓒ ⓓ ⓔ
32. ⓐ ⓑ ⓒ ⓓ ⓔ
33. ⓐ ⓑ ⓒ ⓓ ⓔ
34. ⓐ ⓑ ⓒ ⓓ ⓔ
35. ⓐ ⓑ ⓒ ⓓ ⓔ
36. ⓐ ⓑ ⓒ ⓓ ⓔ
37. ⓐ ⓑ ⓒ ⓓ ⓔ
38. ⓐ ⓑ ⓒ ⓓ ⓔ
39. ⓐ ⓑ ⓒ ⓓ ⓔ
40. ⓐ ⓑ ⓒ ⓓ ⓔ
41. ⓐ ⓑ ⓒ ⓓ ⓔ
42. ⓐ ⓑ ⓒ ⓓ ⓔ
43. ⓐ ⓑ ⓒ ⓓ ⓔ
44. ⓐ ⓑ ⓒ ⓓ ⓔ
45. ⓐ ⓑ ⓒ ⓓ ⓔ
46. ⓐ ⓑ ⓒ ⓓ ⓔ
47. ⓐ ⓑ ⓒ ⓓ ⓔ
48. ⓐ ⓑ ⓒ ⓓ ⓔ
49. ⓐ ⓑ ⓒ ⓓ ⓔ
50. ⓐ ⓑ ⓒ ⓓ ⓔ

PRACTICE TEST 3

Logical Reasoning Test

1. Until the 1930s the majority of all legal immigrants in the United States were male. By the 1990s women made up just over half of all legal immigrants in the United States. Today, legal immigrants are generally younger than the native population of the United States, with the majority being between the ages of 15 and 34. Legal immigrants are more likely to be married and less likely to be divorced than native-born Americans of the same age.

   From the information given here, it CANNOT be validly concluded that:
   a. legal immigrants marry younger than their American counterparts.
   b. legal immigrants are less likely to be divorced than their same-age American counterparts.
   c. Americans are more likely to be divorced than legal immigrants of the same age.
   d. most legal immigrants are between the ages of 15 and 34.
   e. none of the above

2. A federal crime is an act that violates the federal legal code. State crimes are acts that violate state laws. An example of a federal crime is identity theft. An example of a state crime is burglary. Each state has different laws and constitutions, yet some crimes fall under the umbrella of both federal and state crimes.

   From the information given here, it can be validly concluded that:
   a. identity theft violates the federal legal code.
   b. burglary violates the federal legal code.
   c. identity theft can never be considered a federal crime.
   d. burglary can never be considered a federal crime.
   e. none of the above

3. It is possible to obtain U.S. citizenship at birth by being born in the United States or its territories (for example, the U.S. Virgin Islands or Guam), or by inheriting citizenship from parents who are U.S. citizens. Any child born in the United States or its territories while under American jurisdiction is a U.S. citizen at birth. This does not apply to foreign ambassadors; therefore, a child born in the United States to foreign ambassadors does not receive U.S. citizenship at birth. Jonah was not a U.S. citizen at birth.

   From the information given here, it CANNOT be validly concluded that:
   a. Jonah's parents were not foreign ambassadors.
   b. Jonah's parents were not U.S. citizens at the time of his birth.
   c. Jonah was not born in Guam.
   d. Jonah was not born in the U.S. Virgin Islands.
   e. none of the above

4. The officer in charge of the western sector is organizing team coverage of a particular area. She has 12 teams who report to her. Most of her teams are stationed along the border. Several teams are on sites across town. All teams must be available to travel to any station in the western sector.

   From the information given here, it can be validly concluded that:
   a. most of the teams are on sites across town.
   b. few of the teams are located at stations along the western border.
   c. teams on sites across town do not need to be available to travel to any station in the western sector.
   d. no team is exempt from traveling to any station in the western sector.
   e. only the teams located along the border must be available to travel to any station in the western sector.

5. A former employee reported that illegal narcotics were being sold at a certain pharmacy in an urban area. An investigation was conducted and it was determined that all of the illegal sales centered on the Drug Q; however, Drug Q was also prescribed and sold legally. Drug P is sometimes sold illegally, but no sales of Drug P were reported from this pharmacy.
From the information given here, it can be validly concluded that:
   a. Drug P was sold illegally at this pharmacy.
   b. some sales of Drug Q occurred legally at this pharmacy.
   c. some sales of Drug P occurred legally at this pharmacy.
   d. Drug Q was not sold illegally at this pharmacy.
   e. none of the above

6. Statistics show that so-called "border states" (states that lie on the border between the United States and another country) have a disproportionately high level of criminals who are illegal immigrants. Some examples of border states are Texas, New Mexico, and Arizona, among others. Most of the immigrants in New Mexico are legal residents; however, many are illegal.
From the information given here, it can be validly concluded that:
   a. all border states have a higher level of illegal immigrants than legal immigrants.
   b. there is more crime in New Mexico than in Texas.
   c. there are more illegal immigrants in New Mexico than legal immigrants.
   d. there are more legal immigrants in New Mexico than illegal immigrants.
   e. Texas, New Mexico, and Arizona are the only border states in the United States.

7. Agent Mitchell is in charge of all the patrols along the eastern side of the border on weekends. He has at his disposal a helicopter, some ATVs, a sedan, and some motorbikes. He is permitted to allow only experienced drivers to operate these vehicles. If Team 1 contains members with motorbike and helicopter experience; Team 2 contains members with helicopter, ATV, and motorbike experience; Team 3 contains members with helicopter and motorbike experience; and Team 4 contains members with sedan and ATV experience, how can the vehicles be distributed for weekend duty?
From the information given here, it can be validly concluded that the vehicle distribution could occur as follows:
   a. Team 1: motorbike, Team 2: helicopter, Team 3: ATV, Team 4: sedan
   b. Team 1: helicopter, Team 2: motorbike, Team 3: ATV, Team 4: sedan
   c. Team 1: sedan, Team 2: motorbike, Team 3: helicopter, Team 4: ATV
   d. Team 1: helicopter, Team 2: ATV, Team 3: motorbike, Team 4: sedan
   e. none of the above

8. An applicant may not be legally hired for a job until an employer verifies the applicant's identity and eligibility to work. The employer must confirm two things: that the documentation provided by the applicant belongs to the applicant who provides it, and that the applicant is authorized to work in the United States. Acceptable documents are listed on the Employment Eligibility Verification (I-9) form and include, among others, a United States passport, Permanent Resident Card or Alien Registration Receipt Card, or Temporary Resident Card. Employers are not permitted to request more than the number of documents listed on the I-9 or documents that are not listed on the I-9.

From the information given here, it can be validly concluded that:

a. an applicant may be hired for a job if the employer verifies only that she is authorized to work in the United States.
b. an applicant may be hired for a job if the employer verifies only that the identity documentation belongs to the applicant.
c. an applicant may not be legally hired for a job if she provides insufficient documentation.
d. an applicant may not be legally hired for a job if she provides sufficient documentation.
e. an applicant may be hired for a job if she provides an I-9.

9. Specialized education is not required for acceptance into the U.S. Border Patrol, but it is necessary to hold at minimum either a bachelor's degree from an accredited four-year college, or relevant work in law enforcement or the military, or in another stressful workplace where quick decisions need to be made. Alternatively, a combination of college education and relevant work experience may be accepted.

From the information given here, it can be validly concluded that:

a. if a bachelor's degree from an accredited college has not been earned, then relevant work experience may be accepted.
b. if a candidate is accepted into the Border Patrol, then he holds a bachelor's degree.
c. if a candidate has worked in law enforcement, then specialized education is necessary for acceptance.
d. if a candidate is accepted into the Border Patrol, then he does not hold a bachelor's degree.
e. if a bachelor's degree has been earned from a non-accredited college, then no specialized education is necessary for acceptance.

10. Certain skills are required for success as a Border Patrol Agent. One such skill is negotiation; an agent must work with others toward a mutually acceptable agreement that may involve exchanging specific resources or resolving differences, so the agent must be able to build consensus through give-and-take. Teamwork is also an important skill; it is necessary to encourage pride, trust, and group identity within the Border Patrol to foster commitment and to facilitate a sense of cooperation.

From the information given here, it CANNOT be validly concluded that:

a. if an individual is a Border Patrol Agent, then he or she is skilled in negotiating toward an acceptable outcome.
b. if an individual is a Border Patrol Agent, then he or she has developed teamwork skills.
c. if an individual has built consensus through give-and-take, then he or she is a Border Patrol Agent.
d. if an individual is a Border Patrol Agent, then he or she has built consensus through give-and-take.
e. none of the above

11. An employer can sponsor an individual's green card. It is a multi-step process that covers various categories for granting permanent residence to foreign nationals based on employment skills. Step 1 involves the individual's application for a labor certification through the employer to the Department of Labor. Step 2 requires the employer to file an Immigrant Petition for Alien Worker (Form I-140). The Department of State must then assign a current immigrant visa number. Steps 3 and 4 can occur concurrently, and involve the applicant applying for adjustment of status or going through consular processing.

From the information given here, it can be validly concluded that:

a. if the applicant has received processing through the consulate, then he or she has applied for adjustment of status.
b. if the applicant has filed an application for labor certification, then he or she has applied for adjustment of status.
c. if the Department of State has assigned an immigrant visa number, then the individual has filed an application for labor certification.
d. if an employer sponsors an individual's green card, then the multi-step process may be bypassed.
e. none of the above

12. In checking the employment documentation in a certain workplace, an agent uncovered a total of eight male and female illegal workers. Some were from Nicaragua, and some were from Panama. There were more men than women overall, but more men from Nicaragua and more women from Panama. Two women were from Panama.

From the information given here, it can be validly concluded that:

a. if two women were from Panama, then three women were from Nicaragua.
b. if two women were from Panama, then six men were from Nicaragua.
c. if three women were from Nicaragua, then four women were from Panama.
d. if two women were from Panama, then one woman was from Nicaragua.
e. if two men were from Nicaragua, then three women were from Panama.

13. All Border Patrol Agents must speak or learn Spanish to the required level of proficiency at the Border Patrol Academy. It is expected that agents will know the rules of Spanish grammar—for example, which nouns take feminine or masculine articles, when to use which type of pronoun (subject pronouns, direct object pronouns, indirect object pronouns, prepositional pronouns, and reflexive direct and indirect object pronouns), the correct position of words in a sentence, and verb conjugations.

From the information given here, it CANNOT be validly concluded that:

a. if an agent has passed through the Border Patrol program, then a certain level of Spanish language proficiency can be expected.
b. if an agent has a certain level of proficiency in the Spanish language, then he or she has a command of Spanish grammar.
c. if an agent has a certain level of proficiency in the Spanish language, then he or she has passed through the Border Patrol program.
d. if an agent has reached the required level of Spanish language proficiency, then he or she has an understanding of prepositional pronouns.
e. none of the above

14. The only ways for a naturalized U.S. citizen to lose his citizenship are for the individual to expatriate or be denaturalized. Denaturalization can occur if the naturalized U.S. citizen commits certain crimes, misrepresents facts on a legal permanent residence application, or leaves the United States within one year of naturalization to establish permanent residence elsewhere. Kareem is a naturalized U.S. citizen.
From the information given here, it can be validly concluded that:
a. if Kareem loses his U.S. citizenship without being denaturalized, then he must have expatriated.
b. if Kareem has committed no crimes, then he cannot be denaturalized.
c. if Kareem does not expatriate, then he cannot lose his U.S. citizenship.
d. if Kareem is denaturalized, then he must have made a misrepresentation on his legal permanent residence application.
e. none of the above

15. During wartime, Border Patrol Agents may be expected to withdraw from Border Patrol outposts to provide limited assistance to the U.S. Army, which may take over the management of all the border outposts at the international borders that separate the United States from the enemy country. Wartime assistance to the Army is essential, as Border Patrol Agents are familiar with the local terrain from their regular patrols during peacetime. During wartime, border outposts may be reworked into fortified positions in which regular Army units may operate to defend the territorial integrity of the country.
From the information given here, it CANNOT be validly concluded that:
a. if the Border Patrol has withdrawn from the outposts on the international border, then the Army may be operating from the outposts to defend against the enemy country.
b. if the Army is operating from border outposts, then it is likely that they have taken over management from the Border Patrol.
c. if it is wartime, then the Army may take over the management of border outposts.
d. if Border Patrol Agents are asked to provide assistance to the Army, then it is likely that it is wartime.
e. none of the above

16. Officers assigned to conduct a preliminary investigation are instructed to make every effort to obtain as much information as possible. The investigating officer must first ascertain if the suspect is still in the area and armed; proceed to the scene promptly and safely; render assistance to the injured; conduct the arrest of the criminal; locate, identify, and interview witnesses; interrogate the suspect; arrange for the collection of evidence; make an accurate report of the incident; and yield responsibility to the follow-up investigator.

From the information given here, it CANNOT be validly concluded that:
- **a.** if the officer has rendered assistance to the injured, then she has determined whether the suspect is still in the area.
- **b.** if the officer has arranged for the collection of evidence, then she has identified witnesses.
- **c.** if the criminal has been apprehended, then assistance has been rendered to the injured.
- **d.** if witnesses have been interviewed, then a report has been made.
- **e.** none of the above

Spanish Language Proficiency Test

Part I
Read the sentence and then choose the most appropriate synonym for the italicized word or phrase.

1. Muchos refugiados tuvieron que *escoger* entre la vida y la muerte cuando se fueron de su país.
- **a.** decidir
- **b.** escribir
- **c.** aprender
- **d.** caminar
- **e.** correr

2. Debido al peligro que corría en su país, el ciudadano *huyó* durante la noche.
- **a.** llegó
- **b.** entró
- **c.** escapó
- **d.** sacó
- **e.** aprendió

3. En los cincuenta años que lleva trabajando el oficial en la frontera, tiene muchas historias interesantes por *contar*.
- **a.** lograr
- **b.** mentir
- **c.** silenciar
- **d.** compartir
- **e.** hacer

4. El policía *se acercó* al carro con mucho cuidado.
- **a.** llegar
- **b.** vendió
- **c.** se fue
- **d.** manejó
- **e.** se aproximó

5. Cuando los españoles llegaron a América, *conquistaron* muchas tierras indígenas y las proclamaron españolas.
- **a.** se tomaron
- **b.** regalaron
- **c.** perdieron
- **d.** arreglaron
- **e.** pintaron

6. «¡Qué *espanto*!», exclamó la mujer al encontrar a su hijo escondido dentro del armario.
- **a.** susto
- **b.** alegría
- **c.** chiste
- **d.** payaso
- **e.** bonito

PRACTICE TEST 3

7. El *granjero* quiere cambiar la mitad de su cosecha por unos galones de leche.
   a. odontólogo
   b. accionista
   c. camarero
   d. campesino
   e. comerciante

8. La señora llamó a emergencias porque su *marido* se desmayó.
   a. vecino
   b. cuñado
   c. abuelo
   d. esposo
   e. hijo

9. *A veces* jugamos al fútbol entre semana si no tenemos mucha tarea.
   a. Casi siempre
   b. Nunca
   c. Siempre
   d. De vez en cuando
   e. Jamás

10. *Aún* me faltan tres semanas para graduarme del colegio.
   a. Aunque
   b. Sin embargo
   c. Todavía
   d. No obstante
   e. Además

11. Mi hijo tiene mucha *destreza* para jugar al ajedrez.
   a. pereza
   b. ánimo
   c. paciencia
   d. estudio
   e. habilidad

12. Cuando el oficial se dio cuenta del peligro que estaba corriendo, pidió *refuerzos* para protegerse.
   a. consejo
   b. apoyo
   c. su chaleco
   d. un cuaderno
   e. su carro

13. El *lugar* tenía mucho armamento y contrabando cuando la policía lo descubrió.
   a. cajón
   b. robar
   c. sitio
   d. ladrón
   e. ordenador

14. El viajero no tenía *permiso* para llevar armas.
   a. maleta
   b. campo
   c. espacio
   d. licencia
   e. carro

15. El *propietario* del hotel no permite que se hospede ningún mendigo.
   a. dueño
   b. huésped
   c. cocinero
   d. gerente
   e. guía

16. *Abrieron* la caja con mucho cuidado sin saber su contenido.
   a. Taparon
   b. Destaparon
   c. Cerraron
   d. Envolvieron
   e. Armaron

17. La muchacha *supuso* que tenía una deuda sumamente grande en el banco.
   a. asumió
   b. calculó
   c. contó
   d. explicó
   e. eligió

18. El científico *creó* un producto revolucionario para la industria automotriz.
   a. rechazó
   b. vendió
   c. sembró
   d. compró
   e. inventó

19. A cambio de una membrecía de por vida a un club campestre exclusivo, el oficial dejó pasar los *familiares* de un político importante a los Estados Unidos.
   a. conocidos
   b. hijos
   c. parientes
   d. padres
   e. amantes

20. El alumno no pudo *enfocarse* en sus materias porque su mamá estaba muy mal de salud.
   a. enseñar
   b. concentrarse
   c. mentir
   d. comprobar
   e. aprender

Part II, Section I

Read each sentence carefully. Select the appropriate word or phrase to fill each blank space.

21. Fuimos _____ lunes a la embajada a pedir la visa _____ visitar a mi mamá.
   a. en el, por
   b. en el, para
   c. los, por
   d. el, para
   e. en, para

22. Nosotros _____ ido al banco ayer pero empezó a llover a cántaros y _____ tocó quedarnos en casa todo el día.
   a. haber, se
   b. habría, les
   c. hemos, nos
   d. a veríamos, nos
   e. hubiéramos, nos

23. Fueron a _____ a los detenidos en la cárcel pero el oficial no les _____ entrar.
   a. han visitado, dejaron
   b. visitaron, permitieran
   c. visitar, permitió
   d. visitando, quiso
   e. visitarse, permitieron

24. Por favor _____ al tanto de qué sucedió con tu marido _____ la frontera.
   a. ponte, por
   b. poner, para
   c. pongate, cerca de
   d. puesto, por
   e. poneste, en

25. La viuda _____ en portar los documentos _____ encima.
   a. insiste, necesarios
   b. insistida, importante
   c. habías insistido, necesarios
   d. insiste, necesario
   e. insistir, importantes

26. Los oficiales que siguen en capacitación _____ observar la _____ diaria en la frontera.
   a. frecuentemente, tareas
   b. raramente, rutina
   c. a menudo, quehacer
   d. soler, tareas
   e. suelen, rutina

27. El niño abandonado pidió _____ una llamada a su tío para que lo _____.
   a. hiciera, recogieras
   b. llamar, recoger
   c. hizo, recogió
   d. hacer, recoge
   e. hacer, recogiera

28. Ayer mi socio me _____ que la comisión se la _____ por medio de una transferencia bancaria.
   a. pides, envíes
   b. pidió, enviara
   c. pedí, envía
   d. pidió, envió
   e. pidieron, enviaran

29. ¿Oyeron _____ sobre el compañero que fue _____ por sobornar a un inmigrante?
   a. ellos, arrestando
   b. ellas, arrestada
   c. ustedes, arrestado
   d. usted, arrestado
   e. ustedes, arrestados

30. Ella _____ levantó temprano y _____ preparó el desayuno a sus hijos.
   a. se, les
   b. se, los
   c. te, las
   d. le, las
   e. les, le

Part II

Read each sentence carefully. Select the one sentence that is correct.

31.
   a. Busqué para los dos libros pero nunca los encontré.
   b. Busqué por los dos libros pero nunca los encontro.
   c. Busqué los dos libros pero nunca los encontré.
   d. Había buscado por los dos libros pero nunca tuve suerte.
   e. ¿Puedes buscar por mis libros?

32.
   a. El doctor le dio una otra pastilla a su paciente antes del tratamiento.
   b. El doctor le dio otro píldora a su paciente antes del tratamiento.
   c. El doctor lo dio un otro medicamento a su paciente antes del tratamiento.
   d. El doctor le dio un otro medicamento a su paciente antes del tratamiento.
   e. El doctor le dio otra píldora a su paciente antes del tratamiento.

33.
   a. Me duelen las piernas de tanto correr.
   b. Me duelo mis piernas de tanto correr.
   c. Me duele las piernas de tanto correr.
   d. Abrí mis ojos cuando el despertador sonó.
   e. Abro los ojos cuando el despertador sonaba.

PRACTICE TEST 3

34. a. Me gusto mucho el nuevo carro.
b. Me encanta los asientos de cuero en el carro.
c. Les encanto el carro nuevo y quieren uno igual.
d. Les encanta el nuevo carro y quieren uno igual.
e. Me gustan el nuevo carro y quieren uno igual.

35. a. ¿Quién fuiste al teatro contigo?
b. No tengo nadie ir al teatro con.
c. ¿Con quién fuiste al teatro el domingo pasado?
d. ¿Quién fuiste al teatro el domingo pasado?
e. No fui el teatro contigo.

36. a. Un amigo de mío empezó entrenamiento con la DEA pero nunca lo terminó.
b. Un amigo mío empezó entrenamiento con la DEA pero nunca lo terminó.
c. Un amigo de mi empezó entrenamiento por la DEA pero nunca lo terminó.
d. Me amigo empezó entrenamiento para la DEA pero nunca lo terminó.
e. Un mi amigo empezó entrenamiento con la DEA pero nunca lo terminó.

37. a. Soy ingeniero, pero me gusta dibujar en mi tiempo libre.
b. Soy un ingeniero, pero mi gusta dibujar en mi tiempo libre.
c. Estoy ingeniero, pero me gusta dibujar en mi tiempo libre.
d. Estoy un ingeniero, pero me gusta dibujar en mi tiempo libre.
e. Soy un ingeniero, pero me gusta dibujar en mi tiempo libre.

38. a. Les pagan a los traductores cuarenta dólares para hora.
b. El traductor trabaja cuatro días para semana.
c. Ayer los intérpretes pidieron un aumento de cincuenta dólares por hora.
d. Les pagan a los traductores cuarenta dólares con hora.
e. Ayer los intérpretes recibieron un aumento de cincuenta dólares para hora.

39. a. No conozco a la respuesta.
b. El sabe Francia; fue ahí hace tres años.
c. Sabemos a la respuesta porque estudiamos mucho.
d. Conozco todos los países de Suramérica.
e. No conozco a Francia.

40. a. Se recomienda a los visitantes del parque zoológico que no toquen a los animales.
b. Se recomienda a los visitantes del parque zoológico que no tocan a los animales.
c. Recomiendan a los visitantes del parque zoológico no tocando a los animales.
d. Se recomienda a los visitantes del parque zoológico que no tocar a los animales.
e. Recomiendan a los visitantes del parque zoológico que no tocen a los animales.

Part II, Section III

Read each sentence carefully. Select the correct word or phrase to replace the italicized portion of the sentence. In those cases in which the sentence needs no correction, select choice e.

41. El funcionario *los* dijo varias veces a sus oficiales que no se integraran con la gente del pueblo.
a. las
b. les
c. le
d. los se
e. No es necesario hacer ninguna corrección.

42. Los animales que llegaron desde México acaban de *cumpliendo* su cuarentena.
   a. han cumplido
   b. cumplido
   c. cumplir
   d. cumplen
   e. No es necesario hacer ninguna corrección.

43. Para los viajeros que quieren ir a Los Angeles, *tengo* que tomar el bus y el recorrido es de dos horas y media.
   a. he
   b. tener
   c. haber
   d. hay
   e. No es necesario hacer ninguna corrección.

44. El hombre *se reunió* con su hermano menor después de ocho años de no verlo.
   a. se habrán reunido
   b. se reuniste
   c. se reunirán
   d. nos hubiéramos reunido
   e. No es necesario hacer ninguna corrección.

45. Los perros ayudan a proteger a los oficiales cuando los delincuentes *las* atacan.
   a. los
   b. lo
   c. les
   d. le
   e. No es necesario hacer ninguna corrección.

46. La reunión de la junta directiva *es* en la sala de conferencias.
   a. está
   b. hay
   c. haber
   d. son
   e. No es necesario hacer ninguna corrección.

47. Antes de que *irte*, quiero hacerte un par de preguntas sobre tu día.
   a. te ves
   b. te vas
   c. te vayas
   d. te has ido
   e. No es necesario hacer ninguna corrección.

48. Le otorgaron el premio *porque* ser muy responsable y trabajador.
   a. cómo
   b. que
   c. para
   d. por
   e. No es necesario hacer ninguna corrección.

49. *Haber* seis meses que la policía busca nuevos miembros para empezar entrenamiento.
   a. Habían
   b. Había
   c. Hacía
   d. Hace
   e. No es necesario hacer ninguna corrección.

50. El jefe quisiera que *cerráramos* la frontera debido a la amenaza recibida.
   a. se cierra
   b. cierremos
   c. cerramos
   d. cerrar
   e. No es necesario hacer ninguna corrección.

PRACTICE TEST 3

Answers

Logical Reasoning

1. **e.** None of the choices provides information that cannot be obtained from the information in the paragraph, so choice **e** is correct. Choices **a**, **b**, **c**, and **d** restate information provided by the paragraph, so they are incorrect.

2. **a.** Choice **a** restates information given in the first and third sentences within the paragraph, so it is the correct answer. Choice **b** contradicts information given in the first and fourth sentences within the paragraph, so it is incorrect. Identity theft is a federal crime according to the information in the paragraph, so choice **c** is incorrect. It is unclear from the information in the paragraph whether there are circumstances that could cause burglary to be both a state and federal crime, so choice **d** is incorrect. Choice **e** is incorrect because the correct response is found within the answers.

3. **b.** Choice **b** is the only response that provides a condition that would make Jonah not a U.S. citizen according to the paragraph, so this is the correct answer. If Jonah's parents were not foreign ambassadors but he were born in the United States or one of its territories, he would be considered a U.S. citizen. Therefore, Jonah not being a U.S. citizen at birth does not provide information to conclude whether Jonah's parents were foreign ambassadors, so this answer is not correct. If Jonah were born in Guam or the U.S. Virgin Islands, choices **c** and **d**, he would still be a citizen, so these answers are incorrect. The correct answer is provided within the choices, so choice **e** is incorrect.

4. **d.** Choice **d** restates information provided in the last sentence of the paragraph, and is therefore correct. Choices **a** and **b** contradict information presented in the third sentence of the paragraph, and are therefore incorrect. Choices **c** and **e** contradict information provided in the last sentence, and are therefore incorrect.

5. **b.** Choice **b** restates information found in the second sentence of the paragraph, so it is the correct answer. Choices **a** and **c** contradict the last sentence of the paragraph, which states that no sales of Drug P were reported at the pharmacy, so it is not the correct answer. Choice **d** contradicts information in the second sentence in the paragraph, so it is incorrect. Choice **e** is incorrect because the correct response is found within the answers.

6. **d.** Choice **d** restates information given in the last sentence in the paragraph, and is therefore correct. Choice **a** makes an assumption that is not supported by evidence given in the paragraph, and is therefore incorrect. No information is provided in the paragraph on the crime in New Mexico as compared to Texas, so choice **b** is incorrect. Choice **c** contradicts information given in the last sentence in the paragraph, so it is an incorrect answer. The second sentence in the paragraph implies that there are other border states in addition to the ones mentioned (and, indeed, California is one, as well as all the states that border Canada), so choice **e** is incorrect.

7. d. The distribution in choice **d** ensures that experienced members of each team are driving the vehicles according to the information in the paragraph, so it is the correct answer. Choices **a** and **b** distribute an ATV to a team without the relevant experience, so they are incorrect. Choice **c** puts a team without relevant experience in charge of the sedan, so it is incorrect. Choice **e** is incorrect because the correct response is found within the answers.

8. c. Choice **c** is the correct answer, as it restates information provided in the first sentence in the paragraph. Choices **a** and **b** contradict information provided in the second sentence in the paragraph, so they are incorrect. Choice **d** contradicts information provided in the first sentence in the paragraph, so it is incorrect. Choice **e** is incorrect because the applicant needs to provide documentation listed on the I-9, not the I-9 itself.

9. a. Choice **a** restates information from the first sentence in the paragraph, so it is the correct answer. Choices **b**, **c**, **d**, and **e** contain faulty assumptions that could not have been concluded from information in the paragraph, so they are incorrect.

10. c. Choice **c** is a faulty assumption that could not have been concluded from the information in the paragraph, so it is the correct answer.

11. c. Choice **c** restates information found in the third and fifth sentences in the paragraph, and is therefore the correct answer. Choices **a**, **b**, and **d** contradict information found in the paragraph, and are therefore incorrect answers. Because the correct response is found within the answers, choice **e** is incorrect.

12. d. Since there are more men than women, there must be at least five men. Since there are two women from Panama, there must be one from Nicaragua. The only possible scenario is: two women from Panama, one woman from Nicaragua, one man from Panama, and four men from Nicaragua. Choice **d** aligns with this scenario. Choices **a** and **c** have too many women because the total number is eight and there are more men than women. The paragraph states that there are more men from Nicaragua and more women from Panama, which means that there must be at least one man and one woman from each country. Therefore, choice **b** is not possible. Choice **e** contradicts information found in the last sentence of the paragraph, so it is incorrect.

13. c. Although it is true that an agent who has passed through the Border Patrol program is expected to have a certain level of Spanish language proficiency, the opposite is not necessarily true and could not have been concluded from the paragraph, so choice **c** is correct.

14. a. Choice **a** restates information given in the first sentence of the paragraph, and is therefore the correct answer. Choices **b**, **c**, and **d** do not take into account that there is more than one way to be naturalized, and are therefore incorrect. Because the correct response is found in the answers, choice **e** is incorrect.

15. e. Since all the choices contain information that can be concluded from the paragraph, choice **e** is the correct answer.

16. d. Choice **d** confuses the order of investigation and can therefore not be concluded from the information in the paragraph, so it is the correct answer. Choices **a**, **b**, and **c** restate information found within the paragraph, so they are incorrect. Because the correct response is found in the answers, choice **e** is incorrect.

Spanish Language

1. a. *Decidir* in choice **a** means *to decide* and it is the word closest in meaning to *escoger*, which means *to choose*. Choice **b** means *to write*, choice **c** *to learn*, choice **d** *to walk*, and choice **e** *to run*. Choice **a** is the only possible answer.

2. c. Choices **a** (*llegó: he arrived*) and **b** (*entró: he entered*) are the antonyms of *huyó*, which means *he fled*. They are therefore not possible answers. Choices **d** (*sacó: he took out/removed*) and **e** (*aprendió: he learned*) do not make any logical sense in the sentence and their meanings are very different from *huyó*. Therefore, choice **c** (*escapó: he escaped*) is the only possible answer.

3. d. Choice **a** (*lograr: to achieve*) is not a synonym of *contar* (*to tell*), nor is choice **b** (*mentir: to lie*), which changes the meaning of the sentence. Choice **c** (*silenciar: to silent*) means the opposite of *contar* and is therefore not a possible answer either. Choice **e** (*hacer: to do/make*) also conveys a different action. Therefore, choice **d** (*compartir: to share*) is the only possible answer; when a story is *told* to someone, it is *shared* with someone.

4. e. The verb in choice **a** (*llegar: to arrive*) gives a similar meaning to the original word (*se acercó: he approached*) but it is not properly conjugated and therefore not a possible answer. Choices **b** (*vendió: he sold*) and **d** (*manejó: he drove*) convey completely different meanings. Choice **c** (*manejó: he drove*) is a different meaning from *se acercó*. Choice **e** (*se aproximó*) means the same as *se acercó* and is conjugated the same as *se acercó*; therefore, it is the only possible answer.

5. a. Although all choices are in the correct *ellos* form, only choice **a** (*se tomaron: they took*) gives the same meaning as *conquistaron* (*they conquered*). Choices **b** (*regalaron: they gave as a gift/gifted*), **c** (*perdieron: they lost*), **d** (*arreglaron: they fixed*), and **e** (*pintaron: they painted*) all convey very different ideas that would greatly change the action of the subject *los españoles*. Choice **a** means *they took* and is therefore the choice closest in meaning and the only possible answer.

6. a. Although all choices fit in the sentence and are grammatically correct, only choice **a** (*susto: scare*) gives the same meaning as *espanto* (*fright*). Choice **b** (*alegría*) conveys the opposite, meaning *happiness* or *joy*; choice **c** (*chiste*) refers to a joke or something funny; choice **d** (*payaso*) means *clown* and the expression *qué payaso* is used when calling someone a clown. Choice **e** (*bonito*) means *pretty*, which is very different in meaning from the original word *espanto*. Therefore, choice **a** is the only possible answer.

PRACTICE TEST 3

7. d. Although all choices are grammatically correct, only choice **d** (*campesino*) represents the same profession of a *farmer*. All other choices given are executed in a completely different environment. *Odontólogo* in choice **a** is a *dentist*, *accionista* in choice **b** is a *shareholder*, *camarero* in choice **c** is a *waiter*, and *comerciante* in choice **e** is a *trader* or *merchant*. Choice **d** is the only possible answer.

8. d. Choice **d** (*esposo*) is the only word that means the same as *marido* (*husband*). All other choices represent different family members and friends: *vecino* in choice **a** means *neighbor*; *cuñado* in choice **b** means *brother-in-law*; *abuelo* in choice **c** means *grandfather*; *hijo* in choice **e** means *son*. Choice **d** is the only possible answer.

9. d. All choices work grammatically in the sentence and are time expressions, but only choice **d** (*De vez en cuando: Once in a while*) conveys the same time reference as *A veces* (*sometimes*). Choice **a** (*Casi siempre: Almost always*), choice **b** (*Nunca: Never*), choice **c** (*Siempre: Always*), and choice **e** (*Jamás: Never*) are not as close in meaning as choice **d**.

10. c. Only choice **c** (*Todavía: Still*) gives the same meaning as *Aún* (*Still*) in the sentence to convey the idea that the subject *Still has three weeks left before graduating from high school*. All other expressions given in choices **a, b, d,** and **e** change the idea and are therefore not synonyms and not possible answers. *Aunque* in choice **a** means *Although*; *Sin embargo* in choice **b** means *However*; *No obstante* in choice **d** means *Nevertheless* (a synonym of choice **b**, *Sin embargo*), and *Además* in choice **e** means *Furthermore*. Choice **c** is the only synonym.

11. e. Choices **b** (*ánimo: motivation*) and **d** (*estudio: schooling*) can immediately be disqualified because they are masculine nouns, and a feminine noun is needed to agree with *mucha*. Choices **a** (*pereza: laziness*) and **c** (*paciencia: patience*), while they make grammatical and logical sense in the sentence, do not convey the same meaning as *destreza* (*skill*). Choice **e** (*habilidad: ability*) is the only possible synonym of *destreza*.

12. b. Although all choices are grammatically correct, only choice **b** (*apoyo: support*) conveys the same idea and means the same as *refuerzos* (*reinforcement/back-up*). The other choices—**a** (*consejo: advice*), **c** (*su chaleco: his jacket*), **d** (*un cuaderno: a notebook*), and **e** (*su carro: his car*)—would change the meaning of the sentence and are therefore incorrect.

13. c. The word *lugar* (*place*) is a noun and so only another noun can be a synonym. We can therefore eliminate choice **b** (*robar: to rob*), which is a verb and doesn't share the same meaning. Choices **a** (*cajón: drawer*), **d** (*ladrón: thief*), and **e** (*ordenador: computer*) do not convey the same idea as *lugar* either since they represent objects (choices **a** and **e**) and a person (choice **d**); the sentence describes a *place*. Choice **c** (*sitio: site*) is the only possible synonym.

14. d. Although all choices given work grammatically in the sentence, only choice **d** (*licencia: license*) conveys the same idea as *permiso* (*permit*). All the other choices change the idea of the sentence and are therefore incorrect. *Maleta* in choice **a** is a *suitcase*; both choices **b** (*campo*) and **c** (*espacio*) refer to *space* or *room*; choice **e** refers to a *car*. Choice **d** is the only possible answer.

15. a. All choices represent different people who may be found at a hotel, but only choice **a** (*dueño*: owner) gives the same meaning as *propietario* (owner). *Huésped* in choice **b** means *guest*; *cocinero* in choice **c** means *cook*; *gerente* in choice **d** means *manager*; *guía* in choice **e** means *guide*. Therefore, choice **a** is the only possible answer.

16. b. Choices **a** and **c** (*Taparon* and *Cerraron* both mean *They closed*) are antonyms of *abrieron* (*they opened*). Choices **d** and **e** convey a different action: *Envolvieron* in choice **d** means *They wrapped* and *Armaron* in choice **e** means *They assembled*. Choice **b** (*Destaparon: They opened*) is the only possible answer.

17. b. *Asumir* in choice **a** does not mean the same as *suponer* (*to assume*). *Asumir* means *to take charge of/take on*. Choices **c** (*contó*: she told), **d** (*explicó*: she explained), and **e** (*eligió*: she chose) all have different meanings from the verb in question *supuso*. Choice **b** (*calculó*: she figured/calculated) is the only possible answer.

18. e. *Creó* (*he created*) shares its meaning with choice **e** (*inventó*: he invented). Choices **a** (*rechazó*: he rejected), **b** (*vendió*: he sold), **c** (*sembró*: he planted), and **d** (*compró*: he bought) all convey different actions. Only choice **e** is a synonym of the verb *crear*.

19. c. Although choices **b** (*hijos*: children) and **d** (*padres*: parents) do represent family members, they represent specific family members that are not the same as *familiares* (*family members*). Choices **a** (*conocidos*: acquaintances) and **e** (*amantes*: lovers) represent relationships even further from the meaning of *familiares*. Choice **c** (*parientes*: relatives) is the only possible synonym.

20. b. Only choice **b** (*concentrarse*: to concentrate) conveys the same meaning as *enfocarse* (*to focus*). All other choices have different meanings and are therefore not possible answers. *Enseñar* in choice **a** means *to teach*; *mentir* in choice **c** means *to lie*; *comprobar* in choice **d** means *to confirm/prove*; *aprender* in choice **e** means *to learn*.

21. d. Unlike English, where the expression *on Monday* is correct, Spanish does not use *en* before a day of the week. Therefore, choices **a** (*en el, por*), **b** (*en el, para*), and **e** (*en, para*) are not possible answers. Choice **a** is also not an answer because the use of *por* + infinitive verb is used to express an action that has yet to be done (i.e., *la cena está por cocinar*), not a purpose like *para* + infinitive verb expresses. The sentence reads: *We went to the embassy to request a visa to visit my mother.* *Visiting my mother* is the reason why *we went to the embassy*. Only *para* can be used in the second blank. For that same reason, choice **c** (*los, por*) is not a possible answer either. Choice **d** (*el, para*) is the only possible answer.

22. e. The first blank needs to be an auxiliary verb in the *nosotros* form to agree with the subject. With this criterion, we can eliminate choices **a** (*haber, se*) and **b** (*habría, les*) as possible answers because the verb is not in the *nosotros* form. The first answer in choice **d** (*a veríamos, nos*) sounds similar to choice **e** (*hubiéramos, nos*) but the spelling and verb are incorrect. Choice **d** is not possible as it is only phonetically similar to the right answer. The sentence requires a conditional auxiliary verb in the first space; the action didn't end up happening because, as the second part of the sentence indicates, *it began to rain*. We want to convey the idea *we would have*. The first answer *hemos* in choice **c** (*hemos, nos*) is the present perfect, which translates in the sentence as *we have gone*. Choice **c** is therefore not correct. The idea *we would have* is conveyed with choice **e** (*hubiéramos, nos*), the only possible answer.

23. c. An infinitive form of the verb is needed in the first space since it follows an already conjugated verb *fueron*. Therefore, choices **a** (*han visitado, dejaron*), **b** (*visitaron, permitieran*), and **d** (*visitando, quiso*) can be eliminated because the first answer is a conjugated verb. The verb *visitar* is not reflexive so choice **e** (*visitarse, permitieron*) is not a possible answer either; also, the second answer *permitieron* doesn't agree with its singular subject *el oficial*. Choice **c** (*visitar, permitió*) is the only possible answer.

24. a. Choice **c** (*pongate, cerca de*) is incorrect because *ponga* is the formal *Ud.* command and the *te* afterward belongs with the *tú* form; *pongate* is not a correct word or expression in Spanish. The expression *ponerse al tanto* needs the reflexive *se* so we can eliminate choices **b** (*poner, para*) and **d** (*puesto, por*) because they are lacking the reflexive *se* with their form of *poner*. Choice **e** (*poneste, en*) does not consider that *poner* changes to an irregular *pon* when it is a command in the *tú* form; *poneste* is not a word. Choice **a** (*ponte, por*) is the only possible answer since it correctly uses the irregular command of *pon* with the reflexive *te* to form *ponte*, and then uses *por* to signify *by* or *close* to the border.

25. a. Choices **b** (*insistida, importante*), **c** (*habías insistido, necesarios*), and **e** (*insistir, importantes*) do not conjugate the verb *insistir* correctly to agree with the third-person subject *la viuda* (*the widow*). Choice **d** (*insiste, necesario*) conjugates the verb correctly, but the singular adjective *necesario* does not agree with the plural noun *documentos* for the second blank. Only choice **a** (*insiste, necesarios*) is a possible answer because it correctly conjugates *insistir* to *insiste* to agree with the subject *viuda*, and the adjective *necesarios* is both plural and masculine to agree with *documentos*.

26. e. Because the verb *observar* that follows the first blank is in its infinitive form, a conjugated verb is needed before it. Therefore, choices **a** (*frecuentemente, tareas*), **b** (*raramente, rutina*), and **c** (*a menudo, quehacer*) are not possible answers because their first answers are expressions of time, not verbs. Choice **d** (*soler, tareas*) has a verb, but it is in its infinitive form (*soler*) and does not fit in the sentence. The noun for the second blank must agree with the adjective *diaria*. With these two criteria, only choice **e** (*suelen, rutina*) is a possible answer; *suelen* is the conjugated form of *soler* to agree with the subject *los oficiales* and precede *observar*; also, *rutina* is both singular and feminine to agree with the adjective *diaria*.

27. e. The first blank needs to be in the infinitive or gerund form since it follows the conjugated verb *pidió*. Therefore, choices **a** (*hiciera, recogieras*) and **c** (*hizo, recogió*) are not possible answers because their first answers are conjugated verbs. The word choice of *llamar* is redundant in choice **b** (*llamar, recoger*) and the second blank is not conjugated properly. In the second blank, the imperfect subjunctive form is needed because the sentence is in the past and the blank follows the expression *para que*, which will always require the subjunctive. Choice **d** (*hacer, recoge*) provides a simple present conjugation of the second verb *recoger* (not subjunctive). Choice **e** (*hacer, recogiera*) is the only possible answer. Its first blank is in the infinitive form, and the second word *recogiera* is in the imperfect subjunctive.

28. b. The word *ayer* indicates that the sentence refers to the past. Also, the conjugation of the first verb must be in the third person to agree with *mi socio*. Therefore, choices **a** (*pides, envies*), **c** (*pedí, envía*), and **e** (*pidieron, enviaran*) are not possible answers. The verb *pedir + que* requires the use of the subjunctive for the second blank, so choice **d** (*pidió, envió*) with *envió* in the simple past is not correct. Choice **b** (*pidió, enviara*) is the only possible answer; *pidió* agrees with *mi socio*, and *enviara* is correctly conjugated in the imperfect subjunctive.

29. c. The pronoun for the first blank must agree with *oyeron*. Choice **d** (*usted, arrestado*) is incorrect because *usted* does not agree with *oyeron*. Answers for the second blank need to agree with the masculine and singular *compañero*; choices **b** (*arrestada* is feminine) and **e** (*arrestados* is plural and masculine) are therefore not correct. The answer for the second blank must follow the passive voice structure of *fue* + past participle to express *was arrested*. Choice **a** is incorrect because *arrestando* is the gerund form and means *arresting*, not *arrested*. Choice **c** (*ustedes, arrestado*) is the only possible answer. *Ustedes* corresponds with the verb *oyeron* and the singular and masculine *arrestado* agrees with *compañero* to create the passive structure *fue arrestado* (*was arrested*).

30. a. The first verb *levantarse* is reflexive and is referring to the third person *ella*, so only *se* works in the first blank. Therefore, choices **c** (*te, las*), **d** (*le, las*), and **e** (*les, le*) are not possible answers because they do not use *se*. Choices **a** and **b** are left as possible answers. The second space refers to an indirect object *sus hijos* for whom she made breakfast. Choice **b** (*se, los*) uses a direct object pronoun *los* for its second answer and is therefore incorrect. Choice **a** (*se, les*) uses the indirect object pronoun *les* to refer to *her children* and is therefore the only possible answer.

31. c. A very common error in Spanish is putting *por* or *para* after *buscar* to mirror *look for* in English. However, it is incorrect since the verb *buscar* alone conveys this idea. All choices except choice **c** use either *por* or *para* after the conjugated verb and are therefore incorrect. Additionally, *encontro* in choice **b** is not a word; it either needs to stem change to be in the first person present form as *encuentro* or it needs an accent over the *o* to be in the third person past form *encontró*. Choice **c** is the only correct sentence.

32. e. Choices **a**, **c**, and **d** are incorrect because they use *un* or *una* before *otro* or *otra*. The indefinite article *un* or any variation thereof is not needed before any form of *otro* and is incorrect. Choice **b** is incorrect because *píldora* is feminine and requires the feminine form of *otra*, not *otro* as it is given in sentence **b**. Therefore, choice **e** is the only possible answer because it uses *otra* without any indefinite article before it, and *otra* is feminine to agree with *píldora*.

33. a. Body parts almost always use a definite article (*el, la, los, las*) before them instead of possessive adjectives (*my, your*, etc.) like in English. We can therefore eliminate choices **b** (*mis piernas*) and **d** (*mis ojos*) as possible answers since they use possessive adjectives. Choice **b** is also incorrect because the verb *doler* refers to *piernas* and must therefore be plural (*duelen* instead of *duelo*); for that same reason, choice **c** is also incorrect (*duelen* instead of *duele*). Choice **e** incorrectly uses the present tense (*abro*) and the past tense (*sonaba*) in the same sentence. Choice **a** is the only grammatically correct sentence.

34. d. Choices **a**, **b**, **c**, and **e** are incorrectly conjugated with the forms of *gustar* and *encantar* to agree with the objects given in the sentence. *Gustar* and *encantar* must refer to the object(s) the person likes, not the person. In choice **a**, *me gusta* should be used instead of *me gusto* since it refers to *el nuevo carro*. The same principle applies in choices **b**, **c**, and **e**. In choice **b**, the object is *the seats* (*los asientos*), and therefore *encanta* should be *encantan*. In choice **c**, *les encanto* should be *les encanta* since *encanta* refers to the *car* that *delights* or *fascinates them*. In choice **e**, *gustan* should be *gusta* to refer to *el nuevo carro*, and *quieren* should be *quiero* to agree with the subject *yo*. Choice **d** is the only sentence that correctly conjugates its verb to agree with the object *el nuevo carro*.

35. c. A preposition should never end a sentence in Spanish. The preposition in choice **b** must be combined with *quien* and go after *nadie* (it should read *No tengo nadie con quien ir al teatro*); therefore, choice **b** is incorrect. Choice **a** does not make logical sense by using *fuiste* and *contigo* in the same sentence (*Who did you go to the theater with you?*). In choice **d**, the question does not make sense either (*Who did you go to the theater last Sunday?*). Choice **e** is missing *a* after *fui*, which combined with *el*, should read *al* (*I went to the theater* instead of *I went the theater*). Choice **c** is the only possible answer as it correctly puts the preposition at the beginning of the question and includes *a* after *fuiste*.

36. b. Choices **a**, **c**, and **e** all incorrectly express the phrase *a friend of mine* at the beginning of their sentences. Choice **d** should read *mi amigo* at the beginning of its sentence instead of *me amigo*. Choice **b** is the only sentence that forms the phrase *a friend of mine* correctly in Spanish by using *un amigo mío*.

37. a. When describing a profession in Spanish, conjugate the verb *ser* and do not use an article between the form of *ser* and the profession. Choices **b**, **c**, **d**, and **e** do not follow this rule, and choice **b** incorrectly spells *me* as *mi*. Choice **a** does follow this rule and is therefore the only possible answer.

38. c. When expressing frequency, use *por*, not *para*. We can therefore eliminate choices **a**, **b**, and **e** because they use *para* before their time reference (*hora* in choices **a** and **e**, and *semana* in choice **b**). The preposition *con* cannot express frequency either, so choice **d** is not a possible answer. Choice **c** correctly uses *por* before *hora* and is therefore the only possible answer.

39. d. The main point of this question is when to use *saber* and *conocer* and the use of the personal *a*. Choice **a** should not have the personal *a* since it refers to *la respuesta*, not a person. Choice **b** should be a form of *conocer* since it refers to a place. Choice **c** should not have the personal *a* because it is referring to an answer, not a person. Choice **e** also incorrectly uses the personal *a* when referring to a place. Choice **d** is the only possible answer since it correctly uses *conocer* when referring to a place and does not use the personal *a* when a person is not involved.

40. a. The verb *recomendar* followed by *que* requires the use of the subjunctive. Choices **b**, **c**, and **d** are not grammatically correct sentences because they do not use the subjunctive with the second verb *tocar*. Choice **b** uses the simple present (*tocan*), choice **c** uses the gerund (*tocando*), and choice **d** uses the infinitive (*tocar*). Choice **e** (*tocen*) does not consider the stem-changing component of *tocar* when it is changed into its subjunctive form. Therefore, choice **a** (*toquen*) is the only possible answer since it does consider the stem-changing component of *tocar* in the *ellos* subjunctive form.

41. b. When using the verb *decir*, the person to whom the person is speaking is the indirect object. The indirect object, *sus oficiales*, is plural and so the indirect object pronoun must also be plural. Choice **b** is the only possible answer. Choices **a** (*las*) and **e** (*los*) use a direct object pronoun; choice **c** (*le*) uses an indirect object pronoun but it is singular and should be plural; choice **d** (*los se*) incorrectly combines a direct object pronoun (*los*) before a reflexive *se*. Choice **b** correctly uses the plural indirect object pronoun *les* to refer to *sus oficiales* and is therefore the only possible answer.

42. c. After the preposition *de*, the infinitive form of the verb must be used. Choice **c** (*cumplir*) is the only option that correctly uses the infinitive. All other choices incorrectly conjugate the verb. Choice **a** uses the present perfect (*han cumplido*), choice **b** the past participle (*cumplido*), choice **d** the simple present (*cumplen*), and choice **e**, the gerund (*cumpliendo*).

43. d. The structure *hay que + infinitive* is used to express the idea of necessity or obligation. The word *hay* never changes. The phrase is directed toward the travelers, so if the sentence were to use a conjugated verb like *tener*, it needs to be conjugated in the *ellos* form. Therefore, choices **a** (*he*) and **e** (*tengo*) are not correct because they are conjugated in the first person *yo* form. Choices **b** (*tener*) and **c** (*haber*) are not correct either because they have not been conjugated at all. Choice **d** (*hay*) is correct to express necessity with *hay que*.

44. e. The subject in this sentence is *el hombre* so the verb needs to be in the third-person singular *él* form. Choice **a** is conjugated in the *ellos* form (*se habrán reunido: they will have reunited*); choice **b** is an incorrect combination of the third person and the *tú* form (*se reuniste* is an incorrect conjugation); choice **c** is in the *ellos* form (*se reunirán: they will reunite*); and choice **d** is in the *nosotros* form (*nos hubiéramos reunido: we would have reunited*). Choice **e** (*se reunió: he reunited*) is in the third-person form to agree with the subject *el hombre*. It is the only possible answer.

45. a. The object of the verb *atacar* (or the person being attacked) is a direct object so choices **c** (*les*) and **d** (*le*) are incorrect since they represent indirect object pronouns. The correct direct object pronoun needs to be masculine and plural to agree with its object *los oficiales*. Choice **e** is feminine (*las*) and choice **b** is singular (*lo*). Choice **a** (*los*) is the only possible answer.

46. e. Although *estar* is used to denote location in Spanish, *ser* is used to tell where an event is taking place. Therefore, choice **a** (*está*) is incorrect since it uses a form of *estar*. *Hay* as choice **b** does not work when placed in the middle of the sentence after the subject (*la reunión de la junta directiva hay en la sala de conferencias* is incorrect). Choice **c** (*haber*) is also incorrect since it is the infinitive form of choice **b**. Choice **d** (*son*) is incorrect because it is plural and the verb needs to be singular to agree with the subject *la reunión*. Choice **e** (*es*) correctly uses the singular form of *ser* and is therefore the only possible answer.

47. c. The time expression *antes de que* needs the subjunctive form of the verb that follows it. Choice **a** (*te ves*) is not in a correct subjunctive form and represents the verb *verse*, not *irse*. Choice **b** (*te vas*) is the simple *tú* form of *irse*, not in subjunctive form. Choice **d** (*te has ido*) is not in the subjunctive form either but rather in the present perfect form. Choice **e** (*irte*) would be correct if the time expression were *antes de* and not *antes de que* (*antes de irte* is correct, but *antes de que irte* is not). Only choice **c** (*te vayas*) correctly utilizes the subjunctive mood for the *tú* form of *irse*. Therefore, all other choices are incorrect and choice **c** is the only possible answer.

48. d. One of the many uses of *por* is to express the reason or cause for something. When it is immediately followed by a verb, the verb must be in the infinitive form. Choice **d** (*por*) is the only possible answer since *por* precedes an infinitive verb (*ser*) and shows reason (*Le otorgaron el premio por ser muy responsable y trabajador: They gave him the prize for being very responsible and hardworking*). Choice **c** with *para* is not correct since *para + infinitive* expresses a purpose (it would read: *Le otorgaron el premio para ser muy responsable y trabajador: They gave him the prize in order to be very responsible and hardworking*). We want to convey why the prize was given and *para* does not do this. Choice **a** (*cómo*) is a question word meaning *how* and it would not make sense in the sentence, nor would choice **b** since *que* does not correctly join the fragments of the sentence. Choice **e** (*porque*) would be correct if the verb following *porque* were conjugated (e.g., *Le otorgaron el premio porque era muy responsable y trabajador*). However, the verb is the infinitive *ser* and *porque* does not work. Choice **d** is the only possible answer.

49. d. The expression *hace + period of time* with a verb in the present tense is used to express an action that began however long ago and continues today. Since *busca* is in the present tense, we know that the action continues into the present time. Choices **a** (*Habían*), **b** (*Había*), and **c** (*Hacía*) refer to the past tense and are therefore not possible answers. Choice **e** (*Haber*) is not conjugated and can therefore not be considered a possible answer. Choice **d** (*Hace*) is the only possible answer that exemplifies the use of *hace + period of time*.

50. e. The combination of the verb *querer + que* calls for the subjunctive mood. We can therefore eliminate choices **a** (*se cierra*), **c** (*cerramos*), and **d** (*cerrar*) since they do not employ the subjunctive. Choice **b** (*cierremos*) is not correctly conjugated to represent the *nosotros* subjunctive form; *cerremos* is the correct *nosotros* present subjunctive form, not *cierremos*. Choice **e** (*cerráramos*) represents the imperfect subjunctive and is the only possible answer.

Practice Test 3: Scoring and Diagnostic Chart

To evaluate how you did on this practice exam, start by totaling the number of correct responses on the two sections of this practice exam. First, find the number of questions you got right in each part. Questions you skipped or got wrong don't count; just add up the number of correct answers.

If at least 70% of your responses on the two parts are correct (47 correct), you are most likely prepared to pass the Border Patrol Exam. However, because the entrance process is competitive, you may need a higher score on the official exam to get accepted into the Border Patrol Academy.

In addition to seeing how you performed overall, you can use the following scoring chart to help diagnose your strengths and weaknesses in the different skills assessed on the exam, to better focus your study preparation.

PRACTICE TEST 3

LOGICAL REASONING SECTION

SKILL	QUESTION
Reasoning about Groups and Categories	1–8
Reasoning about Events or Situations	9–16

SPANISH LANGUAGE SECTION

SKILL	QUESTION
Part I	1, 2, 3, 4, 5, 6, 7, 8, 9, 10, 11, 12, 13, 14, 15, 16, 17, 18, 19, 20
Part II, Section I	21, 22, 23, 24, 25, 26, 27, 28, 29, 30
Part II, Section II	31, 32, 33, 34, 35, 36, 37, 38, 39, 40
Part II, Section III	41, 42, 43, 44, 45, 46, 47, 48, 49, 50

CHAPTER

PRACTICE TEST 4

This practice test assesses your logical reasoning abilities. However, instead of Spanish language questions, you will be tested on artificial language abilities. For this exam, you should simulate the actual test-taking experience as closely as you can. Find a quiet place to work where you won't be disturbed. Tear out the answer sheet on the next page if you own this book, or photocopy it if not, and find some No. 2 pencils to fill in the circles. After the exam, use the answer explanations to see how you did, and to find out why the right answers are right and the wrong ones are wrong.

LEARNINGEXPRESS ANSWER SHEET

PRACTICE TEST 4

Logical Reasoning Test

1. Over the years, the priorities of the Border Patrol have changed. After information showed that readily available jobs were attracting high numbers of illegal immigrants to the country, in 1986 the Immigration Reform and Control Act focused their attention on employers suspected of hiring illegal immigrants. The Border Patrol increased enforcement of employment laws and escalated inspections of employment documentation, hoping to cut down on illegal employment of immigrants.

   From the information given here, it can be validly concluded that:

   a. employers are less willing to hire illegal than legal immigrants.
   b. employers are more willing to hire illegal than legal immigrants.
   c. the Border Patrol focused just as strongly on employers suspected of hiring illegal immigrants prior to 1986 as they did after 1986.
   d. the Border Patrol did not focus as strongly on employers suspected of hiring illegal immigrants prior to 1986.
   e. the Border Patrol will focus solely on employers suspected of hiring illegal immigrants in the future.

2. The investigating agent, who speaks only English, needs to talk with several witnesses about a possible crime. Two of the witnesses speak only Spanish, one witness speaks Spanish and English, one witness speaks only English, and two witnesses speak only Italian. The agent must pay overtime if his interpreters work more than six hours in one day, and all the interviews must be completed within five business days. The agent has access to two interpreters; one speaks Spanish and English, and one speaks Italian and English. It will take four hours to interview each person.

   From the information given here, it can be validly concluded that:

   a. some witnesses will require fewer than four hours to question.
   b. some witnesses will require more than four hours to question.
   c. the agent will not need to pay his interpreters overtime.
   d. the agent will only need to pay overtime for one interpreter.
   e. the agent will need to hire an additional interpreter.

3. Federal crimes are crimes that violate federal law; state crimes violate state law. State laws vary from state to state, but most crimes committed are categorized as state crimes. Examples of state crimes include robbery, domestic violence, and drug trafficking, among others. Justine is accused of computer fraud.

   From the information given here, it can be validly concluded that:

   a. the crime Justine is accused of is categorized as a state crime.
   b. the crime Justine is accused of is categorized as a federal crime.
   c. Justine is guilty of computer fraud.
   d. Justine is not guilty of computer fraud.
   e. none of the above

4. In the past, green cards were issued by the Immigration and Naturalization Service (INS). During a reorganization, that office was absorbed into the Bureau of Citizenship and Immigration Service (BCIS), which is part of the Department of Homeland Security (DHS). Eventually, the BCIS was renamed U.S. Citizenship and Immigration Services (USCIS). Xavier holds a green card issued by the INS.
From the information given here, it can be validly concluded that:
   a. Xavier's green card is now invalid.
   b. Xavier's green card was reissued by the USCIS.
   c. Xavier received his green card before the BCIS was renamed USCIS.
   d. Xavier received his green card after the BCIS was renamed USCIS.
   e. none of the above

5. *Forcible entry* is a term used to define entry into a residence or other real estate property by military, police, or emergency personnel. When departing after forcible entry has been employed, officers must ensure that the property is properly secured. If the property is not secured, the officers may be held liable for damage or theft that occurs after they depart. If forcible entry is employed, measures must be taken to minimize damage to the property. Officer Z is authorized to enter a residence using forcible entry.
From the information given here, it CANNOT be validly concluded that:
   a. Officer Z will be required to secure the home unless she does not force entry.
   b. if Officer Z is not required to ensure that the home is secure upon leaving, then she did not force entry into the home.
   c. if Officer Z forces entry and fails to secure the home, then she may be liable for loss of items resulting from leaving the home unsecured.
   d. if Officer Z must physically force entry into the home, then she is not required to ensure that the home is secure upon leaving.
   e. none of the above

6. In the United States, federal and state governments generally consider a crime punishable with incarceration for one year or less to be a *misdemeanor*. All other crimes are considered *felonies*. Some examples of misdemeanors are vandalism, trespassing, and disorderly conduct, among others. Some examples of felonies include treason, terrorism, and kidnapping, among others. The rationale for the degree of punishment is the degree to which a crime affects others or society in general.

From the information given here, it CANNOT be validly concluded that:

a. treason is a felony.
b. trespassing is a misdemeanor.
c. individuals convicted of vandalism are generally incarcerated for less than a year.
d. the crime of disorderly conduct affects society less than the crime of kidnapping.
e. the crime of disorderly conduct affects society more than the crime of kidnapping.

7. An officer heard an explosion on the north side of the sector. He radioed for assistance and found four guards who could respond to the disturbance: Guard M, who is two miles from the north side of the sector; Guard N, who is seven miles from the north side; Guard O, who is five miles from the north side; and Guard P, who is four miles from the north side. The officer wants the available guard closest to the north side to respond. Guard P is sent to the scene.

From the information given here, it can be validly concluded that:

a. the guard closest to the north side was able to respond.
b. the guard closest to the north side was unable to respond.
c. the guard farthest from the north side was unable to respond.
d. the guard farthest from the north side was able to respond.
e. the officer sent two guards.

8. Pepper spray, also known as OC (oleoresin capsicum) spray, OC gas, or capsicum spray, is a chemical compound that has proven effective in riot and crowd control. Pepper spray irritates the eyes, often causing tears, pain, and temporary blindness. The temporary blindness pepper spray causes enables arresting officers to restrain subjects without using deadly force. Although pepper spray is considered a less-than-lethal substance, on rare occasions it may have been a contributing factor to death.

From the information given here, it CANNOT be validly concluded that:

a. pepper spray is sometimes used in riot control.
b. oleoresin capsicum spray causes temporary blindness.
c. temporary blindness allows arrestees to be more easily apprehended.
d. the use of pepper spray is considered deadly force.
e. pepper spray is an alternative to deadly force.

9. The U.S. Border Patrol utilizes various teams for search and rescue, to locate concealed illegal aliens, and to detect the presence of narcotics. There are six teams in a particular sector; two of each are assigned to a specific duty. Teams 1 and 4 have the same specialty. Team 2 does not specialize in narcotics. Teams 3 and 5 both specialize in either search and rescue or narcotics. Team 4 specializes in narcotics, and Team 6 specializes in the location of concealed illegal aliens.

From the information given here, it CANNOT be validly concluded that:

a. if Team 4 specializes in narcotics, then Team 1 specializes in narcotics.
b. if Team 3 specializes in search and rescue, then Team 5 specializes in search and rescue.
c. if Team 6 specializes in the location of concealed illegal aliens, then Team 2 specializes in search and rescue.
d. if Team 3 specializes in search and rescue, then Team 5 specializes in narcotics.
e. if Team 1 specializes in narcotics, then Team 4 specializes in narcotics.

10. One way in which an individual can obtain a green card is through the diversity visa lottery. The State Department holds this lottery every year and chooses winners randomly from all qualified entries. Individuals selected under this lottery are given the opportunity to apply for permanent residence (green card). Once permanent residence is granted, the individual is authorized to live and work permanently in the United States. Green card holders are also allowed to bring a spouse and any unmarried children under the age of 21 to the United States.

From the information given here, it CANNOT be validly concluded that:

a. if an individual wins the diversity visa lottery, then he or she may apply for a green card.
b. if a green card is granted, then the individual is permitted to live in the United States.
c. if an individual is authorized to work in the United States, then he or she holds a green card.
d. if a green card holder's child is married, then he or she is not eligible to be brought to the United States.
e. none of the above

11. When investigating a crime, it is essential to record certain information. This information includes, in order: the time of arrival on the scene; the weather conditions (if pertinent to the investigation); the approximate time of crime, as well as when it was discovered, and by whom; the identity of other officers present; contact information of the victim(s) and/or witnesses; the time, date, and location of the interview; and a thorough description of the suspect.

From the information given here, it CANNOT be validly concluded that:

a. if the identity of the other officers present has been recorded, then the time of arrival has been recorded.
b. if the weather is being recorded, then the time of the crime has not yet been recorded.
c. if the time and date of the interview has been recorded, then the time of the crime has been recorded.
d. if the weather has been recorded, then this information is applicable to the investigation.
e. none of the above

12. Section I of the Fourteenth Amendment to the U.S. Constitution reads, "All persons born or naturalized in the United States, and subject to the jurisdiction thereof, are citizens of the United States and of the State wherein they reside. No State shall make or enforce any law which shall abridge the privileges or immunities of citizens of the United States; nor shall any State deprive any person of life, liberty, or prosperity, without due process of law; nor deny to any person within its jurisdiction the equal protection of the laws."
From the information given here, it can be validly concluded that:
   a. if a naturalized citizen has had a right revoked, then due process of law is unnecessary.
   b. if a U.S.-born citizen resides in a state, then he or she is not subject to its jurisdiction.
   c. if a naturalized citizen resides in a state, then he or she is subject to its jurisdiction.
   d. if a state enforces a law, then it will infringe on the privileges of U.S. citizens.
   e. if due process of law has occurred, then U.S. citizens have received privileges from the state.

13. In 1904, the U.S. Immigration Service assigned a few mounted inspectors to patrol the border to prevent illegal crossings. Because these inspectors had no real training in border patrol, they were effectively just a token force. They were unable to stem the tide of illegal aliens crossing U.S. borders. In 1915, Congress authorized a new group of 75 inspectors, called mounted guards or mounted inspectors.
From the information given here, it CANNOT be validly concluded that:
   a. if the first inspectors were ineffective, then it's because they had no real training in border patrol.
   b. if the first inspectors were unable to prevent illegal aliens from crossing the borders, then it's because they were just a token force.
   c. if the first inspectors were a token force, then it's because they had no real training in border patrol.
   d. if the new group of mounted guards was authorized in 1915, then it is likely because of the ineffectiveness of the initial inspectors.
   e. none of the above

14. Evidence has many different roles in the investigation of a crime. It can link a suspect to a crime scene if, for example, a footprint matching the shoe of the suspect is found. Evidence can eliminate a suspect, as well; if the shoe size of the suspect is not a positive match for the footprint evidence, the suspect cannot be linked to the crime scene. Evidence can also back up or contradict a witness statement, which may help guide officers in further investigations. Evidence such as DNA or fingerprints is also valuable in providing a firm identification of a perpetrator or suspect.
From the information given here, it CANNOT be validly concluded that:
   a. if a witness's statement is contradicted by evidence found at the crime scene, then the officer may trust the validity of the statement.
   b. if a footprint matching the shoe of a suspect is found at a crime scene, then that suspect is linked to the crime scene.
   c. if a witness's statement is contradicted by evidence found at the crime scene, then the officer may not trust the validity of the statement.
   d. if the shoe size of the suspect does not match that of footprint evidence, then those prints do not tie the suspect to the crime scene.
   e. none of the above

15. After September 11, 2001, the Department of Homeland Security created two immigration enforcement agencies out of the Immigration and Naturalization Service (INS): U.S. Immigration and Customs Enforcement (ICE) and the U.S. Customs and Border Protection (CBP). ICE was made responsible for investigations, detention and removal of illegal immigrants, and interior law enforcement. CBP was made responsible for inspections at U.S. ports of entry and for preventing illegal entries between the port of entry, transportation check, and entries on the coastal borders of the United States.
From the information given here, it CANNOT be validly concluded that:
   a. two separate agencies were created to give each a more specific focus.
   b. the INS held responsibility for immigration law enforcement prior to September 11.
   c. changes to the INS were made as a result of the attacks on September 11.
   d. ICE is better suited to prevent illegal entries on the coast.
   e. CBP is better suited to conduct inspections at U.S. ports of entry.

16. The U.S. government has identified seven core skill sets that are important to the success of a border agent. One of these is the appropriate integration of technology (for example, computers) into the workplace. Agents must be able to use computer applications to effectively analyze data and communicate information. Agents must also be able to use technology to work more efficiently and to improve work processes. The focus is on the most commonly used computer applications: the Windows XP operating system with Microsoft Word, Excel spreadsheets, and Microsoft Outlook.

From the information given here, it can be validly concluded that:

a. if an agent has strong computer skills, she will not be able to work in Microsoft Outlook.
b. if an agent does not have appropriate computer skills, then she will be able to effectively analyze data.
c. if an agent does not have the skills to use Windows XP, then she will be able to work with Excel.
d. if the border agent is to succeed, then she need not effectively analyze data.
e. if an agent is to use Microsoft Word, then she must have skills in computer technology.

Artificial Language Review

Artificial Language Supplemental Booklet

To answer the Artificial Language questions, refer to the sections that follow: Vocabulary Lists and Grammatical Rules.

Some of the words given in the following Vocabulary Lists are not the same as those that will be given in the actual Border Patrol Exam. Therefore, it is best not to memorize them before taking the actual test. The Grammatical Rules are the same as those used in the actual test, except that some of the prefixes (word beginnings) and suffixes (word endings) used in the real test differ from those used here.

VOCABULARY LISTS FOR THE ARTIFICIAL LANGUAGE ARRANGED ALPHABETICALLY BY THE ENGLISH WORD			
ENGLISH	**ARTIFICIAL LANGUAGE**	**ENGLISH**	**ARTIFICIAL LANGUAGE**
a, an	bex	skillful	autile
alien	huslek	that	velle
and	rua	the	lac
boy	ekaplek	this	volle
country	failek	to be	syntur
difficult	froble	to border	regtur
enemy	avelek	to cross	chontur
friend	kometlek	to drive	artur

English	Artificial Language	English	Artificial Language
from	mor	to escape	pirtur
government	almanlek	to guard	bontur
he, him	yev	to have	tultur
jeep	dunlek	to identify	kalentur
legal	colle	to injure	liatur
loyal	inle	to inspect	zeltur
man	kaplek	to shoot	degtur
of	quea	to spy	tattur
paper	trenedlek	to station	lextur
river	browlek	to work	frigtur

ARRANGED ALPHABETICALLY BY THE ARTIFICIAL LANGUAGE WORD

Artificial Language	English	Artificial Language	English
almanlek	government	kaplek	man
artur	to drive	kometlek	friend
autile	skillful	lac	the
avelek	enemy	lextur	to station
bex	a, an	liatur	to injure
bontur	to guard	mor	from
browlek	river	pirtur	to escape
chontur	to cross	quea	of
colle	legal	regtur	to border
degtur	to shoot	rua	and
dunlek	jeep	syntur	to be
ekaplek	boy	tattur	to spy
failek	country	trenedlek	paper
frigtur	to work	tultur	to have
froble	difficult	velle	that
huslek	alien	volle	this
inle	loyal	yev	he, him
kalentur	to identify	zeltur	to inspect

Grammatical Rules for the Artificial Language

The Grammatical Rules given here are the same as those used in the Border Patrol Exam, except that the prefixes (word beginnings) and suffixes (word endings) used in the exam differ from those used here.

During the exam, you will have access to the rules at all times. Consequently, it is important that you understand these rules, but it is not necessary that you memorize them. In fact, memorizing them will hinder rather than help you, because the beginnings and endings of words are different in the version of the Artificial Language that appears in this manual than the one that appears in the actual test.

You should note that Part Three of the official Artificial Language Manual contains a glossary of grammatical terms to assist you if you are not thoroughly familiar with the meanings of these grammatical terms.

Rule 1

To form the feminine singular of a noun, a pronoun, an adjective, or an article, add the suffix *-til* to the masculine singular form. Only nouns, pronouns, adjectives, and articles take feminine endings in the Artificial Language. When gender is not specified, the masculine form is used.

> **Examples**
> If a *male eagle* is a *verlek*, then a *female eagle* is a *verlektil*.
>
> If an *ambitious* man is a *tosle* man, an *ambitious* woman is a *tosletil* woman.

Rule 2

To form the plural of nouns, pronouns, and adjectives, add the suffix *-id* to the correct singular form.

> **Examples**
> If one *male eagle* is a *verlek*, then several *male eagles* are *verlekid*.
>
> If an *ambitious* woman is a *tosletil* woman, several *ambitious* women are *tosletilid* women.

Rule 3

Adjectives modifying nouns and pronouns with feminine and/or plural endings must have endings that agree with the words they modify. In addition, an article (*a*, *an*, and *the*) preceding a noun must also agree with the noun in gender and number.

> **Examples**
> If an *active male eagle* is a *sojle verlek*, then an *active female eagle* is a *sojletil verlektil* and several *active female eagles* are *sojletilid verlektilid*.
>
> If *this male eagle* is *volle verlek*, *these female eagles* are *volletilid verlektilid*.
>
> If *the male eagle* is *lac verlek*, *the female eagle* is *lactil verlektil*, and *the female eagles* are *lactilid verlektilid*.
>
> If *a male eagle* is *bex verlek*, several *male eagles* are *bexid verlekid*.

Rule 4

The stem of the verb is obtained by omitting the suffix *-tur* from the infinitive form of the verb.

> **Example**
> The stem of the verb *syntur* is *syn*.

Rule 5

All subjects and their verbs must agree in number; that is, singular subjects require singular verbs and plural subjects require plural verbs. (See Rules 6 and 7.)

Rule 6

To form the present tense of a verb, add the suffix *-ex* to the stem for the singular form or the suffix *-ux* to the stem for the plural.

> **Example**
> If *to bark* is *naltur*, then *nalex* is the present tense for the singular (the dog *barks*) and *nalux* is the present tense for the plural (the dogs *bark*).

Rule 7

To form the past tense of a verb, first add the suffix *-rem* to the stem, and then add the suffix *-ot* if the verb is singular or the suffix *-et* if it is plural.

> **Example**
> If *to bark* is *naltur*, then *nalremot* is the past tense for the singular (the dog *barked*), and *nalremet* is the past tense for the plural (the dogs *barked*).

Rule 8

To form the past participle of a verb, add to the stem of the verb the suffix *-to*. It can be used to form compound tenses with the verb *to have*, as a predicate with the verb *to be*, or as an adjective. In the last two cases, it takes masculine, feminine, singular, and plural forms in agreement with the noun to which it refers.

> **Example of use in a compound tense with the verb *to have***
> If *to bark* is *naltur* and *to have* is *tultur*, then *tulex nalto* is the present perfect for the singular (the dog *has barked*) and *tulux nalto* is the present perfect for the plural (the dogs *have barked*). Similarly, *tulremot nalto* is the past perfect for the singular (the dog *had barked*) and *tulremet nalto* is the past perfect for the plural (the dogs *had barked*).

> **Example of use as a predicate with the verb *to be***
> If *to adopt* is *raptur* and *to be* is *syntur*, then a *boy was adopted* is an *ekaplek synremot rapto* and many *girls were adopted* is *ekaplektilid synremet raptotilid*.

> **Example of use as an adjective**
> If *to delight* is *kastur*, then a *delighted boy* is a *kasto ekaplek* and many *delighted girls* are *kastotilid ekaplektilid*.

Rule 9

To form a noun from a verb, add the suffix *-lek* to the stem of the verb.

> **Example**
> If *longtur* is *to write*, then a *writer* is a *longlek*.

Rule 10

To form an adjective from a noun, substitute the suffix *-le* for the suffix *-lek*.

> **Example**
> If *pellek* is *beauty*, then a *beautiful male eagle* is a *pelle verlek*, and a *beautiful female eagle* is a *pelletil verlektil*. (Note the feminine ending *-til*.)

Rule 11

To form an adverb from an adjective, add the suffix *-de* to the masculine form of the adjective. (Note that adverbs do not change their form to agree in number or gender with the word they modify.)

> **Example**
> If *pelle* is *beautiful*, then *beautifully* is *pellede*.

Rule 12

To form the possessive of a noun or pronoun, add the suffix *-oe* to the noun or pronoun after any plural or feminine suffixes.

> **Examples**
> If a *boglek* is a *dog*, then a *dog's* collar is a *boglekoe* collar.
>
> If *he* is *yev*, then *his* book is *yevoe* book.
>
> If *she* is *yevtil*, then *her* book is *yevtiloe* book.

Rule 13

To make a word negative, add the prefix *da-* to the correct affirmative form.

Examples

If an *active male eagle* is a *sojle verlek*, then an *inactive male eagle* is a *dasojle verlek*.

If the *dog barks* is *boglek nalex*, then the *dog does not bark* is *boglek danalex*.

Artificial Language

Use the Vocabulary Lists and Grammatical Rules to help you answer these questions.

For each sentence, decide which words have been translated correctly. Use scratch paper to list each numbered word that is correctly translated into the Artificial Language. When you have finished listing the words that are correctly translated in sentences 1 through 20, select your answer according to the following instructions:

Mark:
- **a.** if *only* the word numbered 1 is correctly translated.
- **b.** if *only* the word numbered 2 is correctly translated.
- **c.** if *only* the word numbered 3 is correctly translated.
- **d.** if *two or more* of the numbered words are correctly translated.
- **e.** if *none* of the numbered words is correctly translated.

Be sure to list only the *numbered* words that are *correctly* translated.

Study the sample question before going on to the test questions.

Sample Sentence
This woman crossed the river.

Sample Translation
Bex kaplektil chonremet lac browlek.
 1   2   3

The word numbered 1, *bex*, is incorrect because the translation of *bex* is *a*. The word *volletil* should have been used. The word numbered 2 is correct. *Kaplektil* has been correctly formed by adding the feminine ending to the masculine noun, applying Rule 1. The word numbered 3, *chonremet*, is incorrect because the singular form, *chonremot*, should have been used. Because the word numbered 2 is correct, the answer to the sample question is **b**.

Now go on with questions 1 through 20 and answer them in the manner indicated. Be sure to record your answers on the separate answer sheet found at the beginning of the test.

Sentence
1. She drives the jeep.

2. He is a friend.

3. The woman is an enemy.

Translation
Velle arex lac failek.
 1   2   3

Yev syntu bex kometlektil.
 1   2   3

Lac kaplektil synex bextil avelektil.
 1   2   3

PRACTICE TEST 4

4. The men crossed the river. Lacid <u>kaplek</u> <u>chonremot</u> lac <u>browlek</u>.
                                                              1   2   3

5. This alien is loyal. Volle <u>huslektil</u> <u>syn</u> <u>inletil</u>.
                                1   2   3

6. The boys and girls crossed the river. Lacid <u>ekaplektilid</u> rua <u>ekaplekid</u> chonremet lac <u>browlek</u>.
                                            1   2   3

7. The spy's enemy identified him. Lac <u>tatlekoe</u> avelek <u>kalenremot</u> <u>yev</u>.
                            1   2   3

8. That paper is from this government. <u>Velle</u> trenedlek <u>synex</u> <u>quea</u> velle almanlek.
                            1   2   3

9. These are legal papers. <u>Volleid</u> synux <u>colle</u> <u>trenedlekid</u>.
                            1   2   3

10. Enemies are difficult. <u>Avelektilid</u> <u>synux</u> <u>frobletilid</u>.
                        1   2   3

11. She was a loyal friend. Yevtil synremot <u>bexot</u> <u>inletilot</u> <u>kometlektilot</u>.
                            1   2   3

12. These spies are not friends of the country. <u>Velleid</u> tatlekid <u>dasynex</u> <u>kometlekid</u> quea lac failek.
                             1   2   3

13. Governments have to shoot disloyal spies. <u>Almanlekid</u> tulux degtur <u>inleid</u> <u>datatlekid</u>.
                             1   2   3

14. The jeep injured those boys. Lac <u>dunlekex</u> <u>liaremex</u> velleid <u>ekaplekex</u>.
                        1   2   3

15. They drove the jeep unskillfully. <u>Yevidet</u> arrem lac dunlek <u>daautileidde</u>.
                      1   2   3

16. The women's work was legal. Lactilid <u>kaplektiloeid</u> <u>friglek</u> <u>synremot</u> colle.
                          1   2   3

17. The inspector drove unskillfully. Lac <u>zellek</u> <u>arot</u> <u>daautilede</u>.
                         1 2   3

18. These spies have illegal papers from their friends. <u>Volletilid</u> tatlekid tulux <u>dacolleid</u> trenedlek mor.
                                                             1   2
yevidoe <u>kometlektilid</u>.
                3

19. The guards shot her. Lacid <u>bonid</u> <u>degremid</u> <u>yevtilid</u>.
                       1   2   3

20. The enemies identified the disloyal spies. Lacid avelekid kalenremet <u>lacid</u> <u>dainleid</u> <u>tatturlekid</u>.
                                                    1   2   3

For each question in this group, select one of the five suggested choices that correctly translates the italicized word or group of words into the Artificial Language.

Choice **c** is the correct translation of the italicized words, *the friends*, because the definite article, *lac*, must change its ending to agree with the noun (see Rule 3), and the noun *kometlekid* has the proper plural suffix (Rule 2).

Sample Question
Where are the friends?
a. bex kometlek
b. lac kometlek
c. lacid kometlekid
d. lac kometlekid
e. bex kometlekid

Paragraph

Both *men and women* work as our *country's spies*. They are trained to overcome difficult situations.
          21   22

They have to cross borders with *illegal identification*. They must act like a *loyal friend* in *enemy country*.
          23   24   25   26

They might need *to drive a jeep skillfully* over dangerous ground or even *to shoot a guard* if their identity
                          27   28

is exposed. They can be tempted to accept money *from an unfriendly government* and must constantly
                                                          29

strive to maintain their loyalty to *their country*.
                                          30

21. a. kaplektil rua kaplektilid frigux
    b. kaplekid rua kaplektilid frigux
    c. kaplektilid rua kaplekid frigux
    d. kaplekid rua kaplektilid frigex
    e. kaplektilid rua kaplekid frigex

22. a. failekid tatlekid
    b. failekid tatturlekid
    c. failekde tatlekid
    d. failekoe tatlekid
    e. failekoe tatturlekid

23. a. Yev tulex chontur reglekid
    b. Yevid tulux chontur reglekid
    c. Yevtilid tulux chontur reglekid
    d. Yevid tulux chonux reglekid
    e. Yev tulex chontur regturid

24. a. collede kalenlekde
    b. collede kalenlek
    c. dacollede kalenlek
    d. dacolle dakalenlek
    e. dacolle kalenlek

PRACTICE TEST 4

25. a. dainleid kometlekid
    b. dainle kometlek
    c. inle kometlek
    d. inletil kometlektil
    e. dainletil kometlektil

26. a. avele failek
    b. avelek failek
    c. avele faile
    d. avelekoe failek
    e. avelekoe faile

27. a. arex bex dunlek daautile
    b. arex bex dunlekid autileid
    c. artur bex dunlek daautile
    d. artur bex dunlek autilede
    e. artur bex dunlekid autileid

28. a. degux bex bonlek
    b. degux bex bonturlek
    c. degex bex bonlekid
    d. degtur bex bonturlek
    e. degtur bex bonlek

29. a. mor bex dakometle almanlek
    b. mor bex kometle daalmanlek
    c. mor bex dakometle daalmanlek
    d. bex mor dakometle daalmanlek
    e. bex mor dakometle almanlek

30. a. yev failek
    b. yevid failek
    c. yevidoe failek
    d. yevidoe failekid
    e. yevidoe failekidoe

For this group of questions, select the one response option that is the correct translation of the English word or words in parentheses. You should translate the entire sentence in order to determine what form should be used.

Sample Question
Lacid almanlekoe tatlekid (crossed the border).
   a. chonremet bex reglek
   b. chonremot lac reglek
   c. chonremet lac reglek
   d. chonremet lac regtir
   e. chonremot bex reglek

Lacid almanlekoe tatlekid chonremet lac reglek means *The government's spies crossed the border.*

Because *chonremet lac reglek* is the only one of these expressions that means *they* (plural) *crossed the border*, choice **c** is the correct answer to the sample question.

31. Yevtil kalenremot (her enemies' jeep).
    a. yev avelekid dunlek
    b. yevtil avelekidoe dunlekid
    c. yevtilid avelekid dunlekid
    d. yevtiloe avelekidoe dunlek
    e. yevtiloe avelekidoe dunlekoe

32. Yevid (crossed the border legally).
    a. *chonremet lac reglek collede*
    b. *chonremet lacid reglekid collede*
    c. *chonremot lac reglek collede*
    d. *chonremot lac reglek colle*
    e. *chonremot lac reglek dacollede.*

33. (The spies of those governments) synremet avelekid.
    a. *Lac tatlek quea velle almanlek*
    b. *Lac tatlekid quea velle almanlek*
    c. *Lacid tatlekid quea velle almanlekid*
    d. *Lacid tatlekid quea velleid almanlekid*
    e. *Lacid tatlekid quea volleid almanlekid*

34. (These women shot) lacid avelekid.
  a. Volletilid kaplektilid degremot
  b. Volletilid kaplektilid degremet
  c. Vollelid kaplektilid degremet
  d. Vollelid kaplektilid degremot
  e. Volletilid kaplektilid degrem

35. Yevid degremet (skillfully from their jeeps).
  a. autile mor yevid dunlekid
  b. daautile mor yevid dunlekid
  c. autilede mor yevoe dunlekid
  d. autilede mor yevid dunlekid
  e. autilede mor yevidoe dunlekid

36. (The stations of the disloyal men) synremet kalento.
  a. Lac lexlekid quea lac dainleid kaplekid
  b. Lac lexid quea lac inleidda kaplekid
  c. Lacid lexlekid quea lacid dainleid kaplekid
  d. Lacid lexleid quea lacid dainleid kaplekid
  e. Lacid lexlekid quea dalacid dainleid kaplekid

37. (Those station inspectors) kalenremet lacid tatlekid.
  a. Velle lexle zellek
  b. Velleid lexleid zellekid
  c. Velleid lexlekid zellekid
  d. Volleid lexlekid zellekid
  e. Velletilid lexletilid zellektilid

38. Lacid bonlekid (inspected the stations).
  a. zelremet lacid lexlekid
  b. zelremet lacid lexleid
  c. zelet lacid lexlekid
  d. zelremot lacid lexlekid
  e. zelremot lac lexlek

39. (The escaped enemies) chonremet lac reglek.
  a. Lac pirle avelek
  b. Lac pirle avelekid
  c. Lacid pirleid avelekid
  d. Lac pirto avelekid
  e. Lacid pirtoid avelekid

40. (The girl and the boys) synremet kometlekid.
  a. Lac ekaplek rua lactilid ekaplektilid
  b. Lactilid ekaplektilid rua lac ekaplek
  c. Lactil ekaplektil rua lac ekaplekid
  d. Lactil ekaplektil rua lacid ekaplekid
  e. Lactilid ekaplektilid rua lacid ekaplekid

41. Lacid tatlekid (shot from the station).
  a. degremot quea lac lexlek
  b. degremet quea lac lexlek
  c. degremet mor lac lexlek
  d. degremet mor lac lexturlek
  e. degremot mor lac lexlek

42. Lacid lexlekid rua (the borders were guarded).
  a. lacid reglekid synremet bontoid
  b. lacid regleid synremet bonto
  c. lacid regleid synremot bonto
  d. lacid reglekid synremet bonle
  e. lacid reglekid synremot bonle

For the last group of questions, select one of the five suggested choices that is the correct form of the italicized expression as it is used in the sentence. At the end of the sentence, you will find instructions in parentheses telling you which form to use. In some sentences you will be asked to supply the correct forms of two or more expressions. In this case, the instructions for these expressions are presented consecutively in the parentheses and are separated by a dash (for example, past tense—adverb). Be sure to translate the entire sentence before selecting your answer.

PRACTICE TEST 4

Sample Question
Yev *bontir* lac browlek. (present tense)
a. bonremot
b. bonremet
c. boneux
d. bonux
e. bonex

Choices **a** and **b** are incorrect because they are in the past tense. Choice **c** is misspelled. Choice **d** is in the present tense, but it, too, is incorrect because the subject of the sentence is singular and therefore takes a verb with a singular rather than a plural ending. Choice **e** is the answer to the sample question.

43. Lacid kometlekid *inle* bonremet lac lexlek. (adverb)
    a. dainlede
    b. inlede
    c. inlededa
    d. inleidde
    e. dainledeid

44. Lactilid ekaplektilid *syntur kometlek*. (plural past tense—negative plural adjective)
    a. synrem—dakometletil
    b. synremot—dakometletilid
    c. synremet—dakometlektilid
    d. synremet—dakometletil
    e. synremet—dakometletilid

45. Lacid *lextur* bonlekid frigremet inlede. (plural adjective)
    a. lexturid
    b. lexlekid
    c. lexlek
    d. lexleid
    e. lexle

46. Lacid ekaplekid *kalentur* lac *pirtur*. (plural past tense verb—singular noun)
    a. kalenremet—pirlek
    b. kalenremot—pirlek
    c. kalenet—pirturlek
    d. kalenremet—pirturlek
    e. kalenremot—pirlektil

47. Lactilid *tattur colle* chonremet lac reglek. (feminine plural noun—negative adverb)
    a. tattilid—dacollede
    b. tatleklid—dacollede
    c. tatlektilid—dacollede
    d. tatlektilid—dacolleid
    e. tatlektilid—collede

48. Lactil *lextur zeltur tultur* bex avelek. (feminine singular adjective—feminine singular noun—negative singular present tense verb)
    a. *lexle zellek datulex*
    b. *lexlektil zellektil datulex*
    c. *lexletil zellektil datulex*
    d. *lexletil zellek datulux*
    e. *lexletil zellektil tuldaremot*

49. *Yev* avelekid *synux autile*. (feminine singular possessive—masculine plural adjective)
    a. *Yevoe—autileid*
    b. *Yevtil—autileid*
    c. *Yevtiloe—autiletilid*
    d. *Yevtiloe—autile*
    e. *Yevtiloe—autileid*

50. Lactilid *almanlek zeltur tultur* lacid trenedlekid. (plural feminine adjective—plural feminine noun—negative plural past tense verb)
    a. *almanletilid—zellektilid—datulremet*
    b. *almanletil—zellektil—datulremot*
    c. *almanlektilid—zellektilid—datulremet*
    d. *almanletilid—zelletilid—datulremet*
    e. *almanletilid—zellektilid—tuldaremet*

PRACTICE TEST 4

Answers

Logical Reasoning

1. **d.** The information provided in the first and second sentences of the paragraph shows that the Border Patrol focused on employers after 1986; choice **d** restates this information, and is therefore the correct answer. Choices **a** and **b** state information that cannot be concluded from the information in the paragraph, and are therefore invalid. Choice **c** presents information that is contradicted by the information in the first and second sentences, and is therefore invalid. Information on the Border Patrol's future priorities is not provided in the paragraph, rendering choice **e** invalid.

2. **c.** The agent has only four total witnesses who require interpretation, as three of them speak English, the language he himself is fluent in. The two interpreters can interview one witness per day for two days, which does not result in overtime—so choice **c** is correct. Choices **a** and **b** contradict information provided in the last sentence of the paragraph, so they are incorrect. Choices **d** and **e** misinterpret the situation presented in the paragraph, so they are incorrect.

3. **e.** Although computer fraud is generally categorized as a federal crime, the paragraph does not provide this information, so choice **e** is the correct answer. Choices **a** and **b** are incorrect because the paragraph does not state whether computer fraud is considered a federal or state crime. The paragraph states only what Justine is accused of, not what she was convicted of, so there is no way to know if she is guilty or not guilty. Therefore, choices **c** and **d** are incorrect.

4. **c.** Because Xavier received his green card from the INS and the BCIS was renamed USCIS after the INS was absorbed into it, it can be concluded that Xavier received his green card before the renaming of the BCIS, so choice **c** is correct. Choice **a** is incorrect because office reorganizations would not render a green card invalid. Choice **b** is incorrect because the paragraph provides no information to draw a conclusion that any green cards were reissued by the USCIS. Choice **d** confuses the timing of the office reorganization and is incorrect. The correct answer is provided within the choices, so choice **e** is incorrect.

5. **d.** Choice **d** is the correct answer, because it contradicts information found in the second sentence in the paragraph and cannot therefore be a valid conclusion. Choice **a** is incorrect because it restates information found in the second sentence within the paragraph. Choice **b** is incorrect because it restates information found in the second sentence within the paragraph. Choice **c** is incorrect because it restates information found in the third sentence within the paragraph. The correct answer is provided within the choices, so choice **e** is incorrect.

6. **e.** Choice **e** contradicts the information provided in the sentences and is not a conclusion that can be drawn from reading the paragraph, so it is the correct answer. Choices **a** and **b** support the information provided in the fourth and third sentences, respectively, so they are not the correct answers. Choice **c** supports the information provided in the first and third sentences, so it is an incorrect answer. Choice **d** supports the information provided in the sentences and is a valid conclusion, so it is not the correct answer.

7. b. Choice **b** is the only conclusion that can be validly drawn from the information provided in the paragraph, and is therefore the correct answer. Choice **a** contradicts the information given in the third sentence and is therefore incorrect. Choices **c** and **d** cannot be drawn from information in the paragraph, and are therefore incorrect. Choice **e** contradicts information given in the third sentence and is therefore incorrect.

8. d. Choice **d** contradicts the information found in the third sentence of the paragraph, so it is the correct response. Choices **a**, **b**, **c**, and **e** all contain information that is supported by the paragraph, so they are incorrect.

9. d. Two of the six teams specialize in each area. Since Teams 1 and 4 have the same speciality and Team 4 specializes in narcotics, both Teams 1 and 4 specialize in narcotics. Since Team 6 must specialize in locating concealed illegal aliens, Teams 3 and 5 must therefore specialize in search and rescue. Team 2 is left to specialize in locating concealed illegal aliens. Choice **d** does not align with information found in the fifth sentence, so it is the correct response. Choices **a**, **b**, **c**, and **e** are all conclusions that can be validly drawn from the information in the paragraph, so they are incorrect.

10. c. Choice **c** contains a false assumption—there are many ways one can be authorized to work in the United States, including being a native-born American—so it cannot be concluded from the information in the paragraph, and is therefore the correct answer. Choices **a**, **b**, and **d** restate information found in the paragraph, so they are incorrect answers. Because the correct choice can be found in the answers, choice **e** is incorrect.

11. e. Because choices **a**, **b**, **c**, and **d** correctly restate information found in the paragraph, choice **e** is the correct answer.

12. c. Choice **c** restates information found in the first sentence of the paragraph, so it is the correct answer. Choices **a**, **b**, **d**, and **e** are invalid conclusions, and are therefore the wrong answers.

13. e. Because choices **a**, **b**, **c**, and **d** correctly restate information found in the paragraph, choice **e** is the correct answer.

14. a. Choice **a** makes a conclusion that cannot be inferred from information provided in the fourth sentence in the paragraph, and is therefore correct. Choices **b** and **d** restate information found in the second and third sentences, and are therefore incorrect. Choice **c** makes a conclusion that could be correctly inferred from information provided in the fourth sentence, so it is correct. Because the correct response is found in the answers, choice **e** is incorrect.

15. d. Choice **d** contradicts information presented in the last sentence of the paragraph, so it is the correct answer. Choices **a**, **b**, **c**, and **e** restate information presented in the paragraph, so they are incorrect.

16. e. Choice **e** restates information found in the second and fifth sentences of the paragraph, so it is the correct answer. Choices **a**, **b**, **c**, and **d** make faulty assumptions that could not have been based on information in the paragraph, and are therefore incorrect answers.

Artificial Language

1. **b.** Only the word numbered 2 is correct, so the answer is **b**. The word numbered 1, *velle*, is incorrect because it means *that*, not *she*. Rule 1 states that to form the feminine singular of a pronoun, you have to add the suffix *-til* to the masculine singular form. Consequently, the correct pronoun for *she* is *yevtil*. The word numbered 2, *arex*, is correct. According to Rules 4 and 6, to form the present tense of a verb, you first omit the suffix *-tur* from the infinitive form of the verb and then add the suffix *-ex* to the stem for the singular form of the verb. Note also that according to Rule 5, all subjects and their verbs must agree in number; thus, if the subject is singular, the verb must be in the singular form. The word numbered 3, *failek*, is incorrect. *Failek* means *country*. The correct translation of *jeep* is *dunlek*.

2. **a.** Only the word numbered 1 is correct, so the answer is **a**. The word numbered 1, *yev*, is correct, as it is the correct translation of *he*. The word numbered 2, *syntu*, is incorrect. Although it has been formed from the correct translation of *to be*, *syntur*, the singular form of the present tense is not formed by omitting the final *r* from the infinitive. Instead, the singular form of the present tense is formed by omitting *-tur* from the infinitive and then adding the suffix *-ex*. Thus, the correct verb would be *synex*. The word numbered 3, *kometlektil*, is incorrect. *Kometlektil* has been formed by adding the feminine suffix, *-til*, to the masculine noun, *kometlek*. As the subject of the sentence is the singular masculine pronoun *he*, only the singular masculine translation of friend is needed: *kometlek*.

3. **d.** Both the words numbered 2 and 3 are correct, so the answer is **d**. Word 1, *lac*, is incorrect. *Lac* is the singular masculine form of *the*. As the subject of the sentence is *woman*, a singular feminine article is required. To form it, add the feminine suffix *-til* to the masculine article, *lac*, as shown in Rule 1. The correct translation would therefore be *lactil*. Word 2, *kaplektil*, is correct. To translate *woman*, add the feminine suffix *-til* to *kaplek*, the word for *man*. Word 3, *avelektil*, is also correct. It, too, was formed by adding the feminine suffix *-til* to the masculine singular noun for *enemy*, which is *avelek*.

4. **c.** The only correct word is number 3, so the answer is **c**. Word 1 is incorrect. *Kaplek* is the singular form of *man*. Rule 2 says that to form the plural of a noun add the suffix *-id* to the singular form. The correct translation of *men* would, therefore, be *kaplekid*. Word 2 is also incorrect. Here we need the past tense of *to cross* in the plural as the subject of the sentence is *men*. *Chonremot*, however, has been formed using the singular suffix *-ot*. Instead, the correct translation would be formed, as shown in Rule 7, by first adding the suffix *-rem* to the stem *chon* and then adding the plural suffix *-et*: *chonremet*. *Browlek* is the correct translation of *river*; therefore, the only correct answer is the word numbered 3.

5. e. None of the numbered words has been translated correctly; therefore, the answer is **e**. The first numbered word, *huslektil*, was formed by adding the feminine suffix *-til* to the masculine singular noun *huslek*. We don't know the gender of the word *alien*, however, so, according to Rule 1, when the gender is not specified, the masculine form is used. The correct word choice, then, would be *huslek*. Word 2 involves an incorrect formation of a present tense verb from the infinitive. *Syn* was formed simply by taking the suffix *-tur* from the infinitive, *syntur*. Instead, after omitting *-tur*, the singular suffix *-ex* should have been added to the stem *syn*. The correct word would, therefore, have been *synex*. Word 3 is incorrect because, like word 1, it was created by adding the feminine suffix *-til* to *inle*. Since we don't know the gender of *alien*, the adjective that modifies it, *loyal*, also must take the masculine form, which in this case is *inle*.

6. c. The only correct word is number 3, so the answer is **c**. The first two words to be translated are *boys* and *girls*. To translate *boys*, Rule 2 indicates that the plural suffix *-id* is added to *ekaplek* (*boy*). Word 1, therefore, should be *ekaplekid*. Instead, the feminine suffix *-til* was added after *ekaplek* before adding *-id*. To translate *girls*, Rule 1 shows that we add the feminine suffix *-til* to the end of the masculine singular *ekaplek* and then add the plural suffix *-id*. Word 2, therefore, should be *ekaplektilid*. Instead, word 2 lacks the feminine suffix. *Browlek* is the correct translation of *river*, making word 3 correct.

7. d. All three of the numbered words are correct, so the answer is **d**. To translate *spy's*, we need to do two things. First, as shown in Rule 9, to form a noun from a verb, we add the suffix *-lek* to the stem of the infinitive. The stem of *tattur* (*to spy*) is *tat*, to which we add *-lek*: *tatlek*. Second, according to Rule 12, to make *tatlek* possessive we add the suffix *-oe*: *tatlekoe*. Word 1 is, therefore, correct. To translate *identified*, Rule 7 shows that to form the past tense of a verb in the singular form, we first add the suffix *-rem* to the stem of the infinitive (*kalentur*) and then add the singular suffix *-ot*: *kalenremot*. Word 2 is, therefore, correct. *Yev* is the correct translation of *him*; therefore, word 3 is also correct. Note that in this artificial language *he* and *him* both translate as *yev*.

8. a. Only the word numbered 1 is correct, so the answer is **a**. *Velle* is the correct translation of *that*. Word 1, therefore, is correct. *From* translates as *mor*, not as *quea*, which is *of*. Note that *from* and *of* are distinct in the artificial language. Word 2, therefore, is incorrect. *This* translates as *volle*, making word 3 (*velle*) incorrect.

9. d. Two of the numbered words, words 1 and 3 are correct, so the answer is **d**. To translate *these* we need to create the plural of *volle* (*this*). Rule 2 shows that to form the plural of an adjective, add the suffix *-id* to the singular form: *volle* becomes *volleid*, making word 1 correct. Word 2 is incorrect because it is singular while a plural form is required. Rule 3 indicates that adjectives must agree in number with the nouns they modify. To translate the word correctly, we add the plural suffix *-id* to the singular adjective, *colle*: *colleid*. Note that, even though in English *legal* doesn't change whether it is modifying *paper* or *papers*, in the artificial language the adjective must also be made plural. Word 3 is correct because Rule 2 shows that to translate *papers* we add the plural suffix *-id* to the singular form (*trenedlek*): *trenedlekid*.

10. b. Only the word numbered 2 is correct, so the answer is **b**. Word 1 is incorrect because it includes the feminine suffix *-til*. Rule 1 indicates that if gender is not specified then the masculine formed is used. To translate *enemies*, the plural suffix *-id* is added to the singular noun *avelek*: *avelekid*. Word 2 is correct. As shown by Rule 6, to form the present tense form of a verb in the plural, add the suffix *-ux* to the stem of the infinitive (*syntur*): *synux*. Word 3 is incorrect because, like word 1, it includes the feminine suffix *-til*. It should have been formed by adding only the plural suffix *-id* to the singular adjective *froble*: *frobleid*. Don't be lulled into thinking that an adjective and the noun it modifies are correct because they include the same suffixes. In this case, both *enemies* and *difficult* should have been gender neutral.

11. e. None of the numbered words has been translated correctly; therefore, the answer is **e**. Each of the numbered words is incorrect because it includes the suffix *-ot*. This suffix is added at the end of a past tense verb if it is singular, according to Rule 7, but it is not added to articles, adjectives, or nouns. Word 1 should have been formed by adding the feminine suffix *-til* to *bex* (*a*): *bextil*. Word 2 should have been formed by adding only the feminine suffix *-til* to *inle* (*loyal*): *inletil*. Word 3 should have been created similarly by adding *-til* to *kometlek* (*friend*): *kometlektil*.

12. c. The only correct word is number 3, so the answer is **c**. Word 1 is incorrect: *velleid* is the translation of *those*, not *these*. To translate *these* add the plural suffix *-id* to *volle* (*this*): *volleid*. Word 2 is also incorrect. To translate *are not*, Rule 13 indicates that the prefix *da-* must be added to the correct positive form. The correct positive form of *are*, however, is formed by adding the plural suffix *-ux* to the stem of the infinitive (*syntur*): *synux*. *Da*, then, was added to an incorrect stem, *synex*, which is singular. The correct translation would be *dasynux*. Word 3 is correct. To translate *friends* add the suffix *-id* to *kometlek* (*friend*): *kometlekid*.

13. a. Only the word numbered 1 is correct, so the answer is **a**. Word 1 is correct. To translate *governments* add the plural suffix *-id* to *almanlek* (*government*): *almanlekid*. Both words 2 and 3 are incorrect because the negative prefix *da-* has been used incorrectly. To translate *disloyal*, Rule 13 shows that *da-* must be added to the affirmative form of the word. Therefore, *da-* should have been added to *inleid* (*loyal*), the plural form of *inle*: *dainleid*. Instead, *da-* was added to *tatlekid*. To form *tatlekid*, the correct translation of *spies*, Rule 9 indicates that to form a noun from a verb, add the suffix *-lek* to the stem of the verb (*tattur*): *tatlekid*. A correct translation, then, of *disloyal spies* would be *dainleid tatlekid*.

14. b. The only correct word is word 2, so the answer is **b**. Word 1 is incorrect because it was formed by adding the suffix *-ex* to *dunlek* (*jeep*). The suffix *-ex*, however, is only added to the end of a verb, not a noun. The correct word would have simply been *dunlek*. Word 2 is correct. Rule 2 shows that to form the plural of an adjective, the suffix *-id* is added to the singular form (*velle*): *velleid*. Word 3 is incorrect because, instead of the suffix *-ex*, the suffix *-id* should have been added to *ekaplek* (*boys*): *ekaplekid*.

15. e. None of the numbered words has been translated correctly; therefore, the answer is **e**. Word 1 is incorrect because it includes the suffix *-et*, which is only added to past tense verbs in the plural, not pronouns. To translate *they*, Rule 2 says to add *-id* to the singular form (*yev*): *yevid*. Word 2 is incorrect because, as indicated in Rule 7, to form the past tense of a verb in the plural, not only must the suffix *-rem* be added to the stem of the infinitive (*artur*), the suffix *-et* must be added as well: *arremet*. Word 3 is incorrect because it includes the plural suffix *-id*, whereas Rule 11 says that adverbs do not change their form to agree in number with the word they modify. Instead, to translate *unskillfully*, add the suffix *-de* to *autile* (*skillful*) to create an adverb (*autilede*), and then add the negative prefix *da-*: *daautilede*.

16. d. Words 2 and 3 are correct, so the correct answer is **d**. Word 1 is incorrect. The plural has been formed incorrectly. To translate *women's* first add the feminine suffix *-til* to *kaplek* (*men*) and then the plural suffix *-til*, which gives us *kaplektil* (*women*). Rule 12 shows to form the possessive add the suffix *-oe* after any plural or feminine suffixes: *kaplektilidoe*, which is the correct translation. In word 1, however, *-oe* appears before *-id*. Word 2 is correct. Rule 9 indicates that to form a noun from a verb, add the suffix *-lek* to the stem (*frig*): *friglek*. Word 3 is also correct. To form the past tense of a verb in the singular form, Rule 7 says to first add the suffix *-rem* to the stem (*syn*) of the verb and then add the suffix *-ot*: *synremot*.

17. d. Words 1 and 3 are correct, so the correct answer is **d**. Word 1 is correct. Rule 9 says that to create a noun from a verb add the suffix *-lek* to the stem (*zel*) of the verb: *zellek*. Word 2 is wrong because the past tense of *to drive* in the singular was created incorrectly. To translate *drove* in the singular, Rule 7 says to add the suffix *-rem* to the stem (*ar*) of the verb followed by the suffix *-ot*: *arremot*. As you can see, *-rem* has been omitted in *arot*. Word 3 is correct. To translate *unskillfully*, we first add the suffix *-de* to the adjective *autile*, as shown in Rule 11: *autilede*. To make the word negative, Rule 13 says to add the prefix *da-*: *daautilede*.

18. b. Only word 2 is correct, so the answer is **b**. Word 1 is incorrect because *volletilid* includes the feminine suffix *-til*, which contradicts Rule 1 that says that when gender is not specified the masculine form is used. Rule 2 says to add the suffix *-id* to the singular form of a pronoun to make it plural. To form *these*, add only that suffix to *volle* (*this*): *volleid*. Word 2 is correct. To translate illegal, we must add the negative prefix *da-* to the correct form of the adjective, which in this case needs to be plural because it modifies *papers*. The plural form of *colle* is *colleid*, making the correct translation of *illegal dacolleid*. Word 3 is incorrect for the same reason that word 1 is wrong. It, too, includes the feminine suffix *-til*. Instead, the correct translation would be *kometlekid*.

19. e. None of the numbers are correct, so the answer is **e**. Word 1 is incorrect. Rule 9 says that to form a noun from a verb, add the suffix *-lek* to the stem (*bon*) of the verb. This suffix, however, has been omitted from the translation. The correct translation would be the stem *bon* plus the suffix *-lek* plus the plural suffix *-id*: *bonlekid*. Word 2 is incorrect. It has been created with *-id*, the suffix used to make a noun plural. Instead, Rule 7 shows that to form the past tense of a verb in the plural form, after adding the suffix *-rem* to the stem (*deg*), the suffix *-et* must be added: *degremet*. Word 3 is incorrect because *yevtilid* means *them*, not *her*, as the suffix *-id* indicates that the pronoun is plural. Instead, to translate *her* only add the feminine suffix *-til* to *yev* (*him*): *yevtil*.

20. d. Words 1 and 2 are correct, so the answer is **d**. Word 1 is correct. To translate *the* when it modifies a plural noun, the suffix *-id* must be added to *lac*: *lacid*. Word 2 is also correct. To translate *loyal* when it modifies a plural noun, first add *-id* to *inle* and then, as shown in Rule 13, add the prefix *da-* to make its meaning negative: *dainleid*. Word 3 is incorrect. Rule 9 shows that to form a noun from a verb, add the suffix *-lek* to the stem of the verb. In this case, however, *-lek* was added to the infinitive, *tattur*. To translate *spies* correctly, add the stem *tat* to the suffix *-lek* and then the plural suffix *-id*: *tatlekid*

21. b. This choice is correct because *kaplekid* is formed by adding the suffix *-id* (Rule 2) to *kaplek*; *kaplektilid* is formed by the suffixes *-til* (Rule 1) and *-id* to *kaplek*; *frigux* is formed by adding the suffix *-ux* to the stem of *frigtur* (Rule 6). Choice **a** is incorrect because *men* has been translated with the suffix *-til*, instead of *-id*. Choice **c** is incorrect because this translation means *women and men work*. Choice **d** is incorrect because *work* has been translated with the suffix *-ex*, instead of *-ux*. Choice **e** is incorrect because the first three words mean *women and men* and *work* has been translated with the suffix *-ex*, instead of *-ux*.

22. d. This choice is correct because *failekoe* is formed by adding the possessive suffix *-oe* (Rule 12) to *failek*; *tatlekid* is formed by adding the suffix *-lek* to the stem of *tattur* (Rule 9), then adding the suffix *-id* (Rule 2). Choice **a** is incorrect because *country's* has been translated with the suffix *-id*, instead of *-oe*. Choice **b** is incorrect because *country's* has been translated with the suffix *-id*, instead of *-oe*, and *spies* has been formed by adding the suffixes to the infinitive *tattur* and not its stem. Choice **c** is incorrect because *country's* has been translated with the suffix *-de*, instead of *-oe*. Choice **e** is incorrect because *spies* has been formed by adding the suffixes to the infinitive *tattur* and not its stem.

23. b. This choice is correct because *yevid* is formed by adding the suffix *-id* to *yev* (Rule 2); *tulux* is formed by adding the suffix *-ux* to the stem of *tultur* (Rule 6); *chontur*, as the infinitive form of *to cross*, requires no change; and *reglekid* is formed by adding the suffix *-lek* to the stem of *regtur* (Rule 9), then adding the suffix *-id*. Choice **a** is incorrect because both the words *they* and *have* have been translated in the singular. Choice **c** is incorrect because *they* has been translated with the feminine suffix *-til*. Choice **d** is incorrect because *to cross* has been translated with the suffix *-ux*, instead of maintaining the infinitive form. Choice **e** is incorrect because both the words *they* and *have* have been translated in the singular and *borders* has been translated by adding *-id* to the infinitive form *regtur*.

24. e. This choice is correct because *dacolle* is formed by adding the negative prefix *da-* to *colle* (Rule 13); *kalenlek* is formed by adding the suffix *-lek* to the stem of *kalentur* (Rule 9). Choice **a** is incorrect because the negative prefix *da-* has not been added to *colle* and the adverbial suffix *-de* has been added to each word. Choice **b** is incorrect because the adverbial suffix *-de* has been added to *colle*, instead of the prefix *da-*. Choice **c** is incorrect because *-de* has been added to *colle*. Choice **d** is incorrect because *da-* has been added to both words.

25. c. This choice is correct because *inle* is the correct translation of *loyal* and *kometlek* is the correct translation of *friend*. Both are singular and gender neutral (Rules 1 and 3). Choice **a** is incorrect because the phrase has been translated as *disloyal friends*. Choice **b** is incorrect because the phrase has been translated as *disloyal friend*. Choice **d** is incorrect because the phrase has been translated as *loyal [female] friend*. Choice **e** is incorrect because the phrase has been translated as *disloyal [female] friend*.

26. a. This choice is correct because *avele*, as an adjective, is formed by changing the suffix *-lek* to *-le* (Rule 10); *failek* is the correct translation of *country*. Choice **b** is incorrect because *enemy* has been translated without changing the suffix *-lek* to *-le*. Choice **c** is incorrect because the translation of *country* has included changing the suffix *-lek* to *-le*. Choice **d** is incorrect because *enemy* has been translated by adding the possessive suffix *-oe*. Choice **e** is incorrect because *enemy* has been translated by adding the possessive suffix *-oe* and the translation of *country* has included changing the suffix *-lek* to *-le*.

27. d. This choice is correct because the infinitive *artur* is the correct translation of *to drive*; *dunlek* is the correct translation of *jeep*; and *autilede* is formed by adding the suffix *-de* to *autile* (Rule 11). Choice **a** is incorrect because *to drive* has been translated as a singular verb and the negative prefix *da-* has been added to *autile*, instead of *-de*. Choice **b** is incorrect because *to drive* has been translated as a singular verb, while *jeep* has been made plural and the suffix *-id* has been added to *autile*, instead of *-de*. Choice **c** is incorrect because the negative prefix *da-* has been added to *autile*, instead of *-de*. Choice **e** is incorrect because *jeep* has been made plural and the suffix *-id* has been added to *autile*, instead of *-de*.

28. e. This choice is correct because the infinitive *degtur* is the correct translation of *to shoot*; and *bonlek* is formed by adding the suffix *-lek* to the stem of *bontur* (Rule 9). Choice **a** is incorrect because *to shoot* has been translated as a plural verb. Choice **b** is incorrect because *to shoot* has been translated as a plural verb and *guard* has been translated by adding *-lek* to the infinitive, not the stem. Choice **c** is incorrect because *to shoot* has been translated as a singular verb and *guard* has been translated in the plural. Choice **d** is incorrect because *guard* has been translated by adding *-lek* to the infinitive, not the stem.

29. a. This choice is correct because *mor bex* is the correct translation of *from an*; *dakometle* is formed by first changing the suffix *-lek* to *-le* (Rule 10) in *kometlek*, then adding the negative prefix *da-* (Rule 13); *almanlek* (*government*) doesn't change its form. Choice **b** is incorrect because the prefix *da-* has been added to *almanlek*, not *kometle*. Choice **c** is incorrect because *da-* has been added to *almanlek* as well as *kometle*. Choice **d** is incorrect because *from an* has been translated as *an from* and *da-* has been added to *almanlek* as well as *kometle*. Choice **e** is incorrect because *from an* has been translated as *an from*.

30. c. This choice is correct because *yevidoe* is formed by adding the suffixes *-id* (Rule 2) and *-oe* (Rule 12) to *yev*; *failek* is the correct translation of *country*. Choice **a** is incorrect because *their* has been translated without either of the necessary suffixes. Choice **b** is incorrect because *their* has been translated without *-oe*. Choice **d** is incorrect because *country* has been translated in the plural. Choice **e** is incorrect because *country* has been translated in the plural and possessive.

31. d. *Yevtil kalenremot yevtiloe avelekidoe dunlek* means *She identified her enemies' jeep*. *Yevtiloe* is feminine (Rule 1) and possessive (Rule 12), *avelekidoe* is plural (Rule 2) and possessive (Rule 12), while *dunlek* does not change its singular form. Choice **a** is incorrect because *her* was translated without using the suffixes *-til* or *-oe* and *enemies'* was translated without the suffix *-oe*. Choice **b** is incorrect because *her* was translated without using the suffix *-oe*. Choice **c** is incorrect because *her* was translated using the suffix *-id* instead of *-oe* and *enemies'* was translated without the suffix *-oe*. Choice **e** is incorrect because *jeep* was translated using the suffix *-oe*.

32. a. *Yevid chonremet lac reglek collede* means *They crossed the border legally*. The word *chonremet* is formed by adding the suffixes *-rem* and *-et* to the stem of *chontur* since the verb is in the past tense and *yevid* is plural (Rule 7); *lac* is the singular translation of *the*, *reglek* is formed by adding *-lek* to the stem of *regtur* (Rule 9), and *collede* is formed by adding the suffix *-de* to *colle* (Rule 11). Choice **b** is incorrect because *the border* has been translated in the plural. Choice **c** is incorrect because *crossed* has been translated in the singular. Choice **d** is incorrect because *crossed* has been translated in the singular and *legally* has been translated without the suffix *-de*. Choice **e** is incorrect because *crossed* has been translated in the singular and *legally* has been translated with the negative prefix *da-*.

33. d. *Lacid tatlekid quea velleid almanlekid synremet avelekid* means *The spies of those governments were enemies*. *Lacid* must be plural so the suffix *-id* is added to *lac* (Rule 2), *tatlekid* is formed by adding the suffix *-lek* to the stem of *tattur* (Rule 9) and adding the suffix *-id* (Rule 2), *quea* is the translation of *of* and does not change form, and *velleid* and *almanlekid* are formed by adding the suffix *-id*. Choice **a** is incorrect because none of the words in the phrase has been translated in the plural. Choice **b** is incorrect because *the*, *those*, and *governments* have not been translated in the plural. Choice **c** is incorrect because *those* has not been translated in the plural. Choice **e** is incorrect because *those* has been translated as *these*.

34. b. *Volletilid kaplektilid degremet lacid avelekid* means *These women shot the enemies*. *Volletilid* and *kaplektilid* are formed by adding the suffixes *-til* (Rule 1) and *-id* (Rule 2) to *volle* and *kaplek*, respectively. The word *degremet* is formed by adding the suffixes *-rem* and *-et* (Rule 7) to the stem of *degtur*. Choice **a** is incorrect because *shot* has been translated in the singular. Choice **c** is incorrect because *these* has been translated without the feminine suffix *-til*. Choice **d** is incorrect because *these* has been translated without the feminine suffix *-til* and *shot* has been translated in the singular. Choice **e** is incorrect because *shot* has been translated without the suffix *-et*.

35. e. *Yevid degremet autilede mor yevidoe dunlekid* means *They shot skillfully from their jeeps*. The word *autilede* is formed by adding the suffix *-de* to *autile* (Rule 11), *mor* is the correct translation of *from*, *yevidoe* is formed by adding the suffixes *-id* (Rule 2) and *-oe* (Rule 12) to *yev*, and *dunlekid* is formed by the suffix *-id* to *dunlek*. Choice **a** is incorrect because *skillfully* has been translated without the suffix *-de* and *their* has been translated without the suffix *-oe*. Choice **b** is incorrect because *skillfully* has been translated using the negative prefix *da-* instead of the suffix *-de* and *their* has been translated without the suffix *-oe*. Choice **c** is incorrect because *their* has been translated without the suffix *-id*. Choice **d** is incorrect because *their* has been translated without the suffix *-oe*.

36. c. *Lacid lexlekid quea lacid dainleid kaplekid synremet kalento* means *The stations of the disloyal men were identified*. The two instances of *lacid* are formed by adding the suffix *-id* to *lac* (Rule 2), *lexlekid* is formed by adding the suffixes *-lek* (Rule 9) and *-id*, *quea* is the correct translation of *of*, *dainleid* is formed by adding the prefix *da-* (Rule 13) and suffix *-id* to *inle*, and *kaplekid* is formed by adding the suffix *-id* to *kaplek*. Choice **a** is incorrect because *the* has not been translated into the plural in either of its instances. Choice **b** is incorrect because *the* has not been translated into the plural in either of its instances, *station* has been translated without using the suffix *-lek*, and disloyal has been translated by treating the prefix *da-* as if it were a suffix. Choice **d** is incorrect because stations was formed with the suffix *-le* and not *-lek*. Choice **e** is incorrect because the negative prefix *da-* has been added to the translation of *the*.

37. b. *Velleid lexleid zellekid kalenremet lacid tatlekid* means *Those station inspectors identified the spies*. *Velleid* is formed by adding the suffix *-id* to *velle* (Rule 2); *lexleid* is formed by adding the suffix *-lek* to the stem of *lextur* (Rule 9), substituting the suffix *-le* for *-lek* (Rule 10), and adding the suffix *-id*; *zellekid* is formed by adding the suffixes *-lek* and *-id* to the stem of *zeltur*. Choice **a** is incorrect because none of the words in the phrase have been translated in the plural. Choice **c** is incorrect because *station* has been translated without changing the suffix *-lek* to *-le*. Choice **d** is incorrect because *those* has been translated as *these* and *station* has been translated without changing the suffix *-lek* to *-le*. Choice **e** is incorrect because each word in the phrase includes the feminine suffix *-til*, which violates Rule 1.

38. a. *Lacid bonlekid zelremet lacid lexlekid* means *The guards inspected the stations.* The word *zelremet* is formed by adding the suffixes *-rem* and *-et* to the stem of *zeltur* (Rule 7), *lacid* is formed by adding the suffix *-id* to *lac* (Rule 2), and *lexlekid* is formed by adding the suffixes *-lek* (Rule 9) and *-id* to the stem of *lextur*. Choice **b** is incorrect because *stations* has been translated using the suffix *-le* instead of *-lek*. Choice **c** is incorrect because *inspected* was translated without the suffix *-rem*. Choice **d** is incorrect because *inspected* was translated in the singular. Choice **e** is incorrect because none of the words in the phrase were translated in the plural.

39. e. *Lacid pirtoid avelekid chonremet lac reglek* means *The escaped enemies crossed the border.* *Lacid* is formed by adding the suffix *-id* to *lac* (Rule 2), *pirtoid* is formed by adding the suffixes *-to* (Rule 8) and *-id* to the stem of *pirtur*, and *avelekid* is formed by adding the suffix *-id* to *avelek*. Choice **a** is incorrect because *escaped* has been translated using *-le* instead of *-to* and because none of the words in the phrase are plural. Choice **b** is incorrect because here, too, *escaped* has been translated using *-le* instead of *-to* and because only *enemies* has been translated in the plural. Choice **c** is incorrect because *escaped* has been translated using *-le* instead of *-to*. Choice **d** is incorrect because only *avelekid* is in the plural.

40. d. *Lactil ekaplektil rua lacid ekaplekid synremet kometlekid* means *The girl and the boys were friends.* *Lactil* and *ekaplektil* are formed by adding the suffix *-til* to both *lac* and *ekaplek* (Rule 1); *lacid* and *ekaplekid* are formed by adding the suffix *-id* to both *lac* and *ekaplek* (Rule 2). Choice **a** is incorrect because *the girl* has been translated as *the boy* and *the boys* has been translated as *the girls*. Choice **b** is incorrect because *the girl* has been translated as *the girls* and *the boys* has been translated as *the boy*. Choice **c** is incorrect because the second *the* has not been made plural. Choice **e** is incorrect because *the girl* has been translated as *the girls*.

41. c. *Lacid tatlekid degremet mor lac lexlek* means *The spies shot from the station.* The word *degremet* was formed by adding the suffixes *-rem* and *-et* to the stem of *degtur* (Rule 7), *mor* is the correct translation of *from*, and *lexlek* is formed by adding the suffix *-lek* to the stem of *lextur* (Rule 9). Choice **a** is incorrect because the verb is in the singular and translates *from* as *quea* (*of*). Choice **b** is incorrect because it translates *from* as *quea* (*of*). Choice **d** is incorrect because it translates *station* using the infinitive *lextur*, not its stem. Choice **e** is incorrect because the verb is in the singular.

42. a. *Lacid lexlekid rua lacid reglekid synremet bontoid* means *The stations and the borders were guarded.* The word *reglekid* is formed by adding the suffixes *-lek* (Rule 9) and *-id* (Rule 2) to the stem of *regtur.* The word *synremet* is formed by adding the suffixes *-rem* and *-et* to the stem of *syntur* (Rule 6). The word *bontoid* is formed by adding the suffix *-to* to the stem of *bontur* (Rule 8) and then adding the plural suffix *-id* (Rule 2). Choice **b** is incorrect because *borders* has been translated with the suffix *-le*, not *-lek*. Choice **c** is incorrect because *borders* has been translated with the suffix *-le*, not *-lek*, and *synremet* has been translated with the singular suffix *-ot*. Choice **d** is incorrect because *guarded* has been translated with the suffix *-le*, not *-to*. Choice **e** is incorrect because *synremet* has been translated with the singular *-ot* and *guarded* has been translated with the suffix *-le*.

43. b. *Lacid kometlekid inlede bonremet lac lexlek* means *The friends loyally guarded the station.* To translate *loyally* add the suffix *-de* to the adjective (Rule 11); therefore, *inlede* is correct. Choice **a** is incorrect because the negative prefix *da-* has been added. Choice **c** is incorrect because the negative prefix *da-* has been added, this time at the end of the word. Choice **d** is incorrect because the suffix *-id* has been added after the adjective. Choice **e** is incorrect because it includes not only the prefix *da-* but the suffix *-id*.

44. e. *Lactilid ekaplektilid synremet dakometletilid* means *The girls were unfriendly.* To form *synremet*, add the suffixes *-rem* and *-et* to the stem of *syntur* (Rule 7). To form *dakometletilid*, replace the suffix *-lek* from the noun with *-le* (Rule 10), add the suffixes *-til* (Rule 1) and *-id* (Rule 2), and then the negative prefix *da-* (Rule 13). Choice **a** is incorrect because *were* has been translated without the suffix *-et* and *unfriendly* has been translated without the suffix *-id*. Choice **b** is incorrect because *were* has been translated with the suffix *-ot*. Choice **c** is incorrect because the suffix *-lek* has not been replaced by *-le*. Choice **d** is incorrect because *unfriendly* has been translated without the suffix *-id*.

45. d. *Lacid lexleid bonlekid frigremet inlede* means *The station guards worked loyally.* To form *lexleid*, start by adding *-lek* to the stem of *lextur* (Rule 9), then change *-lek* to *-le* (Rule 10), and add the suffix *-id* (Rule 2). Choice **a** is incorrect because the only change that has been made is to add the suffix *-id* to the infinitive, not the stem. Choice **b** is incorrect because the suffix *-lek* has not been changed to *-le*. Choice **c** is incorrect because the suffix *-lek* has not been changed to *-le* and the suffix *-id* has not been added. Choice **e** is incorrect because the suffix *-id* has not been added.

46. a. *Lacid ekaplekid kalenremet lac pirlek* means *The boys identified the escapee.* To form *kalenremet* add the suffixes *-rem* and *-et* to the stem of *kalentur*. To form *pirlek* add the suffix *-lek* to the stem of *pirtur*. Choice **b** is incorrect because *identified* has been translated with the suffix *-ot*. Choice **c** is incorrect because *identified* has been translated without the suffix *-rem* and the suffix *-lek* has been added to the infinitive *pirtur*, not its stem. Choice **d** is incorrect because the suffix *-lek* has been added to the infinitive *pirtur*, not its stem. Choice **e** is incorrect because *identified* has been translated with the suffix *-ot*, and the feminine suffix has been added to *pirlek*, whereas it should be gender neutral.

47. c. *Lactilid tatlektilid dacollede chonremet lac reglek* means *The [female] spies illegally crossed the border.* The word *tatlektilid* is formed by adding the suffix *-lek* to the stem of *tattur* (Rule 9), then adding the suffixes *-til* (Rule 1) and *-id* (Rule 2). The word *dacollede* is formed by adding the suffix *-de* (Rule 11) and the prefix *da-* (Rule 13) to *colle*. Choice **a** is incorrect because *spies* was translated without the suffix *-lek*. Choice **b** is incorrect because *spies* was translated without the suffix *-til*. Choice **d** is incorrect because *illegally* was translated with the suffix *-id*, instead of *-de*. Choice **e** is incorrect because *illegally* was translated without the prefix *da-*.

48. c. *Lactil lexletil zellektil datulex bex avelek* means *The [female] station inspector does not have an enemy.* The word *lexletil* is formed by adding the suffix *-lek* to the stem of *lectur* (Rule 9), then changing it to the suffix *-le* (Rule 10) and adding the suffix *-til* (Rule 1). The word *zellektil* is formed by adding the suffix *-lek* to the stem of *zeltur* and adding the suffix *-til*. The word *datulex* is formed by adding the suffix *-ex* to the stem of *tultur* (Rule 6) and then adding the negative prefix *da-*. Choice **a** is incorrect because *station* and *inspector* have been translated without the feminine suffix *-til*. Choice **b** is incorrect because *station* has been translated without changing *-lek* to *-le*. Choice **d** is incorrect because *inspector* has been translated without the feminine suffix *-til* and *does not have* has been translated with the suffix *-ux*. Choice **e** is incorrect because *does not have* has been translated with the suffixes *-rem* and *-ot* and the prefix *da-* has been placed after the stem, *tul*.

49. e. *Yevtiloe avelekid synux autileid* means *Her enemies are skillful.* The word *yevtiloe* is formed by adding the suffixes *-til* (Rule 1) and *-oe* (Rule 12) to *yev*. The word *autileid* is formed by adding the suffix *-id* to *autile*. Choice **a** is incorrect because *her* has been translated without the feminine suffix *-til*. Choice **b** is incorrect because *her* has been translated without the possessive suffix *-oe*. Choice **c** is incorrect because *skillful* has been translated with the feminine suffix *-til*, whereas it should be gender neutral. Choice **d** is incorrect because *skillful* has been translated without the plural suffix *-id*.

PRACTICE TEST 4

50. a. *Lactilid almanletilid zellektilid datulremet lacid trenedlekid* means *The government [female] inspectors did not have the papers.* The word *almanletilid* is formed by changing the suffix *-lek* to *-le* (Rule 10), then adding the suffixes *-til* (Rule 1) and *-id* (Rule 2). The word *zellektilid* is formed by adding the suffix *-lek* to the stem of *zeltur* (Rule 9), then adding the suffixes *-til* and *-id*. The word *datulremet* is formed by adding the suffixes *-rem* and *-et* to the stem of *tultur* (Rule 7), then adding the negative prefix *da-*. Choice **b** is incorrect because each word is in the singular form. Choice **c** is incorrect because *government* was translated without changing the suffix *-lek* to *-le*. Choice **d** is incorrect because *inspectors* was translated using the suffix *-le*, instead of *-lek*. Choice **e** is incorrect because *did not have* was translated with the *da-* in the wrong position.

Practice Test 4: Scoring and Diagnostic Chart

To evaluate how you did on this practice exam, start by totaling the number of correct responses on the two sections of this practice exam. First, find the number of questions you got right in each part. Questions you skipped or got wrong don't count; just add up the number of correct answers.

If at least 70% of your responses on the two parts are correct (47 correct), you are most likely prepared to pass the Border Patrol Exam. However, because the entrance process is competitive, you may need a higher score on the official exam to get accepted into the Border Patrol Academy.

In addition to seeing how you performed overall, you can use the following scoring chart to help diagnose your strengths and weaknesses in the different skills assessed on the exam, to better focus your study preparation.

LOGICAL REASONING SECTION	
SKILL	**QUESTION**
Reasoning about Groups and Categories	1–8
Reasoning about Events or Situations	9–16

ARTIFICIAL LANGUAGE SECTION	
SKILL	**QUESTION**
Artificial Language I	1, 2, 3, 4, 5, 6, 7, 8, 9, 10, 11, 12, 13, 14, 15, 16, 17, 18, 19, 20
Artificial Language II	21, 22, 23, 24, 25, 26, 27, 28, 29, 30
Artificial Language III	31, 32, 33, 34, 35, 36, 37, 38, 39, 40, 41, 42
Artificial Language IV	43, 44, 45, 46, 47, 48, 49, 50

C H A P T E R

7 ▶ PRACTICE TEST 5

Similar to the last practice test, this practice test contains questions to challenge your logical reasoning and artificial language abilities. Again, you should simulate the actual test-taking experience as closely as you can.

LEARNINGEXPRESS ANSWER SHEET

1. ⓐ ⓑ ⓒ ⓓ ⓔ
2. ⓐ ⓑ ⓒ ⓓ ⓔ
3. ⓐ ⓑ ⓒ ⓓ ⓔ
4. ⓐ ⓑ ⓒ ⓓ ⓔ
5. ⓐ ⓑ ⓒ ⓓ ⓔ
6. ⓐ ⓑ ⓒ ⓓ ⓔ
7. ⓐ ⓑ ⓒ ⓓ ⓔ
8. ⓐ ⓑ ⓒ ⓓ ⓔ
9. ⓐ ⓑ ⓒ ⓓ ⓔ
10. ⓐ ⓑ ⓒ ⓓ ⓔ
11. ⓐ ⓑ ⓒ ⓓ ⓔ
12. ⓐ ⓑ ⓒ ⓓ ⓔ
13. ⓐ ⓑ ⓒ ⓓ ⓔ
14. ⓐ ⓑ ⓒ ⓓ ⓔ
15. ⓐ ⓑ ⓒ ⓓ ⓔ
16. ⓐ ⓑ ⓒ ⓓ ⓔ

1. ⓐ ⓑ ⓒ ⓓ ⓔ
2. ⓐ ⓑ ⓒ ⓓ ⓔ
3. ⓐ ⓑ ⓒ ⓓ ⓔ
4. ⓐ ⓑ ⓒ ⓓ ⓔ
5. ⓐ ⓑ ⓒ ⓓ ⓔ
6. ⓐ ⓑ ⓒ ⓓ ⓔ
7. ⓐ ⓑ ⓒ ⓓ ⓔ
8. ⓐ ⓑ ⓒ ⓓ ⓔ
9. ⓐ ⓑ ⓒ ⓓ ⓔ
10. ⓐ ⓑ ⓒ ⓓ ⓔ
11. ⓐ ⓑ ⓒ ⓓ ⓔ
12. ⓐ ⓑ ⓒ ⓓ ⓔ
13. ⓐ ⓑ ⓒ ⓓ ⓔ
14. ⓐ ⓑ ⓒ ⓓ ⓔ
15. ⓐ ⓑ ⓒ ⓓ ⓔ
16. ⓐ ⓑ ⓒ ⓓ ⓔ
17. ⓐ ⓑ ⓒ ⓓ ⓔ
18. ⓐ ⓑ ⓒ ⓓ ⓔ
19. ⓐ ⓑ ⓒ ⓓ ⓔ
20. ⓐ ⓑ ⓒ ⓓ ⓔ
21. ⓐ ⓑ ⓒ ⓓ ⓔ
22. ⓐ ⓑ ⓒ ⓓ ⓔ
23. ⓐ ⓑ ⓒ ⓓ ⓔ
24. ⓐ ⓑ ⓒ ⓓ ⓔ
25. ⓐ ⓑ ⓒ ⓓ ⓔ
26. ⓐ ⓑ ⓒ ⓓ ⓔ
27. ⓐ ⓑ ⓒ ⓓ ⓔ
28. ⓐ ⓑ ⓒ ⓓ ⓔ
29. ⓐ ⓑ ⓒ ⓓ ⓔ
30. ⓐ ⓑ ⓒ ⓓ ⓔ
31. ⓐ ⓑ ⓒ ⓓ ⓔ
32. ⓐ ⓑ ⓒ ⓓ ⓔ
33. ⓐ ⓑ ⓒ ⓓ ⓔ
34. ⓐ ⓑ ⓒ ⓓ ⓔ
35. ⓐ ⓑ ⓒ ⓓ ⓔ
36. ⓐ ⓑ ⓒ ⓓ ⓔ
37. ⓐ ⓑ ⓒ ⓓ ⓔ
38. ⓐ ⓑ ⓒ ⓓ ⓔ
39. ⓐ ⓑ ⓒ ⓓ ⓔ
40. ⓐ ⓑ ⓒ ⓓ ⓔ
41. ⓐ ⓑ ⓒ ⓓ ⓔ
42. ⓐ ⓑ ⓒ ⓓ ⓔ
43. ⓐ ⓑ ⓒ ⓓ ⓔ
44. ⓐ ⓑ ⓒ ⓓ ⓔ
45. ⓐ ⓑ ⓒ ⓓ ⓔ
46. ⓐ ⓑ ⓒ ⓓ ⓔ
47. ⓐ ⓑ ⓒ ⓓ ⓔ
48. ⓐ ⓑ ⓒ ⓓ ⓔ
49. ⓐ ⓑ ⓒ ⓓ ⓔ
50. ⓐ ⓑ ⓒ ⓓ ⓔ

Logical Reasoning Test

1. After 9/11, the Border Patrol was merged into the Department of Homeland Security (DHS). Subsequently, the Border Patrol's primary focus shifted toward preventing terrorists and terrorist weapons from entering the United States. However, the Border Patrol's traditional mission—the deterrence, detection, and apprehension of illegal immigrants and individuals involved in the illegal drug trade who attempt to enter the United States other than through designated ports of entry—also stands as an important concern.

   From the information given here, it can be validly concluded that:

   a. the Border Patrol no longer focuses on apprehending illegal immigrants.
   b. the Border Patrol no longer focuses on apprehending terrorists.
   c. the Border Patrol must encourage individuals to enter the United States through designated ports of entry.
   d. the Border Patrol must focus on preventing terrorists and illegal immigrants from entering the United States.
   e. the Border Patrol must review its priorities with the DHS.

2. If a nonimmigrant alien (for example, a student) enters the United States illegally or enters legally but violates her nonimmigrant status, she is considered to be "out of status." A nonimmigrant who remains out of status for at least 180 days may be deported and will be unable to reenter the United States for three years. A nonimmigrant who remains out of status for at least 365 days may be deported and will be unable to reenter the United States for ten years. Esther is a nonimmigrant alien who is living in the United States.

   From the information given here, it can be validly concluded that:

   a. Esther is a student.
   b. Esther is out of status.
   c. Esther will be unable to reenter the United States for at least ten years.
   d. Esther will be unable to reenter the United States for at least three years.
   e. Esther may be in the United States legally.

3. Statistics have shown that more crimes are committed at night than during the day in border states. The agent in charge wishes to increase the number of guards he has stationed along the border during nighttime hours. The northwest sector of the border is six miles long. The agent would like a guard to be stationed every quarter of a mile each evening.

   From the information given here, it CANNOT be validly concluded that:

   a. the northwest sector of the border is more prone to crime than the other sectors.
   b. the agent feels that an effective crime prevention measure is to station a greater number of guards along the border at night.
   c. fewer crimes are committed during the daytime in border states.
   d. the agent is in charge of the northwest sector of the border.
   e. none of the above

4. United States immigration laws contain several grounds upon which non-citizens may be "removed," or deported back to their country of origin. Some examples of grounds upon which removal may occur are: having helped smuggle aliens into the United States, having falsely claimed to be a U.S. citizen in order to gain governmental benefits, or having gained legal status by committing marriage fraud.
From the information given here, it can be validly concluded that:
   a. smuggling aliens into the United States is not a crime that could result in removal.
   b. making false claims is not a serious offense.
   c. a non-citizen in a false marriage may be removed.
   d. smuggling aliens into the United States is a lesser crime than claiming to be a U.S. citizen.
   e. none of the above

5. A Border Patrol Agent has been called upon to perform a farm and ranch check. This check consists of a methodical inspection of farms, ranches, lumber camps, and other potential workplaces that may employ laborers and other unskilled or semi-skilled workers. The agent is performing a thorough review of employment documentation in an attempt to uncover aliens who have escaped detection at U.S. borders or who have violated their immigration status. If an illegal alien is discovered, the agent may begin the process for him or her to be detained or deported, or arrange for him or her to depart voluntarily from the United States.
From the information given here, it can be validly concluded that:
   a. ranches and lumber camps always employ illegal aliens.
   b. an agent's inspection of a workplace should be thorough and methodical.
   c. aliens working on ranches and lumber camps have violated their immigration status.
   d. aliens working on ranches and lumber camps have escaped detection at the U.S. border.
   e. semi-skilled workers on ranches are never aliens.

6. The chief may grant one promotion per year. She commands a team of 15 officers, three of whom are eligible for promotion. She evaluates the officers based on characteristics such as leadership ability, analytical skills, conflict resolution, seniority, and so on. Officer Grant is being promoted this year.

From the information given here, it CANNOT be validly concluded that:
a. Officer Grant exhibits leadership skills.
b. Officer Grant exhibits analytical skills.
c. Officer Grant exhibits skills in conflict resolution.
d. Officer Grant is eligible for promotion this year.
e. Officer Grant has more seniority than the other 14 officers.

7. Border Patrol Agents work for the U.S. Customs and Border Protection Agency (CBP). They enforce the laws of the United States by screening passengers, vehicles, and shipments entering the United States; seizing illegal narcotics, vehicles, and agricultural products; preventing unauthorized entry into the United States; and rescuing individuals who encounter danger when crossing U.S. borders.

From the information given here, it CANNOT be validly concluded that:
a. one of the CBP's priorities is seizure of illegal narcotics.
b. agents strive to prevent illegal entry into the United States.
c. it is always dangerous to cross U.S. borders.
d. agents are sometimes called upon to rescue individuals who are crossing a U.S. border.
e. the CBP works to enforce the laws of the United States.

8. In an ongoing effort to protect the border, the U.S. Border Patrol is building a new substation in the southwest corner of a certain state, which is considered one of the weaker points along the international line. The nearest border patrol station is more than 70 miles away. The area is known for human trafficking and drug smuggling, and is sparsely populated, with approximately two people per square mile. The terrain is difficult to patrol, as the roads are poorly constructed and weeds and sagebrush make passage difficult.

From the information given here, it can be validly concluded that:
a. there is more human trafficking in the southwest corner of the state than in the area of the station 70 miles away.
b. the construction of the new substation is a measure being taken to prevent drug smuggling in the area.
c. guards from the nearest border patrol station do not patrol the southwest corner.
d. human trafficking is not the focus of the nearest border patrol station.
e. the southwest corner of the state is not considered a weak section along the international line.

9. There are two ways to obtain asylum status in the United States: through the affirmative process and through the defensive process. The affirmative process refers to applicants who are in legal status and not in removal proceedings. Applicants simply file Form I-589, Application for Asylum and for Withholding of Removal with USCIS. There is no filing fee required. USCIS will send a notice for a biometrics appointment to the applicant and later schedule them for the asylum interview. A defensive application refers to applicants being in removal proceedings in immigration court.

From the information given here, it CANNOT be validly concluded that:

a. if an applicant does not file Form I-589, then he or she is not participating in the affirmative process.
b. if an applicant files a defensive application, then he or she is not participating in the affirmative process.
c. if an applicant is not in removal proceedings, then he or she cannot file a defensive application.
d. if an applicant files Form I-589, then he or she is participating in the affirmative process.
e. if an applicant files Form I-589, then he or she will pay a fee.

10. Trace evidence may fall into several categories, and includes microscopic evidence such as hair, fibers, paint, and bloodstains. Every contact between a suspect and people or objects at the scene of a crime, including the victim, leaves traces. Evidence is transferred from suspect to scene, and vice versa. The perpetrator may leave his or her own hair behind in a crime scene, for instance. Trace evidence can be a powerful form of evidence that can lead to identification of the perpetrator. Most often, trace evidence is found in the form of textile fibers and paint flakes.

From the information given here, it can be validly concluded that:

a. if there is trace evidence at a crime scene, then it is most likely a bloodstain.
b. if there is trace evidence at a crime scene, then it is most likely paint flakes or fibers.
c. if hair is found at a crime scene, then it is the perpetrator's.
d. if a bloodstain is found at a crime scene, then it is most likely the perpetrator's.
e. none of the above

11. In 2002, Congress passed legislation mandating the Department of Homeland Security (DHS); it became operational in 2003. Most agencies making up the new department merged in March of that year, but some did not. The Border Patrol was one of the agencies folded into the newly created DHS. The DHS merged 22 agencies, including the U.S. Customs Service (which had been part of the Treasury Department) and the INS (which had been part of the Justice Department).

From the information given here, it can be validly concluded that:

a. if the INS was part of the Justice Department, then it was after 2003.
b. if the Border Patrol was part of the DHS, then it was prior to 2002.
c. if the U.S. Customs Service was part of the DHS, then it was after 2003.
d. if the U.S. Customs Service was part of the Treasury Department, then it was after 2003.
e. none of the above

12. Forensic scientists place evidence into various categories. Direct evidence establishes fact without the need for further analysis. Perhaps the most important form of direct evidence is the eyewitness account. If a witness observed a murder, then there may be nothing to add (although the witness could give false testimony and other evidence may be needed to prove this). Circumstantial evidence is more indirect and it is up to the forensic scientist to provide an explanation for it through his or her investigations. Most of the evidence handled in the forensic lab is circumstantial evidence. Although more objective than direct evidence, there is always the danger of losing or contaminating circumstantial evidence.

From the information given here, it can be validly concluded that:

a. if direct evidence has established fact, then further analysis is unnecessary.
b. if evidence is being handled in the forensic lab, it is direct evidence.
c. if a witness saw a murder occur, then no additional evidence is necessary.
d. if evidence is being handled in the forensic lab, it is circumstantial evidence.
e. none of the above

13. During a routine traffic check, an agent discovered a sizable amount of contraband secreted in the false bottom of a van by a smuggler. On investigating further, she found four other vans that she suspected of cooperating with the smuggler, as well. Three of the vans had false bottoms, but only one of the vans contained contraband.
    From the information given here, it can be validly concluded that:
    a. if a van contains contraband, it does not have a false bottom.
    b. if a van has a false bottom, it contains contraband.
    c. if a van contains contraband, it has a false bottom.
    d. if a van has a false bottom, it does not contain contraband.
    e. none of the above

14. In order to become a U.S. Border Patrol Agent, applicants must meet specific criteria; they must be a U.S. citizen who is under the age of 40 at the time of application and in possession of a valid state driver's license, among others. Ingrid is not eligible to become a U.S. Border Patrol Agent.
    From the information given here, it can be validly concluded that:
    a. if Ingrid is 39, she is not a U.S. citizen and/or does not have a valid driver's license.
    b. if Ingrid has a valid driver's license, she is 41.
    c. if Ingrid is a U.S. citizen, she is 41.
    d. if Ingrid has a valid driver's license and is 39, she is a U.S. citizen.
    e. if Ingrid is a U.S. citizen and is 39, she has a valid driver's license.

15. The Fourth Amendment prohibits the government from conducting unreasonable searches and seizures while investigating criminal activity and building a case against a particular suspect. The Fifth Amendment prohibits the government from compelling individuals to incriminate themselves, from denying individuals due process of law, from subjecting individuals to multiple punishments or prosecutions for a single offense, and from being prosecuted in federal court without first being indicted by a grand jury. The Sixth Amendment guarantees defendants the right to a speedy and public trial by an impartial jury, the right to be informed of all charges against them, the right to confront adverse witnesses, the right to subpoena favorable witnesses, and the right to an attorney. The Eighth Amendment prohibits the government from requiring excessive bail to be posted for pre-trial release, from imposing excessive fines, and from inflicting cruel and unusual punishments.
    From the information given here, it CANNOT be validly concluded that:
    a. if an individual is being prosecuted in federal court, then he or she has been indicted by a grand jury.
    b. if the government has imposed an excessive fine, then the Sixth Amendment has been violated.
    c. if due process has been denied, then the Fifth Amendment has been violated.
    d. if an individual has been informed of all charges, then the Sixth Amendment has been upheld.
    e. none of the above

16. Aliens may qualify as Special Immigrants, who are given green card priority, if they meet certain conditions. These individuals are able to invest $1 million and create at least ten new full-time jobs in the U.S. economy. In certain situations, an investment of $500,000 may be acceptable, if this investment creates at least five new jobs. Further consideration may be given to investors who will create jobs in certain targeted areas.

From the information given here, it CANNOT be validly concluded that:

a. if an individual qualifies as a Special Immigrant, then he or she can invest at least $500,000 and create at least five new jobs.
b. if an individual can create jobs in certain targeted areas, can invest $1 million, and will create at least ten new jobs, then he or she may be given priority.
c. if an individual is given priority, he or she can invest at least $500,000 and create at least five new jobs.
d. if an individual can invest less than $500,000 in the U.S. economy, he or she will be given special consideration.
e. none of the above

Artificial Language Review

Artificial Language Supplemental Booklet

To answer the Artificial Language questions, refer to the sections that follow: Vocabulary Lists and Grammatical Rules.

Some of the words given in the following Vocabulary Lists are not the same as those that will be given in the actual Border Patrol Exam. Therefore, it is best not to memorize them before taking the actual test. The Grammatical Rules are the same as those used in the actual test, except that some of the prefixes (word beginnings) and suffixes (word endings) used in the real test differ from those used here.

Vocabulary Lists for the Artificial Language

ARRANGED ALPHABETICALLY BY THE ENGLISH WORD

ENGLISH	ARTIFICIAL LANGUAGE	ENGLISH	ARTIFICIAL LANGUAGE
a, an	bex	skillful	autile
alien	huslek	that	velle
and	cre	the	ric
boy	ekaplek	this	volle
car	tenlek	to be	synkir
country	failek	to border	regkir
danger	gonlek	to cross	chonkir
difficult	brale	to document	clegkir
enemy	avelek	to escape	pirkir
friend	kometlek	to guard	bonkir
from	mor	to have	tulkir
government	almanlek	to identify	kalenkir
he, him	yev	to inspect	zelkir
land	ponlek	to patrol	linkir
legal	colle	to question	pafkir
man	kaplek	to report	fonkir
on	qua	to station	lexkir
river	browlek	to work	frigkir

ARRANGED ALPHABETICALLY BY THE ARTIFICIAL LANGUAGE WORD

ARTIFICIAL LANGUAGE	ENGLISH	ARTIFICIAL LANGUAGE	ENGLISH
almanlek	government	kalenkir	to identify
autile	skillful	kometlek	friend
avelek	enemy	lexkir	to station
bex	a, an	linkir	to patrol
bonkir	to guard	mor	from
brale	difficult	pafkir	to question

browlek	river	pirkir	to escape
chonkir	to cross	ponlek	land
clegkir	to document	qua	on
colle	legal	regkir	to border
cre	and	ric	the
ekaplek	boy	synkir	to be
failek	country	tenlek	car
fonkir	to report	tulkir	to have
frigkir	to work	velle	that
gonlek	danger	volle	this
huslek	alien	yev	he, him
kaplek	man	zelkir	to inspect

Grammatical Rules for the Artificial Language

The Grammatical Rules given here are the same as those used in the Border Patrol Exam, except that the prefixes (word beginnings) and suffixes (word endings) used in the exam differ from those used here.

During the exam, you will have access to the rules at all times. Consequently, it is important that you understand these rules, but it is not necessary that you memorize them. In fact, memorizing them will hinder rather than help you, because the beginnings and endings of words are different in the version of the Artificial Language that appears in this manual than the one that appears in the actual test.

You should note that Part Three of the official Artificial Language Manual contains a glossary of grammatical terms to assist you if you are not thoroughly familiar with the meanings of these grammatical terms.

Rule 1

To form the feminine singular of a noun, a pronoun, an adjective, or an article, add the suffix -lif to the masculine singular form. Only nouns, pronouns, adjectives, and articles take feminine endings in the Artificial Language. When gender is not specified, the masculine form is used.

Examples

If a *male eagle* is a *verlek*, then a *female eagle* is a *verleklif*.

If an *ambitious* man is a *tosle* man, an *ambitious* woman is a *toslelif* woman.

Rule 2

To form the plural of nouns, pronouns, and adjectives, add the suffix -ob to the correct singular form.

Examples

If one *male eagle* is a *verlek*, then several *male eagles* are *verlekob*.

If an *ambitious* woman is a *toslelif* woman, several *ambitious* women are *toslelifob* women.

Rule 3
Adjectives modifying nouns and pronouns with feminine and/or plural endings must have endings that agree with the words they modify. In addition, an article (*a*, *an*, and *the*) preceding a noun must also agree with the noun in gender and number.

Examples
If an *active male eagle* is a *sojle verlek*, then an *active female eagle* is a *sojlelif verleklif* and several *active female eagles* are *sojlelifob verleklifob*.

If *this male eagle* is *volle verlek*, *these female eagles* are *vollelifob verleklifob*.

If *the male eagle* is *ric verlek*, *the female eagle* is *riclif verleklif* and *the female eagles* are *riclifob verleklifob*.

If *a male eagle* is *bex verlek*, *several male eagles* are *bexob verlekob*.

Rule 4
The stem of the verb is obtained by omitting the suffix -*kir* from the infinitive form of the verb.

Example
The stem of the verb *synkir* is *syn*.

Rule 5
All subjects and their verbs must agree in number; that is, singular subjects require singular verbs and plural subjects require plural verbs. (See Rules 6 and 7.)

Rule 6
To form the present tense of a verb, add the suffix -*ot* to the stem for the singular form or the suffix -*et* to the stem for the plural.

Example
If *to bark* is *nalkir*, then *nalot* is the present tense for the singular (the dog *barks*) and *nalet* is the present tense for the plural (the dogs *bark*).

Rule 7
To form the past tense of a verb, first add the suffix -*rem* to the stem, and then add the suffix -*ot* if the verb is singular or the suffix -*et* if it is plural.

Example
If *to bark* is *nalkir*, then *nalremot* is the past tense for the singular (the dog *barked*), and *nalremet* is the past tense for the plural (the dogs *barked*).

Rule 8
To form the past participle of a verb, add to the stem of the verb the suffix -*to*. It can be used to form compound tenses with the verb *to have*, as a predicate with the verb *to be*, or as an adjective. In the last two cases, it takes masculine, feminine, singular, and plural forms in agreement with the noun to which it refers.

Example of use in a compound tense with the verb *to have*
If *to bark* is *nalkir* and *to have* is *tulkir*, then *tulot nalto* is the present perfect for the singular (the dog *has barked*) and *tulet nalto* is the present perfect for the plural (the dogs *have barked*). Similarly, *tulremot nalto* is the past perfect for the singular (the dog *had barked*) and *tulremet nalto* is the past perfect for the plural (the dogs *had barked*).

Example of use as a predicate with the verb *to be*
If *to adopt* is *rapkir* and *to be* is *synkir*, then *a boy was adopted* is *ekaplek synremot rapto* and many *girls were adopted* is *ekapleklifob synremet raptolifob*.

Example of use as an adjective
If *to delight* is *kaskir*, then a *delighted boy* is *kasto ekaplek* and many *delighted girls* are *kastolifob ekapleklifob*.

Rule 9

To form a noun from a verb, add the suffix *-lek* to the stem of the verb.

Example
If *longkir* is *to write*, then a *writer* is a *longlek*.

Rule 10

To form an adjective from a noun, substitute the suffix *-le* for the suffix *-lek*.

Example
If *pellek* is *beauty*, then a *beautiful male eagle* is a *pelle verlek*, and a *beautiful female eagle* is a *pellelif verleklif*. (Note the feminine ending *-lif*.)

Rule 11

To form an adverb from an adjective, add the suffix *-de* to the masculine form of the adjective. (Note that adverbs do not change their form to agree in number or gender with the word they modify.)

Example
If *pelle* is *beautiful*, then *beautifully* is *pellede*.

Rule 12

To form the possessive of a noun or pronoun, add the suffix *-oe* to the noun or pronoun after any plural or feminine suffixes.

Examples
If a *boglek* is a *dog*, then a *dog's* collar is a *boglekoe* collar.

If *he* is *yev*, then *his* book is *yevoe* book.

If *she* is *yevlif*, then *her* book is *yevlifoe* book.

Rule 13

To make a word negative, add the prefix *mu-* to the correct affirmative form.

Examples
If an *active male eagle* is a *sojle verlek*, then an *inactive male eagle* is a *musojle verlek*.

If the *dog barks* is *boglek nalot*, then the *dog does not bark* is *boglek munalot*.

Artificial Language

Use the Vocabulary Lists and Grammatical Rules to help you answer these questions.

For each sentence, decide which words have been translated correctly. Use scratch paper to list each numbered word that is correctly translated into the Artificial Language. When you have finished listing the words that are correctly translated in sentences 1 through 20, select your answer according to the following instructions:

Mark:
a. if *only* the word numbered 1 is correctly translated.
b. if *only* the word numbered 2 is correctly translated.
c. if *only* the word numbered 3 is correctly translated.
d. if *two or more* of the numbered words are correctly translated.
e. if *none* of the numbered words is correctly translated.

Be sure to list only the *numbered* words that are *correctly* translated.

Study the sample question before going on to the test questions.

PRACTICE TEST 5

Sample Sentence
This woman crossed the river.

Sample Translation
Bex kapleklif chonremet lac browlek.
 1   2   3

The word numbered 1, *bex*, is incorrect because the translation of *bex* is *a*. The word *vollelif* should have been used. The word numbered 2 is correct. *Kapleklif* has been correctly formed by adding the feminine ending to the masculine noun, applying Rule 1. The word numbered 3, *chonremet*, is incorrect because the singular form, *chonremot*, should have been used. Because the word numbered 2 is correct, the answer to the sample question is **b**.

Now go on with questions 1 through 20 and answer them in the manner indicated. Be sure to record your answers on the separate answer sheet found at the beginning of the test.

Sentence

1. The patrol questions the aliens.

2. These boys are friends.

3. The enemies are on the border.

4. The friendly workers do not have those documents.

5. These women are station guards.

6. An alien was reported to be on the land.

7. The women escaped from the guards.

8. The boys identified them.

9. Those girls are not illegal aliens.

10. They are difficult women to identify.

11. The patrol identified the enemies.

12. The governmental inspectors work from the station.

13. They have to cross the border.

14. The inspectors questioned her work.

15. Those reporters inspected the documents.

Translation

Ric linlek pafkot ricob husleklifob.
     1   2   3

Velleob ekapleob synet kometlekob.
   1   2   3

Ric avelekob synet qua ric reglek.
 1   2   3

Ricob kometlekob friglekob mutulet
         1   2
vellekob cleglekob.
   3

Vollelifob kapleklifob synet lexleklifob bonleklifob.
     1   2   3

Bex huslek synremot fonto synkir qua ric ponlek.
 1   2   3

Riclifob kapleklifob pirkirremet mor riclifob bonlekob.
            1   2   3

Ricob ekaplekob kalenremot yevob.
          1   2   3

Velleob ekapleklifob musynet mucolleob husleklifob.
   1   2   3

Yevlifob synet bralelifob kapleklifob kalenkirlifob.
   1   2   3

Ric linlek kalenot ricob aveleklifob.
     1   2   3

Ricob almanleob zellekob friget
          1   2
mor ric lexlek.
 3

Yevob tulkir chonet ric reglek.
        1   2   3

Ricob zellekob pafremet yevoe friglek.
                  1   2   3

Ricob fonlekob zelremet ricob cleglekob.
         1   2   3

PRACTICE TEST 5

16. The woman and boy did not have difficult questions.
Riclif kapleklif <u>creob</u> ekaplek <u>mutulremet</u>
          1   2
braleob <u>pafkirlekob</u>.
              3

17. The women have illegally crossed the land.
Riclifob kapleklifob <u>tulet</u> <u>mucolleoe</u> <u>chonkirto</u> ric ponlek.
                        1   2   3

18. That man skillfully escaped from the guards.
<u>Volle</u> kaplek <u>autilede</u> <u>pirremot</u> mor ricob bonklekob.
   1   2   3

19. The dangerous land was not patrolled.
Ric <u>gonlek</u> ponlek <u>synremotmu</u> <u>linto</u>.
       1   2   3

20. Those women are the governmental inspectors.
Vellelifob kapleklifob <u>synet</u> riclifob <u>almanlelifob</u>
                          1   2
<u>zelleklifob</u>.
        3

For each question in this group, select one of the five suggested choices that correctly translates the italicized word or group of words into the Artificial Language.

Sample Question
Where are *the friends*?
a. bex kometlek
b. ric kometlek
c. ricob kometlekob
d. ric kometlekob
e. bex kometlekob

Choice **c** is the correct translation of the italicized words, *the friends*, because the definite article, *ric*, must change its ending to agree with the noun (see Rule 3), and the noun *kometlekob* has the proper plural suffix (Rule 2).

Paragraph

The nation's *border patrol* is made up of determined *men and women*. Dedicated to safeguarding
                          21   22
their country, they work under *difficult and dangerous* conditions. *To guard the border*
           23   24   25
from the government's enemies, they often *have to cross* rough terrain in freezing or scorching
                26   27
temperatures. Frequently they *are stationed* far from the conveniences they grew up with. An important
                                    28
aspect of their job is that they *identify and question illegal aliens.* They must also carefully prepare
                                              29
governmental documents to report their findings.
                30

159

PRACTICE TEST 5

21. a. regkirlek linkirlek
    b. regkirle linkirle
    c. regle linlek
    d. regle linle
    e. regkirle linlek

22. a. kaplek cre kapleklif
    b. kapleklifob creob kaplekob
    c. kaplekob creob kapleklifob
    d. kapleklifob cre kaplekob
    e. kaplekob cre kapleklifob

23. a. yevoboe failek, yevob friget
    b. yevoboe failekob, yevob friget
    c. yevob failekob, yevob frigetob
    d. yevob failek, yevoboe frigetob
    e. yevoeob failek, yevob friget

24. a. braleob creob gonleob
    b. braleob cre gonleob
    c. braleob cre gonlekob
    d. bralekob cre gonlekob
    e. bralekob creob gonlekob

25. a. bonto ric reglek
    b. bonet ric regle
    c. bonet ric reglek
    d. bonkir ric reglek
    e. bonkir ric regle

26. a. mor ricob almanlekoe avelekob
    b. mor ricoboe almanlekoe avelekob
    c. mor ricob almanlekob avelekob
    d. qua ricob almanlekoe avelekoboe
    e. qua ricoboe almanlekoe avelekoboe

27. a. tulot chonkir
    b. tulkir chonkir
    c. tulkir chonet
    d. tulet chonet
    e. tulet chonkir

28. a. synot lexto
    b. synot lextoob
    c. synet lextoob
    d. synet lexto
    e. synto lexremet

29. a. kalenot cre pafot mucolleob huslekob
    b. kalenet cre pafet mucolleob huslekob
    c. kalenot bex pafot collemuob husklekob
    d. kalenet bex pafet collemuob huslekob
    e. kalenot bex pafot colleobmu huslekob

30. a. almanlekob cleglekob fonkirob
    b. almanleob clegleob fonkirob
    c. almanleob clegleob fonkir
    d. almanleob cleglekob fonkir
    e. almanlekob cleglekob fonkir

For this group of questions, select the one response option that is the correct translation of the English word or words in parentheses. You should translate the entire sentence in order to determine what form should be used.

Sample Question
Ricob almanlekoe tatlekob (crossed the border).
  a. chonremet bex reglek
  b. chonremot ric reglek
  c. chonremet ric reglek
  d. chonremet ric regkir
  e. chonremot bex reglek

Ricob almanlekoe tatlekob chonremet ric reglek means *The government's spies crossed the border.*

Because *chonremet ric reglek* is the only one of these expressions that means *they* (plural) *crossed the border*, choice **c** is the correct answer to the sample question.

31. (These girls did not have) kometlekob mor ric failek.
 a. Vellelifob ekapleklifob tulremotmu
 b. Velleob ekaplekob mutulremot
 c. Volleob ekaplekob tulremetmu
 d. Vollelifob ekapleklifob mutulremet
 e. Vollelifob ekapleklifoe mutulkirremet

32. Yevlif kalenremot (this illegal document).
 a. volle mucolle cleglek
 b. volle collemu cleglek
 c. volle mucolle clegkirlek
 d. velle collemu clegkirlek
 e. velle mucolle cleglek

33. Ric fonlek synot mor (an identified enemy).
 a. ric kalento avelek
 b. ric kalenkirto avelek
 c. bex kalen avelekto
 d. bex kalenkirto avelek
 e. bex kalento avelek

34. Velle fonlek synot (from the station guards).
 a. mor ric lexleob bonlekob
 b. mor ricob lexleob bonlekob
 c. mor ricob lexlekob bonlekob
 d. mor ric lexleob bonleob
 e. mor ricob lexlekob bonleob

35. (The border patrol) chonremot ric browlek.
 a. Ric regle linkirlek
 b. Ric reglek linle
 c. Ric regle linlek
 d. Ric reglek linlek
 e. Ric regkirle linkirlek

36. (The inspector's station) synremot bonto.
 a. Ric zelkiroe lexkirlek
 b. Ric zellekoe lexkirlek
 c. Ric zellekob lexle
 d. Ric zellekob lexlek
 e. Ric zellekoe lexlek

37. (That inspector questioned) ricob lexleob friglekob.
 a. Velle zellek pafremot
 b. Velle zellek pafremet
 c. Velle zelkirlek pafremot
 d. Volle zelkirlek pafremet
 e. Volle zelle pafremot

38. Vollelif kometlelif (woman does not have the document).
 a. kaplelif mutulet ric clegle
 b. kapleklif mutulot ric cleglek
 c. kapleklif mutulkirot ric clegkirlek
 d. kaplelif tulotmu ric clegkirlek
 e. kaplelif tulotmu ric cleglek

39. (The guard's report) synremot pafto.
 a. Ric bonkirleklifoe fonkirlek
 b. Ric bonkirlekoe fonkirlek
 c. Ric bonleklifoe fonlek
 d. Ric bonlekoe fonlek
 e. Ric bonlekob fonlek

40. (This dangerous woman was) pafto qua ric reglek.
 a. Vellelif gonlelif kapleklif synremet
 b. Vellelif gonlelif kapleklif synremot
 c. Vollelif gonlelif kapleklif synremot
 d. Vollelif gonleklif kapleklif synremet
 e. Volle gonle kaplek synremet

41. Ric fonlek kalenremot (the girls on the land).
 a. riclifob ekapleklifob qua ric ponlek
 b. ric ekapleklifob qua ric ponlek
 c. riclif ekapleklif qua riclif ponleklif
 d. riclif ekapleklif qua ric ponlek
 e. ricob ekaplekob qua ricob ponlekob

42. (Her friendly questions) synremet mor ric cleglek.
  a. Yevlifoe kometlekob pafleob
  b. Yevlifoboe kometlekob paflekob
  c. Yevlifoboe kometleob paflekob
  d. Yevlifob kometleob paflekob
  e. Yevoboe kometleob pafleob

For the last group of questions, select one of the five suggested choices that is the correct form of the italicized expression as it is used in the sentence. At the end of the sentence, you will find instructions in parentheses telling you which form to use. In some sentences you will be asked to supply the correct forms of two or more expressions. In this case, the instructions for these expressions are presented consecutively in the parentheses and are separated by a dash (for example, past tense—adverb). Be sure to translate the entire sentence before selecting your answer.

Sample Question
Yev *bonkir* ric browlek. (present tense)
  a. bonremot
  b. bonremet
  c. boneet
  d. bonet
  e. bonot

Choices **a** and **b** are incorrect because they are in the past tense. Choice **c** is misspelled. Choice **d** is in the present tense, but it too is incorrect because the subject of the sentence is singular and therefore takes a verb with a singular rather than a plural ending. Choice **e** is the answer to the sample question.

43. Ricob *almanlek* zellekob synremet *kometlek*. (masculine plural adjective—negative masculine plural adjective)
  a. almanle—mukometle
  b. almanle—kometlemu
  c. almanleob—mukometleob
  d. almanleob—kometleobmu
  e. almanlekob—mukometlekob

44. Ricob bonlekob *fsrigkir* qua ric reglek. (past plural verb)
  a. frigrem
  b. frigot
  c. frigremot
  d. frigremet
  e. frigkirremet

45. Riclifob *ekaplek* paflekob synremet *brale*. (feminine plural possessive noun—negative plural adjective)
  a. ekapleklifoe—bralemu
  b. ekapleklifoboe—mubraleob
  c. ekapleklifob—mubraleob
  d. ekapleklifoboe—mubrale
  e. ekapleklifoe—braleobmu

46. Ric *bonkir autile* pafremot ric huslek. (feminine singular noun—adverb)
  a. bonlek—autile
  b. bonlek—autilede
  c. bonleklif—autilelif
  d. bonleklif—autilede
  e. bonleklif—autilelifde

47. *Volle* kapleklif synremot *pafkir* qua ric reglek. (feminine singular article—feminine singular past participle)
  a. Velle—pafkirto
  b. Vellelif—paftolif
  c. Vellelif—pafto
  d. Vollelif—pafto
  e. Vollelif—paftolif

48. Riclif ekapleklif *synkir* ric ekaplekoe *kometlek*.
(negative singular past tense verb—feminine singular noun)
   a. synremotmu—kometlek
   b. musynremot—kometleklif
   c. musynremet—kometleklif
   d. synremetmu—kometlek
   e. musynkirremot—kometleklif

49. Riclif *lexkir* frigleklif *clegkir* ricob huslekob.
(feminine singular adjective—negative singular past tense verb)
   a. lexlelif—muclegremot
   b. lexlelif—muclegremet
   c. lexleklif—muclegremot
   d. lexleklif—muclegremet
   e. lexle—clegmuremot

50. Ricob zellekob *tulkir clegkir yev* friglek.
(negative plural present tense verb—past participle—plural male possessive adjective)
   a. mutulet—clegkirto—yevob
   b. tuletmu—clegkirto—yevlifoe
   c. tulmuot—clegto—yevoe
   d. mutulot—clegtoob—yevoboe
   e. mutulet—clegto—yevoboe

Answers

Logical Reasoning

1. d. Choice **d**, which highlights both important concerns on which the Border Patrol must focus as given in the paragraph, is the correct answer. Choices **a** and **b** contradict information given in the paragraph, so they are incorrect. Choices **c** and **e** are conclusions that cannot be drawn from information given in the paragraph, so they are incorrect.

2. e. As the paragraph does not provide information on whether Esther has violated her non-immigrant status or entered the country illegally, it may be concluded that she may be in the country legally; therefore, choice **e** is correct. Choices **a**, **b**, **c**, and **d** are not proved valid through information provided in the paragraph, so they are not correct.

3. a. Choice **a** contains information that cannot be concluded from the paragraph, so this is the correct answer. Choices **b**, **c**, and **d** restate information given in the paragraph, so they are incorrect. Choice **e** is incorrect because the correct answer is provided in the choices.

4. c. Choice **c** restates information provided in the paragraph, and is therefore the correct answer. Choices **a**, **b**, and **d** cannot be concluded from the information provided in the paragraph, so they are incorrect. The correct answer is provided within the choices, so choice **e** is incorrect.

5. b. Choice **b** is the only answer that can be validly concluded from the sentences in the paragraph. Choice **a** is an incorrect assumption, and is therefore the wrong answer. Choices **c**, **d**, and **e** make assumptions that are not supported by the paragraph, and are therefore incorrect answers.

6. e. Choice e states that Officer Grant has more seniority than all the other officers on the team, but that is not necessarily true based on the information given in the paragraph, so this is the correct answer. Choices a, b, c, and d all contain information that can be concluded from the information provided in the paragraph, so they are incorrect.

7. c. Choice c makes an assumption—that crossing the border is always dangerous—that is not supported by the paragraph, and is therefore the correct answer. Choices a, b, d, and e all restate information contained within the paragraph, so they are incorrect answers.

8. b. Choice b, which restates information provided in the first and third sentences, is the correct answer. Choices a, c, and d are conclusions that cannot be drawn from the information provided in the paragraph, so they are incorrect answers. Choice e contradicts information provided in the first sentence of the paragraph, so it is an incorrect answer.

9. e. Choice e contradicts information in the third and fourth sentences in the paragraph, so it is the correct response. Choices a, b, c, and d restate information found in the paragraph, so they are incorrect choices.

10. b. Choice b restates information found in the last sentence of the paragraph, so it is the correct answer. Choices a, c, and d are faulty conclusions that could not have been drawn from the information in the paragraph, so they are incorrect. The correct answer is provided within the choices, so choice e is incorrect.

11. c. Choice c restates information found in the second and third sentences in the paragraph, so it is the correct answer. Choices a, b, and d confuse information provided in the paragraph, so they are incorrect. Because the correct response is found in the answers, choice e is incorrect.

12. a. Choice a restates information found in the second sentence, so it is correct. Choices b and d confuse information found in the sixth sentence, so they are incorrect. Choice c confuses information found in the second sentence, so it is incorrect. Because the correct response is found in the answers, choice e is incorrect.

13. e. Answers a, b, c, and d make false assumptions that are not based on the information given, so choice e is the correct answer.

14. a. Applicants must meet all three of the criteria outlined in the paragraph, so if Ingrid meets the age limit requirement she must fail one or both of the others, so choice a is correct. Choices b and c cannot be concluded because information on the third criteria is missing. Ingrid's age cannot be concluded from her meeting the first criterion in each response, so they are not correct. Choices d and e are not correct because she meets all three criteria in both scenarios, which contradicts the information given in the last sentence.

15. b. Choice b confuses information provided in the last sentence because the Eighth Amendment actually deals with excessive fines, so b is not a valid conclusion and is the correct answer. Choices a, c, and d restate information found in the paragraph, so they are incorrect answers. The correct response is found within the answers, so choice e is incorrect.

16. d. Choice **d** confuses information provided in the third sentence and cannot be concluded from the paragraph, so it is the correct answer.

Artificial Language

1. a. Only the word numbered 1 is correct, so the answer is **a**. *Patrol* is translated by adding the suffix *-lek* to the stem (Rule 9) of *linkir* (*to patrol*). Word 2 is incorrect because, instead of adding the suffix *-ot* (Rule 6) to the stem, *-paf*, of the infinitive *pafkir* (*to question*), the suffix was added to *pafk-*. The word should have been *pafot*. Word 3 is incorrect because, even though it does include the plural suffix *-ob* (Rule 2), it unnecessarily includes the feminine suffix *-lif*, which is only used if the gender of the word is specified (Rule 1). The word should have been *huslekob*.

2. c. Only the word numbered 3 is correct, so the answer is **c**. *Friends* is translated by adding the plural suffix *-ob* (Rule 2) to *kometlek* (*boys*). Even though it includes the suffix *-ob*, word 1 is incorrect because *these* should have been translated by beginning with the word *this* and then making it plural; instead, the word *velle* (*that*) was used. The word should have been *volleob*. Word 2 is incorrect because it is missing the *k*; to be formed correctly the suffix *-ob* should be added to *ekaplek*. The correct word, then, would have been *epaplekob*.

3. d. Words 2 and 3 are correct, so the answer is **d**. *Are* is translated by adding the plural verb suffix *-et* to the stem (Rule 6) of *synkir* (*to be*). Since *border* is a noun formed from a verb, it is translated by adding the suffix *-lek* to the stem (Rule 9) of *regkir* (*to border*). *The* has been incorrectly translated. It should be plural as it modifies *enemies* (Rule 3). The gender-neutral translation of *the* is formed by adding the suffix *-ob* to *ric* (Rule 2). The correct word would be *ricob*.

4. b. Only the word numbered 2 is correctly translated, so the answer is **b**. *Workers* is translated by adding the suffix *-lek* to the stem (Rule 9) of *frigkir* (*to work*) and then adding the plural suffix *-ob* (Rule 2). *Friendly* should translated by changing the suffix *-lek* in *kometlek* (*boys*) to *-le* (Rule 10) and then adding the plural suffix *-ob*. Word 2, however, includes *-lek*. The correct word would be *kometleob*. *Those* should be translated by adding the suffix *-ob* to *velle* (*that*) to form *velleob*; it is incorrect because it includes an unnecessary *k*.

5. d. Words 1 and 2 are correct, so the answer is **d**. *These* is translated by adding the feminine suffix *-lif* (Rule 1) and the plural suffix *-ob* (Rule 2) to *volle* (*this*). *Are* is translated by adding the plural verb suffix *-et* to the stem (Rule 6) of *synkir* (*to be*). *Station* is an adjective formed from a noun. The noun is formed from the verb *lexkir* (Rule 9) by adding suffix *-lek* to the stem; to create an adjective, *-lek* is substituted by the suffix *-le* (Rule 10). Then, as *women* is feminine and plural, the suffixes *-lif* and *-ob* are added to form *lexlelifob*. Word 3 is incorrect because *-lek* has not been changed to *-le*.

6. d. All three numbered words are correct, so the answer is **d**. *Bex* is the correct translation of *an*. *Was* is translated by adding the suffixes *-rem* and *-ot* to the stem (Rule 7) of *synkir* because it is in the past tense and singular. *Reported* is translated by adding the suffix *-to* to the stem (Rule 8) of *fonkir* (*to report*) because it is a past participle.

7. a. Only word 1 is correct, so the answer is **a**. *Women* is translated by adding the feminine suffix *-lif* (Rule 1) and the plural suffix *-ob* (Rule 2) to *kaplek* (*men*). *Escaped* should be translated by adding the suffixes *-rem* and *-et* to the stem (Rule 7) of *pirkir* (*to escape*) to form *pirremet*. Instead, the suffixes were added to the infinitive. *The* should be translated by adding the plural suffix *-ob* to *ric* (Rule 2) to form *ricob*. Instead, the feminine suffix *-lif* has been added unnecessarily to the words; *guards* is gender neutral, so *the* should be, too.

8. d. The words numbered 1 and 3 are correct, so the answer is **d**. *Boys* is translated by adding the plural suffix *-ob* (Rule 2) to *epaplek* (*boys*). *Them* is translated by added the suffix *-ob* to *yev* (*him*). *Identified* should have been translated by adding the suffixes *-rem* and *et* to the stem (Rule 7) of *kalenkir* (*to identify*) because the verb is in the past tense and plural to form *kalenremet*. Instead, the singular verb suffix *-ot* has been used.

9. b. Only word 2 is correct, so the answer is **b**. *Girls* is translated by adding the feminine suffix *-lif* (Rule 1) and the plural suffix *-ob* (Rule 2) to *ekaplek* (*boys*). *Those* should be translated by adding the suffixes *-lif* and *-ob* to *velle* (*that*); instead, the word is missing *-lif*. *Illegal* should be translated by the negative prefix *mu-* (Rule 13) and the suffixes *-lif* and *-ob* to *colle* (*legal*); instead, the word is missing *-lif*, as was the case with *those*.

10. d. Words 1 and 2 are correct, so the answer is **d**. *They* is translated by adding the feminine suffix *lif* (Rule 1), since *they* refers to women, and the plural suffix *-ob* (Rule 2) to *yev* (*he*). *Are* is translated by adding the suffix *-et* to the stem (Rule 6) of *synkir* (*to be*) because it is plural. *To identify* should be translated simply as the infinitive *kalenkir*; instead, the word includes the suffixes *-lif* and *-ob*.

11. a. Only word 1 is correct, so the answer is **a**. *Patrol* is translated by adding the suffix *-lek* to the stem (Rule 9) of *linkir* (*to patrol*). *Identified* should be translated by adding the suffixes *-rem* and *-ot* to the stem (Rule 7) of *kalenkir* (*to identifiy*) because the verb is in the past tense and singular, to form *kalenremot*; instead, the word is missing *-rem*. *Enemies* should be translated by adding the plural suffix *-ob* to *avelek* (*enemy*) to form *avelekob*. Instead, the word also includes the feminine suffix *-lif*, which it doesn't need since the word is gender neutral.

12. d. All three words are correct, so the answer is **d**. *Governmental* is translated by, first, changing the suffix *-lek* in *almanlek* (*government*) to the suffix *-le* (Rule 9) since it functions as an adjective, and then by adding the plural suffix *-ob* (Rule 2). *Inspectors* is translated by adding the suffix *-lek* to the stem (Rule 9) of *zelkir* (*to inspect*) and then adding the suffix *-ob*. *Mor* is the correct translation of *from*.

13. c. Only word 3 is correct, so the answer is **c**. *Border* is translated by adding the suffix *-lek* to the stem (Rule 9) of *regkir* (*to border*). *Have* should be translated by adding the suffix *-et* to the stem (Rule 6) of *tulkir* (*to have*) because the verb is in the present tense and plural to form *tulet*. *To cross* should have been translated simply as the infinitive *chonkir*.

14. d. Words 1 and 3 are correct, so the answer is **d**. *Questioned* is translated by adding the suffixes *-rem* and *-et* to the stem (Rule 7) of *pafkir* (*to question*) because it is in the past tense and plural. *Work* is translated by adding the suffix *-lek* to the stem (Rule 9) of *frigkir* (*to work*) because it is a noun formed from a verb. *Her* should be translated by adding the feminine suffix *-lif* (Rule 1) and the possessive suffix *-oe* (Rule 13) to *yev* (*he*) to form *yevlifoe*; instead, it is missing *-lif*.

15. d. Words 2 and 3 are correct, so the answer is **d**. *Inspected* is translated by adding the suffixes *-rem* and *-et* to the stem (Rule 7) of *zelkir* (*to inspect*) because the verb is in the past tense and is plural. *Documents* is translated by adding the suffix *-lek* to the stem (Rule 9) of *clegkir* (*to document*) because it is a noun formed from a verb, and then by adding the plural suffix *-ob* (Rule 2). *Those* should be translated by adding the plural suffix *-ob* (Rule 2) to *velle* (*that*) to form *velleob*; instead, *-ob* has been added to *ric* (*the*).

16. b. Only word 2 is correct, so the answer is **b**. *Did not have* is translated by adding the suffixes *-rem* and *-et* to the stem (Rule 7) of *tulkir* because the verb is in the past tense and is plural, and then by adding the negative prefix *mu-* (Rule 13). The correct translation of *and* is *cre*; this word, instead, includes the suffix *-ob*. *Questions* should be translated by adding the suffix *-lek* to the stem (Rule 9) of *pafkir* since it is a noun formed from a verb and then adding the plural suffix *-ob* (Rule 2) to form *paflekob*; instead, the suffixes were added to the infinitive of the verb.

17. a. Only word 1 is correct, so the answer is **a**. *Have* is translated by adding the suffix *-et* to the stem (Rule 6) of *tulkir* since the verb is in the present tense and is plural. *Illegally* should be translated by adding the suffix *-de* to form an adverb from the adjective *colle* (*legal*), and then adding the negative prefix *mu-* to form *mucollede*; instead, the possessive suffix *-oe* has been added. *Crossed* should be translated by adding the suffix *-to* to the stem of *chonkir* (*to cross*) to form the past participle (Rule 8); instead, the suffix has been added to the infinitive form of the verb.

18. d. Words 2 and 3 are correct, so the answer is **d**. Since it is an adverb, *skillfully* is translated by adding the suffix *-de* (Rule 10) to *autile* (*skillful*). *Escaped* is translated by adding the suffixes *-rem* and *-ot* to the stem (Rule 7) of *pirkir* (*to escape*). *Volle* means *this*; the correct translation of *that* is *velle*.

19. c. Only word 3 is correct, so the answer is **c**. Since *patrolled* is a past participle, it is translated by adding the suffix *-to* to the stem (Rule 8) of *linkir* (*to patrol*). Because it is an adjective formed from a noun, *dangerous* should be translated by changing the suffix *-lek* in *gonlek* (*danger*) to *-le*, which would give *gonle*; instead, the suffix has not been changed. *Was not* should be translated by adding the suffixes *-rem* and *-ot* to the stem (Rule 7) of *synkir* because the verb is in the past tense and is singular; the negative suffix *mu-* would then be added to give *musynremot*. Instead, *mu-* has been added to the end of the word.

20. d. All three words are correct, so the answer is **d.** *Are* is translated by adding the suffix *-et* to the stem (Rule 6) of *synkir* (*to be*) because the verb is in the present tense and is singular. *Governmental* is translated by changing the suffix *-lek* in *almanlek* (*government*) to *-le* since it is functioning as an adjective, then by adding the feminine suffix *-lif* (Rule 1) and the plural suffix *-ob* (Rule 2). *Inspectors* is translated by adding the suffix *-lek* to the stem (Rule 9) of *zelkir* (*to inspect*) because it is a noun formed from a verb, then by adding the suffixes *-lif* and *-ob*.

21. c. This choice is correct because *border* is translated by, first, adding the suffix *-lek* to the stem (Rule 9) of *regkir* (*to border*) and, then, because it modifies *patrol*, *-le* is substituted for *-lek* (Rule 10); *patrol* is translated by adding the suffix *-lek* to the stem of *linkir* (*to patrol*). Choice **a** is incorrect because both words still include the infinitive and because *border* has also been translated without changing *-lek* to *-le*. Choice **b** is incorrect because both words still include the infinitive and because *patrol* has also been translated using *-le*, instead of *-lek*. Choice **d** is incorrect because *patrol* has been translated using *-le*, instead of *-lek*. Choice **e** is incorrect because the translation of *border* still includes the infinitive.

22. e. This choice is correct because *men* is translated by adding the plural suffix *-ob* (Rule 2) to *kaplek* (*man*); *cre* means *and*; and *women* is translated by adding the feminine suffix *-lif* (Rule 1) to *kaplek* and then by adding the plural suffix *-ob*. Choice **a** is incorrect because this choice means *man and woman*. Choice **b** is incorrect because *man* has been translated using the feminine suffix *-lif*; the translation of *and* unnecessarily includes the suffix *-ob*; and the translation of *women* lacks *-lif*. Choice **c** is incorrect because the translation of *and* unnecessarily includes the suffix *-ob*. Choice **d** is incorrect because *man* has been translated using *-lif* and because the translation of *women* lacks *-lif*.

23. a. This choice is correct because *their* is translated by adding the plural suffix *-ob* (Rule 2) to *yev* (*he*), then adding the possessive suffix *-oe* (12); *country* is translated as *failek*; *they* is translated by adding *-ob* to *yev*; and *work* is translated by adding the suffix *-et* to the stem (Rule 6) of *frigkir* (*to work*) because the verb is in the present tense and is singular. Choice **b** is incorrect because the translation of *country* unnecessarily includes the plural suffix *-ob*. Choice **c** is incorrect because *their* has been translated without the possessive suffix *-oe* and because the translations of both *country* and *work* unnecessarily include the plural suffix *-ob*. Choice **d** is incorrect because *their* has been translated without the possessive suffix *-oe*; *they* has been translated using the possessive suffix *-oe*; and *work* has been translated using the plural suffix *-ob*. Choice **e** is incorrect because in the translation of *their*, the suffixes *-oe* and *-ob* are in the wrong positions in the word.

24. b. This choice is correct because *difficult* is formed by adding the plural suffix *-ob* to *brale* (*difficult*); *cre* means *and*; and *dangerous* is translated by changing the suffix *-lek* in *gonlek* (*danger*) to *-le* (Rule 10) and then adding the plural suffix *-ob*. Choice **a** is incorrect because the suffix *-ob* has been added unnecessarily to *cre*. Choice **c** is incorrect because *dangerous* has been translated without changing the suffix *-lek* to *-le*. Choice **d** is incorrect because the translations of both *difficult* and *dangerous* include the suffix *-lek*, instead of *-le*. Choice **e** is incorrect because the translations of both *difficult* and *dangerous* include the suffix *-lek* and because the suffix *-ob* has been added unnecessarily to *cre*.

25. d. This choice is correct because *to guard* is translated simply as the infinitive, *bonkir*; *ric* is the translation of *the*; and *border* is translated by adding the suffix *-lek* to the stem (Rule 9) of *regkir* (*to border*). Choice **a** is incorrect because *bonto* is a past participle. Choice **b** is incorrect because *bonet* is a plural verb, not an infinitive, and because *border* has been translated with the suffix *-le*, instead of *-lek*. Choice **c** is incorrect because *bonet* is a plural verb. Choice **e** is incorrect because *border* has been translated with the suffix *-le*, instead of *-lek*.

26. a. This choice is correct because *mor* is the correct translation of *from*; *the* is translated by adding the plural suffix *-ob* (Rule 2) to *ric* (*the*); *government's* is translated by adding the possessive suffix *-oe* (Rule 12) to *almanlek* (*government*); and *enemies* is translated by adding the suffix *-ob* to *avelek* (*enemy*). Choice **b** is incorrect because the translation of *the* unnecessarily includes the possessive suffix *-oe*. Choice **c** is incorrect because *government's* has been translated using the plural suffix *-ob*, instead of *-oe*. Choice **d** is incorrect because *qua* means *on* and because the translation of *enemies* unnecessarily includes the suffix *-oe*. Choice **e** is incorrect because *qua* means *on* and because the translations of *the* and *enemies* unnecessarily include the suffix *-oe*.

27. e. This choice is correct; *have* is translated by adding the suffix *-et* to the stem (Rule 6) of *tulkir* (*to have*) because the verb is in the present tense and is plural, and *to cross* is translated simply as the infinitive, *chonkir*. Choice **a** is incorrect because *have* has been translated using the singular suffix *-ot*. Choice **b** is incorrect because *have* has been translated as the infinitive. Choice **c** is incorrect because *have* has been translated as the infinitive and *to cross* has been translated as a plural, present-tense verb, instead of as the infinitive. Choice **d** is incorrect because *to cross* has been translated as a plural, present-tense verb.

28. c. This choice is correct because *are* is translated by adding the suffix *-et* to the stem (Rule 6) of *synkir* (*to be*) because the verb is in the present tense and is plural; *stationed* is translated by adding the suffix *-to* to the stem (Rule 8) of *lexkir* (*to station*), and then by adding the plural suffix *-ob* (Rule 2) because it functions as a predicate with the verb *to be*. Choice **a** is incorrect because *are* has been translated using the singular suffix *-ot* and because *lexto* lacks the plural suffix *-ob*. Choice **b** is incorrect because *are* has been translated using *-ot*. Choice **d** is incorrect because *lexto* lacks the plural suffix *-ob*. Choice **e** is incorrect because the suffix *-to* has been added to the stem of the verb *synkir*, instead of *-et*, and because *station* has been translated as a past-tense verb, not as a past participle.

29. b. This choice is correct because the words *identify* and *question* are translated by adding the suffix *-et* to the stem (Rule 6) of *kalenkir* (*to identify*) and *pafkir* (*to question*), respectively, because the verbs are in the present tense and are plural; *cre* is the translation of *and*; *illegal* is translated by adding the plural suffix *-ob* and the negative prefix *mu-* (Rule 13) to *colle* (*legal*); *aliens* is translated by adding *-ob* to *huslek* (*aliens*). Choice **a** is incorrect because *identify* and *question* have been translated using the singular suffix *-ot*, instead of the plural *-et*. Choice **c** is incorrect because *identify* and *question* have been translated using the suffix *-ot*; *bex* means *a/an*, not *and*; and *illegal* has been translated by putting *mu-* in the wrong position. Choice **d** is incorrect because *and* has been translated using *bex* (*a/n*) and *illegal* has been translated by putting *mu-* in the wrong position. Choice **e** is incorrect because *identify* and *question* have been translated using the suffix *-ot*; *and* has been translated using *bex*; and *illegal* has been translated by putting *mu-* in the wrong position.

30. d. This choice is correct because *governmental* is translated by changing the suffix *-lek* to *-le* (Rule 10) and then adding the plural suffix *-ob* (Rule 2); *documents* is translated by adding the suffix *-lek* to the stem (Rule 9) of *clegkir* (*to document*) and then adding *-ob*; *to report* is translated simply as the infinitive, *fonkir*. Choice **a** is incorrect because *governmental* has been translated with *-lek* and because the translation of *to report* includes the suffix *-ob*. Choice **b** is incorrect because *documents* has been translated using *-le*, instead of *-lek*, and *to report* has been translated using *-ob*. Choice **c** is incorrect because *documents* has been translated using *-le*, instead of *-lek*. Choice **e** is incorrect because *governmental* has been translated with *-lek*.

31. d. *Vollelifob ekapleklifob mutulremet kometlekob mor ric failek* means *These girls did not have friends from the country*. *These* is translated by adding the feminine suffix *-lif* (Rule 1) and the plural suffix *-ob* (Rule 2) to *volle* (*this*). *Girls* is translated similarly by adding *-lif* and *-ob* to *ekaplek* (*boy*). *Did not have* is translated by adding the suffixes *-rem* and *-et* to the stem of *tulkir* (*to have*) because the verb is in the past tense and plural (Rule 7); it is made negative by adding the prefix *mu-*. Choice **a** is incorrect because *these* was translated using *velle*, which means *that*, and because the verb was incorrectly formed, both by using the singular suffix *-ot* and putting the negative prefix *mu-* at the end of the word. Choice **b** is incorrect because *these* was translated using *velle* and the suffix *-lif* was omitted; *girls* was also translated without *-lif* and the verb was translated in the singular. Choice **c** is incorrect because both *these* and *girls* were translated without the feminine *-lif* and because the verb was formed with *mu-* placed at the end of the word. Choice **e** is incorrect because *girls* was translated with the possessive suffix *-oe*, instead of *-ob*, and because the verb was formed without changing the infinitive to the stem before adding the suffixes and prefix.

32. a. *Yevlif kalenremot volle mucolle cleglek* means *She identified this illegal document*. *Volle* is the correct translation of *this*. *Illegal* is translated by adding the negative prefix *mu-* (Rule 13) to *colle* (*legal*). *Document* is translated by adding the suffix *-lek* (Rule 9) to the stem of *clegkir* (*to document*). Choice **b** is incorrect because *illegal* has been translated by putting the negative prefix *mu-* at the end of *colle*. Choice **c** is incorrect because *document* has been translated by adding the suffix *-lek* to the infinitive of the verb, instead of its stem. Choice **d** is incorrect because *velle* means *that*, *illegal* has been translated by putting the negative prefix *mu-* at the end of *colle*, and *document* has been translated by adding the suffix *-lek* to the infinitive of the verb, instead of its stem. Choice **e** is incorrect because *velle* means *that*.

33. e. *Ric fonlek synot mor bex kalento avelek* means *The report is from an identified enemy*. *Bex* is the correct translation of *an*. *Identified* is translated by adding the suffix *-to* to the stem (Rule 8) of *kalenkir* (*to identify*). *Avelek* is the correct translation of *enemy*. Choice **a** is incorrect because *ric* means *the*. Choice **b** is incorrect because *ric* means *the* and because *identified* was translated using the infinitive, not the stem. Choice **c** is incorrect because the suffix *-to* was added to *avelek* and not to the stem *kalen-*. Choice **d** is incorrect because *identified* was translated using the infinitive, not the stem.

34. b. *Velle fonlek synot mor ricob lexleob bonlekob* means *That report is from the station guards*. *The* is translated by adding the plural suffix *-ob* (Rule 2) to *ric* (*the*). *Station* is translated by first adding the suffix *-lek* (Rule 9) to the stem of *lexkir* (*to station*), then changing *-lek* to the adjectival suffix *-le* (Rule 10) and adding *-ob*. *Guards* is translated by adding the suffix *-lek* to the stem of *bonkir* (*to guard*) and then adding *-ob*. Choice **a** is incorrect because *the* has been translated without the plural suffix. Choice **c** is incorrect because *station* has been translated without changing *-lek* to *-le*. Choice **d** is incorrect because *the* has been translated without the plural suffix, and *guards* has been translated using the suffix *-le*, instead of *-lek*. Choice **e** is incorrect because *station* has been translated without changing *-lek* to *-le*, and *guards* has been translated using the suffix *-le*, instead of *-lek*.

35. c. *Ric regle linlek chonremot ric browlek* means *The border patrol crossed the river*. *Ric* means *the*. As *border* functions as an adjective in this sentence, it is translated by first adding the suffix *-lek* to the stem (Rule 9) of *regkir*, then changing *-lek* to the suffix *-le* (Rule 10). *Patrol* functions as a noun in this sentence; as such, it is translated by adding *-lek* to the stem of *linkir* (*to patrol*). Choice **a** is incorrect because for *patrol*, *-lek* has been translated by adding *-lek* to the infinitive, instead of the stem. Choice **b** is incorrect because *border* has been translated without changing *-lek* to *-le* and *patrol* has been translated incorrectly by using the suffix *-le* instead of *-lek*. Choice **d** is incorrect because *border* has been translated without changing *-lek* to *-le*. Choice **e** is incorrect because both *border* and *patrol* have been translated by adding the suffixes to the infinitives, instead of the stems.

36. e. *Ric zellekoe lexlek synremot bonto* means *The inspector's station was guarded*. *Inspector's* is translated first by adding the suffix *-lek* to the stem (Rule 9) of *zelkir* (*to inspect*), then adding the possessive suffix *-oe* (Rule 12). *Station* is translated by adding *-lek* to the stem of *lexkir* (*to station*). Choice **a** is incorrect because *inspector's* has been translated by adding the possessive suffix *-oe* to the infinitive, instead of to the noun *zellek*, and because *station* has been translated by adding the suffix *-lek* to the infinitive, not the stem. Choice **b** is incorrect because *station* has been translated by adding the suffix to the infinitive, not the stem. Choice **c** is incorrect because *inspector's* has been translated by using the plural suffix *-ob* and *station* with the suffix *-le*. Choice **d** is incorrect because *inspector's* has been translated by using the plural suffix *-ob*.

37. a. *Velle zellek pafremot ricob lexleob friglekob* means *That inspector questioned the station workers*. *Velle* is the correct translation of *that*. *Inspector* is translated by adding the suffix *-lek* to the stem (Rule 9) of *zelkir* (*to inspect*). *Questioned* is translated by adding the suffixes *-rem* and *-ot* to the stem of *pafkir* (*to question*) because it is a singular verb in the past tense (Rule 7). Choice **b** is incorrect because *questioned* has been translated using the plural suffix *-et*, instead of the singular *-ot*. Choice **c** is incorrect because *inspector* has been translated by adding *-lek* to the infinitive rather than the stem. Choice **d** is incorrect because *volle* means *this*; *inspector* has been translated by adding *-lek* to the infinitive rather than the stem; and *questioned* has been translated using the plural suffix *-et*. Choice **e** is incorrect because *volle* means *this* and *inspector* has been translated by adding the suffix *-le*, instead of *-lek*.

38. b. *Vollelif kometlelif kapleklif mutulot ric cleglek* means *This friendly woman does not have the document*. *Woman* is translated by adding the feminine suffix *-lif* (Rule 1) to *kaplek* (*man*). *Does not have* is formed by adding the suffix *-ot* to the stem of *tulkir* (*to have*) because the verb is singular and in the present tense (Rule 6); it is made negative by adding the prefix *mu-* (Rule 13). *The* translates as *ric*. *Document* is translated by adding the suffix *-lek* to the stem (Rule 9) of *clegkir* (*to document*). Choice **a** is incorrect because both *woman* and *document* have been translated using the suffix *-le*, instead of *-lek*, and because the verb has been translated using the plural suffix *-et*, instead of the singular *-ot*. Choice **c** is incorrect because both *does not have* and *document* have been translated using the infinitive, not the stem. Choice **d** is incorrect because *woman* has been translated using the suffix *-le*, instead of *-lek*; the verb has the prefix *mu-* placed at the end of the word; and *document* has been translated using the infinitive, not the stem. Choice **e** is incorrect because *woman* has been translated using the suffix *-le*, instead of *-lek*, and because the verb has the prefix *mu-* placed at the end of the word.

39. d. *Ric bonlekoe fonlek synremot pafto* means *The guard's report was questioned.* *The* translates as *ric*. *Guard's* is translated by adding the suffix *-lek* (Rule 9) to the stem of *bonkir* (*to guard*) and then adding the possessive suffix *-oe* (Rule 12). *Report* is translated by adding *-lek* to the stem of *fonkir* (*to report*). Choice **a** is incorrect because *guard's* has been translated by adding the suffix *-lek* to the infinitive, instead of the stem, as well as unnecessarily adding the feminine suffix *-lif*, and *report* has also been translated by adding *-lek* to the infinitive. Choice **b** is incorrect because both *guard's* and *report* have been translated by adding the suffix *-lek* to the infinitive, instead of the stem. Choice **c** is incorrect because the feminine suffix *-lif* has been unnecessarily added in the translation of *guard's*. Choice **e** is incorrect because *guard's* has been incorrectly translated using the plural suffix *-ob,* instead of the possessive suffix.

40. c. *Vollelif gonlelif kapleklif synremot pafto qua ric reglek* means *This dangerous woman was questioned on the border.* *This* is translated by adding the feminine suffix *-lif* (Rule 1) to *volle* (*this*). *Dangerous* is translated by first changing the suffix *-lek* to *-le* (Rule 10), then adding *-lif*. *Woman* is formed by adding *-lif* to *kaplek* (*man*). *Was* is translated by adding the suffixes *-rem* and *-ot* to the stem of *synkir* (*to be*) because the verb is in the past tense and singular (Rule 7). Choice **a** is incorrect because *this* has been translated as *that* (*velle*) and because the verb has been translated with the plural suffix *-et*. Choice **b** is incorrect because *this* has been translated as *that*. Choice **d** is incorrect because *dangerous* has been translated without changing the suffix *-lek* to *-le* and because the verb has been translated with the plural suffix *-et*. Choice **e** is incorrect because *this, dangerous,* and *woman* have been translated without the feminine suffix *-lif* and because the verb has been translated with the plural suffix *-et*.

41. a. *Ric fonlek kalenremot riclifob ekapleklifob qua ric ponlek* means *The report identified the girls on the land*. *Riclifob ekapleklifob* (*the girls*) is formed by adding the feminine suffix *-lif* (Rule 1) and the plural suffix *-ob* (Rule 2) to both *ric* (*the*) and *ekaplek* (*boy*). *The land* is translated simply as *ric ponlek* as its gender is neutral and it is singular. Choice **b** is incorrect because *the* has not been translated in either the feminine or plural forms. Choice **c** is incorrect because *the girls* has been translated without the plural suffix, and *the land* has been incorrectly translated using the feminine suffix. Choice **d** is incorrect because *the girls* has been translated without the plural suffix. Choice **e** is incorrect because *the girls* has been translated without the feminine suffix and *the land* has been incorrectly translated using the plural suffix.

42. c. *Yevlifoboe kometleob paflekob synremet mor ric cleglek* means *Her friendly questions were from the document*. *Her* is translated by adding the feminine suffix *-lif* (Rule 1), the plural suffix *-ob* (Rule 2), and the possessive suffix *-oe* (Rule 12) to *yev* (*he*). *Friendly* is translated by changing the suffix *-lek* in *kometlek* (*friend*) to *-le* (Rule 10) and then adding *-ob*. *Questions* is translated by omitting *-kir* from the infinitive *pafkir* and adding the suffixes *-lek* (Rule 9) and *-ob*. Choice **a** is incorrect because *her* has been translated without the plural suffix, *friendly* has been translated without changing the suffix *-lek* to *-le*, and *questions* has been translated using the suffix *-le* instead of *-lek*. Choice **b** is incorrect because *friendly* has been translated without changing the suffix *-lek* to *-le*. Choice **d** is incorrect because *her* has been translated without the possessive suffix. Choice **e** is incorrect because *her* has been translated without the feminine suffix and *questions* has been translated using the suffix *-le* instead of *-lek*.

43. **c.** *Ricob almanleob zellekob synremet mukometleob* means *The governmental inspectors were unfriendly.* Since *governmental* functions as an adjective, it is translated by changing the suffix *-lek* to *-le* (Rule 10) in *almanlek* (*government*); the suffix *-ob* (Rule 2) is then added to make the adjective plural to match the noun *inspectors* (Rule 3). *Unfriendly* is translated by replacing *-lek* with *-le* and then adding the suffix *-ob* and the negative prefix *mu-* (Rule 13). Choice **a** is incorrect because both translations lack the plural suffix *-ob*. Choice **b** is incorrect because both translations lack *-ob* and because the prefix *mu-* has been placed at the end of the word. Choice **d** is incorrect because *unfriendly* has been translated with *mu-* at the end of the word. Choice **e** is incorrect because neither translation included changing *-lek* for *-le*.

44. **d.** *Ricob bonlekob frigremet qua ric reglek* means *The guards worked on the border.* *Frigremet* is formed by adding the suffixes *-rem* and *-et* to the stem (Rule 7) of the infinitive. Choice **a** is incorrect because it doesn't include the suffix *-et*. Choice **b** is incorrect because the suffix *-ot* is singular and the suffix *-rem* is missing. Choice **c** is incorrect because the suffix *-ot* is singular. Choice **e** is incorrect because the suffixes were added to the infinitive, instead of the stem.

45. **b.** *Riclifob ekapleklifoboe paflekob synremet mubraleob* means *The girls' questions were not difficult.* *Girls'* is translated by, first, adding the feminine suffix *-lif* (Rule 1) to *ekaplek* (*boy*), then adding the plural suffix *-ob* (Rule 2) and the possessive suffix *-oe* (Rule 12). *Not difficult* is translated by adding the plural suffix *-ob* and the negative prefix *mu-* (Rule 13). Choice **a** is incorrect because both *girls'* and *not difficult* have been translated without *-ob* and because *not difficult* has been translated with *mu-* at the end of the word. Choice **c** is incorrect because *girls'* has been translated without *-oe*. Choice **d** is incorrect because *not difficult* has been translated without *-ob*. Choice **e** is incorrect because *girls'* has been translated without *-ob* and because *not difficult* has been translated with *mu-* at the end of the word.

46. **d.** *Ric bonleklif autilede pafremot ric huslek* means *The [female] guard skillfully questioned the alien.* *[Female] guard* is translated, first, by adding the suffix *-lek* to the stem (Rule 9) of *bonkir* (*to guard*), then by adding the feminine suffix *-lif* (Rule 1). *Skillfully* is translated by adding the suffix *-de* to the *masculine* form (Rule 11) of the adjective, *autile* (*skillful*). Choice **a** is incorrect because *guard* has been translated without the suffix *-lif*, and because *skillfully* has been translated without the suffix *-de*. Choice **b** is incorrect because *guard* has been translated without *-lif*. Choice **c** is incorrect because *skillfully* has been translated with *-lif* at the end of the word, instead of *-de*. Choice **e** is incorrect because the suffix *-lif* has been added in the translation of *skillfully*.

47. e. *Vollelif kapleklif synremot paftolif qua ric reglek* means *This woman was questioned on the border.* Since *this* is feminine, the suffix *-lif* (Rule 1) is added to *volle* (*this*). *Questioned* is translated by adding the suffix *-to* to the stem of *pafkir* (*to question*) to form the past participle, and then by adding the feminine suffix *-lif* (Rule 8). Choice **a** is incorrect because *velle* means *that* and because *questioned* has been translated using the infinitive. Neither word includes the feminine suffix *-lif*. Choice **b** is incorrect because *this* has been translated as *that*. Choice **c** is incorrect because *this* has been translated as *that* and because *questioned* has been translated without *-lif*. Choice **d** is incorrect because *questioned* has been translated without *-lif*.

48. b. *Riclif ekapleklif musynremot ric ekaplekoe kometleklif* means *The girl was not the boy's friend.* *Was not* is translated, first, by adding the suffixes *-rem* and *-ot* to the stem (Rule 7) of *synkir* (*to be*) because it is in the past tense and singular and, then, by adding the negative prefix *mu-* (Rule 13). *Friend* was translated by adding the feminine suffix (Rule 1) to *kometlek* (*friend*). Choice **a** is incorrect because *was not* has been translated with the negative prefix *mu-* placed at the end of the word and because *friend* has been translated without the feminine suffix *-lif*. Choice **c** is incorrect because *was not* has been translated with the plural suffix *-et*. Choice **d** is incorrect because *was not* has been translated with *-et* and with *mu-* at the end of the word, and because *friend* has been translated without *-lif*. Choice **e** is incorrect because the translation of *was not* was formed with the infinitive, instead of the stem.

49. a. *Riclif lexlelif frigleklif muclegremot ricob huslekob* means *The [female] station worker did not document the aliens.* To translate *station*, the suffix *-lek* is added to the stem (Rule 9) of *lexkir* (*to station*), but, as this word is functioning as an adjective, *-lek* is replaced by *-le* (Rule 10); as the adjective must be feminine, the suffix *-lif* is added (Rule 1). *Did not document* is translated by adding the suffixes *-rem* and *-ot* to the stem (Rule 7) since the verb is in the past tense and is singular, and then by adding the negative suffix *mu-* (Rule 13). Choice **b** is incorrect because *did not document* has been translated with the plural suffix *-et*. Choice **c** is incorrect because *station* has been translated without changing the suffix *-lek* to *-le*. Choice **d** is incorrect because *station* has been translated without changing *-lek* to *-le* and because *did not document* has been translated with *-et*. Choice **e** is incorrect because *station* has been translated without the feminine suffix *-lif* and *did not document* has been translated with *mu-* in the wrong position.

50. e. *Ricob zellekob mutulet clegto yevoboe friglek* means *The inspectors have not documented their work*. *Have not* is translated by adding the plural suffix *-et* to the stem (Rule 6) of *tulkir* (*to have*), and then adding the negative prefix *mu-* (Rule 13). The past participle *documented* is translated by adding the suffix *-to* to the stem (Rule 8) of *clegkir* (*to document*). *Their* is translated by adding the plural suffix *-ob* (Rule 2) to *yev* (*he*) to form *they*, and then adding the possessive suffix *-oe* (Rule 12). Choice **a** is incorrect because *documented* has been formed with the infinitive, instead of the stem, and because *their* has been translated without the possessive suffix *-oe*. Choice **b** is incorrect because *have not* has been translated with the negative prefix *mu-* at the end of the word; *documented* has been formed with the infinitive; and *their* has been formed with the feminine suffix *-lif*, instead of the plural suffix *-ob*. Choice **c** is incorrect because *have not* has been translated with *mu-* in the wrong position and with the singular suffix *-ot*, and because *their* has been translated without *-ob*. Choice **d** is incorrect because *have not* has been translated with *-ot*, and because *documented* has been translated with *-ob* unnecessarily added to it.

Practice Test 5: Scoring and Diagnostic Chart

To evaluate how you did on this practice exam, start by totaling the number of correct responses on the two sections of this practice exam. First, find the number of questions you got right in each part. Questions you skipped or got wrong don't count; just add up the number of correct answers.

If at least 70% of your responses on the two parts are correct (47 correct), you are most likely prepared to pass the Border Patrol Exam. However, because the entrance process is competitive, you may need a higher score on the official exam to get accepted into the Border Patrol Academy.

In addition to seeing how you performed overall, you can use the following scoring chart to help diagnose your strengths and weaknesses in the different skills assessed on the exam, to better focus your study preparation.

LOGICAL REASONING SECTION	
SKILL	**QUESTION**
Reasoning about Groups and Categories	1–8
Reasoning about Events or Situations	9–16

ARTIFICIAL LANGUAGE SECTION	
SKILL	**QUESTION**
Artificial Language I	1, 2, 3, 4, 5, 6, 7, 8, 9, 10, 11, 12, 13, 14, 15, 16, 17, 18, 19, 20
Artificial Language II	21, 22, 23, 24, 25, 26, 27, 28, 29, 30
Artificial Language III	31, 32, 33, 34, 35, 36, 37, 38, 39, 40, 41, 42
Artificial Language IV	43, 44, 45, 46, 47, 48, 49, 50

CHAPTER 8

PRACTICE TEST 6

This is the final practice test, and it contains logical reasoning and artificial language questions. Again, you should simulate the actual test-taking experience as closely as you can, including giving yourself four and a half hours to complete the test.

LEARNINGEXPRESS ANSWER SHEET

1. ⓐ ⓑ ⓒ ⓓ ⓔ
2. ⓐ ⓑ ⓒ ⓓ ⓔ
3. ⓐ ⓑ ⓒ ⓓ ⓔ
4. ⓐ ⓑ ⓒ ⓓ ⓔ
5. ⓐ ⓑ ⓒ ⓓ ⓔ
6. ⓐ ⓑ ⓒ ⓓ ⓔ
7. ⓐ ⓑ ⓒ ⓓ ⓔ
8. ⓐ ⓑ ⓒ ⓓ ⓔ
9. ⓐ ⓑ ⓒ ⓓ ⓔ
10. ⓐ ⓑ ⓒ ⓓ ⓔ
11. ⓐ ⓑ ⓒ ⓓ ⓔ
12. ⓐ ⓑ ⓒ ⓓ ⓔ
13. ⓐ ⓑ ⓒ ⓓ ⓔ
14. ⓐ ⓑ ⓒ ⓓ ⓔ
15. ⓐ ⓑ ⓒ ⓓ ⓔ
16. ⓐ ⓑ ⓒ ⓓ ⓔ

1. ⓐ ⓑ ⓒ ⓓ ⓔ
2. ⓐ ⓑ ⓒ ⓓ ⓔ
3. ⓐ ⓑ ⓒ ⓓ ⓔ
4. ⓐ ⓑ ⓒ ⓓ ⓔ
5. ⓐ ⓑ ⓒ ⓓ ⓔ
6. ⓐ ⓑ ⓒ ⓓ ⓔ
7. ⓐ ⓑ ⓒ ⓓ ⓔ
8. ⓐ ⓑ ⓒ ⓓ ⓔ
9. ⓐ ⓑ ⓒ ⓓ ⓔ
10. ⓐ ⓑ ⓒ ⓓ ⓔ
11. ⓐ ⓑ ⓒ ⓓ ⓔ
12. ⓐ ⓑ ⓒ ⓓ ⓔ
13. ⓐ ⓑ ⓒ ⓓ ⓔ
14. ⓐ ⓑ ⓒ ⓓ ⓔ
15. ⓐ ⓑ ⓒ ⓓ ⓔ
16. ⓐ ⓑ ⓒ ⓓ ⓔ
17. ⓐ ⓑ ⓒ ⓓ ⓔ
18. ⓐ ⓑ ⓒ ⓓ ⓔ
19. ⓐ ⓑ ⓒ ⓓ ⓔ
20. ⓐ ⓑ ⓒ ⓓ ⓔ
21. ⓐ ⓑ ⓒ ⓓ ⓔ
22. ⓐ ⓑ ⓒ ⓓ ⓔ
23. ⓐ ⓑ ⓒ ⓓ ⓔ
24. ⓐ ⓑ ⓒ ⓓ ⓔ
25. ⓐ ⓑ ⓒ ⓓ ⓔ
26. ⓐ ⓑ ⓒ ⓓ ⓔ
27. ⓐ ⓑ ⓒ ⓓ ⓔ
28. ⓐ ⓑ ⓒ ⓓ ⓔ
29. ⓐ ⓑ ⓒ ⓓ ⓔ
30. ⓐ ⓑ ⓒ ⓓ ⓔ
31. ⓐ ⓑ ⓒ ⓓ ⓔ
32. ⓐ ⓑ ⓒ ⓓ ⓔ
33. ⓐ ⓑ ⓒ ⓓ ⓔ
34. ⓐ ⓑ ⓒ ⓓ ⓔ
35. ⓐ ⓑ ⓒ ⓓ ⓔ
36. ⓐ ⓑ ⓒ ⓓ ⓔ
37. ⓐ ⓑ ⓒ ⓓ ⓔ
38. ⓐ ⓑ ⓒ ⓓ ⓔ
39. ⓐ ⓑ ⓒ ⓓ ⓔ
40. ⓐ ⓑ ⓒ ⓓ ⓔ
41. ⓐ ⓑ ⓒ ⓓ ⓔ
42. ⓐ ⓑ ⓒ ⓓ ⓔ
43. ⓐ ⓑ ⓒ ⓓ ⓔ
44. ⓐ ⓑ ⓒ ⓓ ⓔ
45. ⓐ ⓑ ⓒ ⓓ ⓔ
46. ⓐ ⓑ ⓒ ⓓ ⓔ
47. ⓐ ⓑ ⓒ ⓓ ⓔ
48. ⓐ ⓑ ⓒ ⓓ ⓔ
49. ⓐ ⓑ ⓒ ⓓ ⓔ
50. ⓐ ⓑ ⓒ ⓓ ⓔ

Logical Reasoning Test

1. Border Patrol Agents may voluntarily retire at any age after completing 25 years of service, or at age 50 or older with 20 years of service. The mandatory retirement age is 57 with 20 years of service. However, if an agent has fewer than 20 years of service by the age of 57, she may work beyond the age of 57 and retire when she meets the combination of age and service requirements. Agents must be under the age of 40 when they apply for the program. Jordan will retire in ten years.
From the information given here, it CANNOT be validly concluded that:
   a. the maximum age at which Jordan can retire is 60.
   b. Jordan may retire after completing 25 years of service.
   c. Jordan may retire after completing 20 years of service as long as she is 50 years of age or older at time of retirement.
   d. Jordan is 30.
   e. there is no minimum age at which Jordan can retire once she has completed 25 years of service.

2. An individual seeking admission to the United States, including both seeking entry at the border and seeking the right to stay in the country legally (such as with a green card) must meet specific eligibility requirements. Some characteristics that may make an individual inadmissible include: having entered the United States without permission, having committed fraud in order to gain an immigration benefit, and having helped smuggle other foreign-born individuals into the United States, for example.
From the information given here, it can be validly concluded that:
   a. some individuals who enter the United States without permission are eligible to stay in the country.
   b. all individuals who enter the United States without permission are eligible to stay in the country.
   c. no individuals who enter the United States without permission are eligible to stay in the country.
   d. most individuals who seek to stay in the country have entered the United States without permission.
   e. most individuals who seek to stay in the country have committed fraud.

3. An officer stationed on the southeastern sector has uncovered 12 individuals attempting to enter the country illegally in the past two years. Another officer stationed on the southwestern sector has uncovered 19 individuals attempting to enter the country illegally in the past two years. A total of 17 individuals have attempted to enter the country illegally from the southwestern and southeastern sectors this year. One of the officers on the sector is senior to the other.

From the information given here, it can be validly concluded that:
a. more individuals have attempted to enter the country illegally from the senior officer's sector than from the junior officer's sector.
b. fewer individuals have attempted to enter the country illegally from the senior officer's sector than from the junior officer's sector.
c. fewer than 20 individuals have attempted entry in these sectors this year.
d. more than 20 individuals have attempted entry in these sectors this year.
e. none of the above

4. Veterans of the U.S. Armed Forces have been given some preference in federal jobs applications. The Department of Labor highlights laws that were enacted to prevent veterans who are seeking federal employment from being penalized because of the time they spent in their military service, and to recognize that those who have served in the military have made sacrifices that nonveterans have not. Therefore, veterans who served on active duty for a period of more than 180 consecutive days receive a hiring preference determined by a point score when they apply for jobs with the Border Patrol.

From the information given here, it can be validly concluded that:
a. no veterans receive a preference determined by a point score when applying for a federal job.
b. all veterans who have not served more than 180 consecutive days receive a preference when applying for a federal job.
c. no veterans who have served more than 180 consecutive days receive a preference when applying for a federal job.
d. some veterans are penalized when applying for a federal job for having served time in the military.
e. none of the above

5. Investigators have discovered a trafficking ring that operated through an exclusive restaurant and nightclub in a heavily populated area. It was discovered that most illegal activity was conducted through the restaurant on Saturday nights; however, some illegal activity also occurred on Fridays. On certain Tuesdays illegal activity occurred, as well, but trafficking was never conducted through this restaurant on Thursdays.

From the information given here, it can be validly concluded that:

a. illegal activity occurred at this restaurant only on weekends.
b. illegal activity occurred at this restaurant only on weekdays.
c. most illegal activity occurred at this restaurant on the weekend.
d. no illegal activity occurred at this restaurant on the weekend.
e. no illegal activity occurred at this restaurant on weekdays.

6. A business owner in a border state claimed that all her South American (for example, Argentinean and Bolivian) employees were working for her legally. However, officers investigated and found that many of her workers were not legally employed. The officers systematically reviewed the employees' documentation and found that all the employees over 30 years of age were working in the United States legally, and none of the illegal workers were from Bolivia.

From the information given here, it can be validly concluded that:

a. some of the workers over 30 were from Bolivia.
b. some of the workers over 30 were illegally employed.
c. none of the workers from Bolivia were over 30.
d. all the workers from Bolivia were employed legally.
e. some of the Argentinean workers were over 30.

7. In recent times the U.S. Border Patrol employed over 20,200 agents who were specifically responsible for patrolling the 6,000 miles of international land borders near Mexico and Canada and 2,000 miles of coastal waters surrounding the peninsula of Florida and the island of Puerto Rico. Most agents were assigned to the U.S.-Mexico border to prevent drug trafficking and illegal immigration, but many agents are assigned to Canada. A smaller number is assigned to Florida and Puerto Rico.
From the information given here, it can be validly concluded that:
a. more agents are concentrated in Mexico than in Canada.
b. drug trafficking and illegal immigration are not major concerns on the U.S.-Canada border.
c. drug trafficking and illegal immigration are not major concerns in Puerto Rico.
d. more agents are concentrated in Florida and Puerto Rico than in Canada.
e. none of the above

8. Horse and bike patrols are often used to supplement regular vehicle and foot patrols in the U.S. Border Patrol. Horse units patrol areas along the international boundaries that are difficult to access using standard vehicles or ATVs because of their exceedingly rough terrain. Bike patrols are employed in areas that pose problems for vehicles, such as roads with tight turns or small alleyways. Patrols on horseback have increased in recent years because smugglers have made their bases in secluded, mountainous areas that are difficult to monitor with modern devices and strategies.
From the information given here, it CANNOT be validly concluded that:
a. horse patrols have increased in number to control smuggling in remote areas.
b. horse and bike units are utilized to access areas that are difficult for other patrols.
c. horse patrols are utilized in lesser numbers than vehicle and foot patrols.
d. bike patrols are utilized in lesser numbers than vehicle and foot patrols.
e. none of the above

9. To apply for handgun ownership in many states, a specific procedure must be followed. An official form must be obtained and completed. To be official, the form must be typewritten, the applicant's signature must be notarized, and the application must contain the following: recent photographs; a copy of the application's passport, birth certificate, or military record; proof of citizenship or alien registration card and good conduct certificate; proof of residence (such as a real estate tax bill, ownership shares in a cooperative or condominium, or copy of a lease); and arrest information, in addition to other documents.

From the information given here, it CANNOT be validly concluded that:

a. if a real estate tax bill is submitted, then a copy of a lease is not required.
b. if the signature is notarized, then the application is complete.
c. if the form is not typewritten, then the application is not complete.
d. if a military record is provided, then a birth certificate is not required.
e. if an alien registration card is provided, then a good conduct certificate is required.

10. After an incarcerated defendant has exhausted all appeals, he may file a writ of habeas corpus. This is a civil suit against the warden of the prison, challenging the constitutionality of the incarceration. The only basis for granting relief to a habeas corpus petitioner is the deprivation of a constitutional right. For example, an inmate might claim that he was denied the assistance of counsel guaranteed by the Sixth Amendment on grounds that his attorney was incompetent. Violations of the Fourth Amendment's prohibition against unreasonable searches and seizures are not grounds for granting a writ of habeas corpus.

From the information given here, it can be validly concluded that:

a. if a writ of habeas corpus has been filed, then the petitioner has been victim of an unreasonable search and seizure.
b. if a writ of habeas corpus has been filed, then the petitioner has had a successful appeal.
c. if a petitioner has been denied a constitutional right, then he may not file a writ of habeas corpus.
d. if a petitioner has been represented by an incompetent attorney, then he does not have grounds to file a writ of habeas corpus.
e. none of the above

11. Federal immigration laws determine whether an individual is an alien. Generally, a person born in a foreign country is an alien, but a child born in a foreign nation to parents who are U.S. citizens is a U.S. citizen. The term "alien" also refers to a native-born U.S. citizen who has relinquished U.S. citizenship by living and acquiring citizenship in another country.
From the information given here, it can be validly concluded that:
a. if an individual is born to U.S. citizen parents in a foreign nation, then he is an alien.
b. if an individual has relinquished U.S. citizenship, then he is not an alien.
c. if an individual is an alien, then he was not born to parents who are U.S. citizens.
d. if an individual is an alien, then it is possible that he has acquired citizenship from another country.
e. none of the above

12. A major shift in U.S. immigration policy passed by Congress in 1965 and becoming effective in 1968 led to sharp increases in immigration in the late 1960s and the 1970s. In the 1980s, immigration skyrocketed, reaching totals unparalleled since the first decade of the twentieth century; the trend continued in the 1990s. In the mid-1990s the media began to acknowledge this phenomenon, but even 20 years later it remains a significantly underreported story, one of enormous complexity and far-reaching implications.
From the information given here, it can be validly concluded that:
a. if the policy was passed in 1965, then it would not affect immigration in the 1970s.
b. if immigration increased in the 1980s, it was not due to the policy passed in the 1960s.
c. if immigration was affected by the policy that was passed, the effect was not seen until 20 years later.
d. if the policy was passed in the 1960s, then the increase was almost immediate.
e. none of the above

13. There are two kinds of associative evidence: class and individual. *Class evidence* is defined as items that are mass-produced, and cannot tie a crime to an individual. A gun found at a crime scene, for example, will be of a particular make, but it will not be unique. Similarly, relatively new shoes all make similar footprints if they are the same brand—therefore, they cannot be tied to any one person. However, if the shoe is worn, then the footprint may be particular to an individual, as people wear down their shoes in unique ways. *Individual evidence* refers to evidence that is unique; fingerprints and DNA are the most significant forms of this. While class evidence is important, it usually has to be taken in context with other evidence; individual evidence provides the most information and is therefore the most valued in an investigation.

From the information given here, it can be validly concluded that:

a. if a piece of evidence is categorized as class evidence, it need not be taken in context with other evidence.
b. if a gun is found with no fingerprints on it, then it may be classified as class evidence.
c. if a piece of evidence is categorized as individual evidence, it must be taken in context with other evidence.
d. if traces of blood are found, they may be categorized as class evidence.
e. none of the above

14. Customs procedures for passengers at many international airports (except those in the United States and Canada) may be separated into Red and Green channels. Individuals with goods to declare (for example, those carrying items above the permitted customs limits and/or carrying prohibited items) are directed to the Red channel. Individuals with nothing to declare (for example, those carrying only permitted items that are within the customs limits) are directed to the Green channel. Individuals going through the Green channel who are found to have been carrying prohibited items or items that exceed the customs limit will have made a false declaration to customs, and therefore may be prosecuted.

From the information given here, it can be validly concluded that:

a. if an individual carrying permitted items within the limit is in the Green channel, then he will be prosecuted.
b. if an individual carrying permitted items above the limit is in the Red channel, then he will not be prosecuted.
c. if an individual carrying restricted items above the limit is in the Red channel, then he will be prosecuted.
d. if an individual carrying restricted items above the limit is in the Green channel, then he will not be prosecuted.
e. if an individual carrying prohibited items within the limit is in the Green channel, then he will not be prosecuted.

15. Permanent residents have most of the rights of U.S. citizens, but there are some exceptions. These rights include the right: to live permanently in the United States, provided that no removable (deportable) actions are committed; the right to be employed in the United States at any legal work of one's qualification and choosing; and to be protected by all the laws of the United States, state of residence, and local jurisdiction. However, permanent residents may not vote in elections limited to U.S. citizens, and may not qualify for some jobs due to security concerns.
From the information given here, it CANNOT be validly concluded that:
   a. if an individual may not vote in an election, then he or she is a permanent resident.
   b. if an individual is a permanent resident, then he or she may vote in elections not limited to U.S. citizens.
   c. if an individual is a permanent resident, then he or she may accept any legal work as long as one is qualified.
   d. if an individual is a permanent resident, then he or she may not qualify for certain jobs.
   e. none of the above

16. There are several levels of Border Patrol Agent, including the GS-5, GS-7, GS-9, GS-11, and higher levels. Level GS-5 agents are trainees. Agents working at the GS-7 level detect individuals suspected of violating immigration laws by following up on leads, observing and questioning people, and inspecting documents to determine either U.S. citizenship or alien status. They apprehend and search violators, and recommend to team leaders whether suspects should be held for further questioning or if they should be returned immediately to the country of origin, in addition to other duties.
From the information given here, it can be validly concluded that:
   a. an agent working at level GS-5 is responsible for following up on leads and apprehending and searching violators.
   b. an agent working at level GS-7 is responsible for following up on leads and apprehending and searching violators.
   c. if a suspect is being held for further questioning, he or she was searched.
   d. if a suspect is being returned to his or her country of origin, he or she was searched.
   e. if an agent is inspecting documents to determine U.S. citizenship, he or she is working at level GS-5.

PRACTICE TEST 6

Artificial Language Review

Artificial Language Supplemental Booklet

To answer the Artificial Language questions, refer to the sections that follow: Vocabulary Lists and Grammatical Rules.

Some of the words given in the following Vocabulary Lists are not the same as those that will be given in the actual Border Patrol Exam. Therefore, it is best not to memorize them before taking the actual test. The Grammatical Rules are the same as those used in the actual test, except that some of the prefixes (word beginnings) and suffixes (word endings) used in the real test differ from those used here.

Vocabulary Lists for the Artificial Language

ARRANGED ALPHABETICALLY BY THE ENGLISH WORD			
ENGLISH	ARTIFICIAL LANGUAGE	ENGLISH	ARTIFICIAL LANGUAGE
a, an	bex	river	browlek
alien	huslek	that	velle
and	cre	the	ric
boy	ekaplek	this	volle
brave	gafle	to arrest	hodsur
country	failek	to be	synsur
danger	gonlek	to border	regsur
enemy	avelek	to cross	chonsur
friend	kometlek	to document	clegsur
from	mor	to guard	bonsur
government	almanlek	to have	tulsur
he, him	yev	to identify	kalensur
intelligent	varle	to inspect	zelsur
legal	colle	to patrol	linsur
loyal	inle	to question	pafsur
man	kaplek	to report	fonsur
necessary	munle	to station	lexsur
on	ru	to work	frigsur

191

PRACTICE TEST 6

ARRANGED ALPHABETICALLY BY THE ARTIFICIAL LANGUAGE WORD

ARTIFICIAL LANGUAGE	ENGLISH	ARTIFICIAL LANGUAGE	ENGLISH
almanlek	government	kalensur	to identify
avelek	enemy	kaplek	man
bex	a, an	kometlek	friend
bonsur	to guard	lexsur	to station
browlek	river	linsur	to patrol
chonsur	to cross	mor	from
clegsur	to document	munle	necessary
colle	legal	pafsur	to question
cre	and	regsur	to border
ekaplek	boy	ric	the
failek	country	ru	on
fonsur	to report	synsur	to be
frigsur	to work	tulsur	to have
gafle	brave	varle	intelligent
gonlek	danger	velle	that
hodsur	to arrest	volle	this
huslek	alien	yev	he, him
inle	loyal	zelsur	to inspect

Grammatical Rules for the Artificial Language

The Grammatical Rules given here are the same as those used in the Border Patrol Exam, except that the prefixes (word beginnings) and suffixes (word endings) used in the exam differ from those used here.

During the exam, you will have access to the rules at all times. Consequently, it is important that you understand these rules, but it is not necessary that you memorize them. In fact, memorizing them will hinder rather than help you, because the beginnings and endings of words are different in the version of the Artificial Language that appears in this manual than the one that appears in the actual test.

You should note that Part Three of the official Artificial Language Manual contains a glossary of grammatical terms to assist you if you are not thoroughly familiar with the meanings of these grammatical terms.

Rule 1

To form the feminine singular of a noun, a pronoun, an adjective, or an article, add the suffix *-gid* to the masculine singular form. Only nouns, pronouns, adjectives, and articles take feminine endings in the Artificial Language. When gender is not specified, the masculine form is used.

Examples

If a *male eagle* is a *verlek*, then a *female eagle* is a *verlekgid*.

If an *ambitious* man is a *tosle* man, an *ambitious* woman is a *toslegid* woman.

Rule 2

To form the plural of nouns, pronouns, and adjectives, add the suffix *-ol* to the correct singular form.

Examples

If one *male eagle* is a *verlek*, then several *male eagles* are *verlekol*.

If an *ambitious* woman is a *toslegid* woman, several *ambitious* women are *toslegidol* women.

Rule 3

Adjectives modifying nouns and pronouns with feminine and/or plural endings must have endings that agree with the words they modify. In addition, an article (*a*, *an*, and *the*) preceding a noun must also agree with the noun in gender and number.

Examples

If an *active male eagle* is a *sojle verlek*, then an *active female eagle* is a *sojlegid verlekgid* and several *active female eagles* are *sojlegidol verlekgidol*.

If *this male eagle* is *volle verlek*, then *these female eagles* are *vollegidol verlekgidol*.

If *the male eagle* is *ric verlek*, then *the female eagle* is *ricgid verlekgid* and *the female eagles* are *ricgidol verlekgidol*.

If *a male eagle* is *bex verlek*, then *several male eagles* are *bexol verlekol*.

Rule 4

The stem of the verb is obtained by omitting the suffix *-sur* from the infinitive form of the verb.

Example

The stem of the verb *synsur* is *syn*.

Rule 5

All subjects and their verbs must agree in number; that is, singular subjects require singular verbs and plural subjects require plural verbs. (See Rules 6 and 7.)

Rule 6

To form the present tense of a verb, add the suffix *-ot* to the stem for the singular form or the suffix *-et* to the stem for the plural.

Example

If *to bark* is *nalsur*, then *nalot* is the present tense for the singular (the dog *barks*) and *nalet* is the present tense for the plural (the dogs *bark*).

Rule 7

To form the past tense of a verb, first add the suffix *-rem* to the stem, and then add the suffix *-ot* if the verb is singular or the suffix *-et* if it is plural.

Example

If *to bark* is *nalsur*, then *nalremot* is the past tense for the singular (the dog *barked*), and *nalremet* is the past tense for the plural (the dogs *barked*).

Rule 8

To form the past participle of a verb, add to the stem of the verb the suffix *-to*. It can be used to form compound tenses with the verb *to have*, as a predicate with the verb *to be*, or as an adjective. In the last two cases, it takes masculine, feminine, singular, and plural forms in agreement with the noun to which it refers.

Example of use in a compound tense with the verb *to have*

If *to bark* is *nalsur* and *to have* is *tulsur*, then *tulot nalto* is the present perfect for the singular (the dog *has barked*) and *tulet nalto* is the present perfect for the plural (the dogs *have barked*). Similarly, *tulremot nalto* is the past perfect for the singular (the dog *had barked*) and *tulremet nalto* is the past perfect for the plural (the dogs *had barked*).

Example of use as a predicate with the verb *to be*

If *to adopt* is *rapsur* and *to be* is *synsur*, then a *boy was adopted* is *ekaplek synremot rapto* and many *girls were adopted* is *ekaplekgidol synremet raptogidol*.

Example of use as an adjective

If *to delight* is *kassur*, then a *delighted boy* is a *kasto ekaplek* and many *delighted girls* are *kastogidol ekaplekgidol*.

Rule 9

To form a noun from a verb, add the suffix *-lek* to the stem of the verb.

Example

If *longsur* is *to write*, then a *writer* is a *longlek*.

Rule 10

To form an adjective from a noun, substitute the suffix *-le* for the suffix *-lek*.

Example

If *pellek* is *beauty*, then a *beautiful male eagle* is a *pelle verlek*, and a *beautiful female eagle* is a *pellegid verlekgid*. (Note the feminine ending *-gid*.)

Rule 11

To form an adverb from an adjective, add the suffix *-de* to the masculine form of the adjective. (Note that adverbs do not change their form to agree in number or gender with the word they modify.)

Example

If *pelle* is *beautiful*, then *beautifully* is *pellede*.

Rule 12

To form the possessive of a noun or pronoun, add the suffix *-oe* to the noun or pronoun after any plural or feminine suffixes.

Examples

If a *boglek* is a *dog*, then a *dog's* collar is a *boglekoe* collar.

If *he* is *yev*, then *his* book is *yevoe* book.

If *she* is *yevgid*, then *her* book is *yevgidoe* book.

Rule 13

To make a word negative, add the prefix *ja-* to the correct affirmative form.

Examples

If an *active male eagle* is a *sojle verlek*, then an *inactive male eagle* is a *jasojle verlek*.

If the *dog barks* is *boglek nalot*, then the *dog does not bark* is *boglek janalot*.

Artificial Language

Use the Vocabulary Lists and Grammatical Rules to help you answer these questions.

For each sentence, decide which words have been translated correctly. Use scratch paper to list each numbered word that is correctly translated into the Artificial Language. When you have finished listing the words that are correctly translated in sentences 1 through 20, select your answer according to the following instructions:

PRACTICE TEST 6

Mark:
a. if *only* the word numbered 1 is correctly translated.
b. if *only* the word numbered 2 is correctly translated.
c. if *only* the word numbered 3 is correctly translated.
d. if *two or more* of the numbered words are correctly translated.
e. if *none* of the numbered words is correctly translated.

Be sure to list only the *numbered* words that are *correctly* translated.

Study the sample question before going on to the test questions.

Sample Sentence
This woman crossed the river.

Sample Translation
Bex kaplegid chonremet lac browlek.
 1   2   3

The word numbered 1, *bex*, is incorrect because the translation of *bex* is *a*. The word *vollegid* should have been used. The word numbered 2 is correct. *Kaplekgid* has been correctly formed by adding the feminine ending to the masculine noun, applying Rule 1. The word numbered 3, *chonremet*, is incorrect because the singular form, *chonremot*, should have been used. Because the word numbered 2 is correct, the answer to the sample question is **b**.

Now go on with questions 1 through 20 and answer them in the manner indicated. Be sure to record your answers on the separate answer sheet found at the beginning of the test.

Sentence

1. He questions the guard.

2. She is an inspector.

3. The patrol is loyal.

4. The women guarded the enemy.

5. That country is dangerous.

6. The girls and the boys identified the question.

7. The woman's guard questioned her.

Translation

1. Yevgid pafot ric bonsurlek.
     1   2   3

2. Yevgid synet bexgid zellekgid.
     1   2   3

3. Ricgid linlekgid synot inle.
     1   2   3

4. Ricgidol kaplekgidol bongidolremet ric avelekgid.
               1   2   3

5. Volle failek synsurot gonlek.
     1   2   3

6. Ricgidol ekaplekgidol cre ricol ekaplekol kalenremet ric paflek.
                 1   2   3

7. Ricgid kaplekgidol bonlek pafremot yevgibol.
              1   2   3

195

PRACTICE TEST 6

8. That patrol is on this station.
   <u>Velle</u> <u>linlek</u> synot <u>ru</u> <u>velle</u> lexlek.
     1   2   3

9. These are legal documents.
   <u>Volleol</u> synet <u>colle</u> <u>clegsurol</u>.
     1   2   3

10. The reports are unnecessary.
    Ricol <u>fonsurlekol</u> <u>synet</u> <u>jamunleol</u>.
            1   2   3

11. She was a loyal guard.
    Yevgid synremot <u>bex</u> <u>inle</u> <u>bonlek</u>.
                   1   2   3

12. These patrols do not cross that river.
    <u>Vollelekol</u> <u>linsurlekol</u> <u>jachonet</u> velle browlek.
      1   2   3

13. The patrol has to arrest illegal aliens.
    Ric linlek <u>tulsurot</u> <u>hodot</u> <u>jacolle</u> huslekol.
                1   2   3

14. The inspector reported those women.
    Ric <u>zelle</u> fonremot <u>vellegidol</u> <u>ekaplekgidol</u>.
         1   2   3

15. He disloyally reported his friends.
    Yev <u>jainlede</u> <u>fonremot</u> <u>yevoe</u> kometlekol.
         1   2   3

16. The girls' question was intelligent.
    Ricgidol <u>ekaplekgidoloe</u> <u>paflek</u> synremot <u>varlegid</u>.
              1   2   3

17. The guards bravely crossed the dangerous country.
    Ricol <u>bonlekol</u> <u>gafle</u> <u>chonrem</u> ric gonle failek.
            1   2   3

18. The aliens from that country were arrested.
    <u>Velle</u> huslekol mor <u>ric</u> failek synremet <u>hodtool</u>.
     1   2   3

19. They arrested her.
    <u>Yevgidol</u> <u>hodremet</u> <u>yevgid</u>.
       1   2   3

20. Dangerous borders have to be patrolled.
    <u>Gonle</u> <u>regleol</u> tulet synsur <u>lintool</u>.
      1   2   3

For each question in this group, select one of the five suggested choices that correctly translates the italicized word or group of words into the Artificial Language.

Sample Question
Where are *the friends*?
a. bex kometlek
b. ric kometlek
c. ricol kometlekol
d. ric kometlekob
e. bex kometlekob

Choice **c** is the correct translation of the italicized words, *the friends*, because the definite article, *ric*, must change its ending to agree with the noun (see Rule 3), and the noun *kometlekol* has the proper plural suffix (Rule 2).

PRACTICE TEST 6

The members of the border patrol must be *brave and intelligent* to accomplish *their dangerous work*.
                                              21   22

The country's borders pose dangers that *they loyally guard* against. They *have to arrest* people who may
       23   24   25

have hostile intentions. At *border stations*, they *document aliens* who *have crossed* into the country.
                              26   27   28

These men and these women of the border patrol form the nation's first defense against the threat of
              29

terrorism. Never knowing whether someone is a friend or enemy of the government, they cannot

afford *unnecessary* mistakes.
         30

21. a. gaflegidol cre varlegidol
    b. gaflegid cre varlegid
    c. gaflek cre varlek
    d. gafle cre varle
    e. gafleol cre varleol

22. a. yev gonle friglek
    b. yevol gonle friglekol
    c. yevoe gonle friglek
    d. yevoloe gonle friglek
    e. yevoloe gonleol friglekol

23. a. Ricol failekoe reglekol
    b. Ricol failekoloe reglekol
    c. Ricol failekoe regleol
    d. Ric failekoe reglekol
    e. Ric failekol reglekol

24. a. yev jainle bonet
    b. yevgid jainle bonot
    c. yevol inlede bonet
    d. yevgidol inlede bonot
    e. yevgidol inlede bonet

25. a. tulot hodsur
    b. tulet hodsur
    c. tulot hodot
    d. tulet hodet
    e. tulot hodto

26. a. regleol lexlekol
    b. regleoe lexlekol
    c. reglekol lexlekol
    d. regle lexlekol
    e. regle lexleol

27. a. clegremet huslekol
    b. clegot huslekgidol
    c. clegot huslekol
    d. cleget huslekol
    e. cleget huslekgidol

28. a. tulet chontool
    b. tulot chontool
    c. tulet chonsurto
    d. tulot chonto
    e. tulet chonto

29. a. Volle kaplek cre volle kaplekgid
    b. Volle kaplekol cre vollegid kaplekgidol
    c. Volleol kaplekol cre vollegidol kaplekgidol
    d. Vollegidol kaplekgidol cre volleol kaplekol
    e. Velleol kaplekol cre vellegidol kaplekgidol

30. a. jamunlegidol
    b. jamunleol
    c. jamunle
    d. munleja
    e. munlejaol

PRACTICE TEST 6

For this group of questions, select the one response option that is the correct translation of the English word or words in parentheses. You should translate the entire sentence in order to determine what form should be used.

Sample Question
Ricol almanlekoe tatlekol (crossed the border).
a. chonremet bex reglek
b. chonremot ric reglek
c. chonremet ric reglek
d. chonremet ric regsur
e. chonremot bex reglek

Ricol almanlekoe tatlekol chonremet ric reglek means *The government's spies crossed the border*.

Because *chonremet ric reglek* is the only one of these expressions that means *they* (plural) *crossed the border*, choice **c** is the correct answer to the sample question.

31. (Her country's enemies) synremet ru ric reglek.
    a. Yev failekoe avelekoe
    b. Yevgid failekol avelekgidol
    c. Yevgidoe failekoe avelekol
    d. Yevgidoe failekol avelekol
    e. Yevgid failekoe avelekgidol

32. Ricgid ekaplekgid (bravely crossed) ric browlek.
    a. gaflede chonremot
    b. gafle chonremot
    c. gaflekde chonremot
    d. gaflekde chonremet
    e. gaflegidde chonremet

33. (Their friends from that country) tulet cleglekol.
    a. Yev kometleol mor volle faile
    b. Yevoe kometleol mor volle faile
    c. Yevol kometlekol mor volle failek
    d. Yevoloe kometlekol mor velle failek
    e. Yevolgidoe kometlekgidol mor velle failek

34. (These women guarded) ric ekaplek.
    a. Volleoe kaplekgidol bonsurremet
    b. Volleol kaplekol bonsurremet
    c. Vollegidoe kaplekgidoe bonremet
    d. Vollegidol kaplekgidol bonremot
    e. Vollegidol kaplekgidol bonremet

35. Ricgid zellekgid (unnecessarily reported from the patrol) lexlek.
    a. jamunlekde fonremet mor ric linlek
    b. jamunlede fonremot mor ric linle
    c. jamunle fonremet mor ric linlek
    d. munle fonremot mor ric linle
    e. munlede fonremet mor ric linlek

36. (The reports on the government's dangerous enemies) synremet paftool.
    a. Ric fonlekol ru ricol almanlekol gonleol avelekol
    b. Ricol fonlekol ru ricol almanlekoe gonleol avelekol
    c. Ric fonlekol ru ricol almanlekoe gonle avelekol
    d. Ricol fonleol ru ricol almanleoe gonleol aveleol
    e. Ricol fonlekol ru ric almanlekol gonle avelekol

PRACTICE TEST 6

37. (This border patrol) tulot chonto ric browlek.
  a. Volle regle linlek
  b. Volle reglek linlek
  c. Volle regle linle
  d. Velle regle linlek
  e. Velle reglek linlek

38. Ric kaplek (inspected the documents).
  a. zelremot ricol clegsurlekol
  b. zelremet ric clegleol
  c. zelremot ric cleglekol
  d. zelremet ricol cleglekol
  e. zelremot ricol cleglckol

39. Ric huslek (was arrested and guarded).
  a. synremot hodsurto cre bonsurto
  b. synremet hodto bex bonto
  c. synremot hodto cre bonto
  d. synremet hodde cre bonde
  e. synremot hodde bex bonde

40. Ric bonlek pafremot (the women and the boys).
  a. ric kaplekgidol cre ric ekaplekol
  b. ric kaplekol cre ric ekaplekol
  c. ricol kaplekgidol cre ricol ekaplekol
  d. ricgidol kaplekgidol cre ricol ekaplekol
  e. ricgidol kaplekgidol cre ricgidol ekaplekgidol

41. Ricol zellekol (reported from the station).
  a. fonsurremet mor ricol lexlekol
  b. fonremet mor ric lexle
  c. fonremet mor ric lexlek
  d. fonremot mor ric lexlek
  e. fonremot mor ric lexle

42. Ricol kaplekol synremet ru (the guarded borders).
  a. ric bonto reglekol
  b. ricol bontool reglekol
  c. ric bonsurto regsurlekol
  d. ric bontool reglekol
  e. ricol bonsurol regsurlekol

For the last group of questions, select one of the five suggested choices that is the correct form of the italicized expression as it is used in the sentence. At the end of the sentence, you will find instructions in parentheses telling you which form to use. In some sentences you will be asked to supply the correct forms of two or more expressions. In this case, the instructions for these expressions are presented consecutively in the parentheses and are separated by a dash (for example, past tense—adverb). Be sure to translate the entire sentence before selecting your answer.

Sample Question
Yev *bonsur* ric browlek. (present tense)
  a. bonremot
  b. bonremet
  c. boneet
  d. bonet
  e. bonot

Choices **a** and **b** are incorrect because they are in the past tense. Choice **c** is misspelled. Choice **d** is in the present tense, but it, too, is incorrect because the subject of the sentence is singular and therefore takes a verb with a singular rather than a plural ending. Choice **e** is the answer to the sample question.

43. Ricgidol ekaplekgidol synremet *kometlek*. (plural feminine adjective)
  a. kometle
  b. kometleol
  c. kometlegid
  d. kometlegidol
  e. kometlekgidol

44. Vellegid ekaplekgid *synsur gafle*. (singular past tense verb—singular feminine adjective)
   a. synremot—gaflegid
   b. synremet—gaflegid
   c. synremot—gafle
   d. synremet—gafle
   e. synot—gafle

45. Yevol *inle* fonremet yevoloe kometlekol. (negative adverb)
   a. inlekdeja
   b. deinleja
   c. dejainle
   d. jainlekde
   e. jainlede

46. Ricgidol *lexsur* bonlekgidol synremet *kometlek*. (feminine plural adjective—feminine plural noun)
   a. lexlek—kometlekol
   b. lexle—kometlekol
   c. lexleol—kometlekol
   d. lexlegidol—kometlekgidol
   e. lexlekgidol—kometlekgidol

47. Ricol *frigsur* ru ric *fonsur*. (plural past tense verb—singular noun)
   a. frigremet—fonlek
   b. friget—fonremlek
   c. frigremot—fonlek
   d. frigot—fonremlek
   e. frigsurremet—fonle

48. Ricol *hodsur* synremet *colle*. (plural noun—negative plural adjective)
   a. hodleol—jacollede
   b. hodsurol—jacollede
   c. hodlekol—jacolleol
   d. hodlekol—jacolle
   e. hodsurlekol—jacolle

49. *Yev* paflekol synremet *gonlek*. (singular feminine possessive—plural masculine adjective)
   a. Yevgidol—gonlekol
   b. Yevoe—gonleoe
   c. Yevgidoe—gonleoe
   d. Yevol—gonleol
   e. Yevgidoe—gonleol

50. *Ric kometlek* bonlekgidol *tulsur* ric fonlek. (plural feminine article—negative plural feminine adjective—negative plural past tense verb)
   a. Ricol—jakometleol—tulremet
   b. Ricgidol—jakometlegidol—jatulremet
   c. Ric—kometle—tulremet
   d. Ricgidol—kometlegidol—tulremet
   e. Ric—jakometlegid—jatulremet

PRACTICE TEST 6

Answers

Logical Reasoning

1. **d.** Choice **d** makes a conclusion that is not supported by the information in the paragraph, and is therefore the correct answer. Choices **b**, **c**, and **e** make correct assumptions based on the information in the paragraph, so these answers are incorrect.

2. **c.** Choice **c**, which restates information found in the paragraph, is the correct answer. Choices **a**, **b**, **d**, and **e** rely on faulty conclusions that are not drawn from information in the paragraph, and are incorrect answers.

3. **c.** Choice **c** restates information provided in the third sentence of the paragraph, and is therefore correct. Choices **a** and **b** make conclusions that cannot be drawn from information provided in the paragraph—it is not known which officer is senior to the other—so they are incorrect. Choice **d** contradicts information provided in the third sentence of the paragraph, and is incorrect. Because the correct answer is found in the choices, choice **e** is incorrect.

4. **e.** None of the previous answers presents valid conclusions drawn from the information in the paragraph, so choice **e** is the correct answer. Choices **a**, **b**, and **c** contradict information given in the third sentence of the paragraph, so they are incorrect. Choice **d** contradicts information given in the second sentence of the paragraph, so it is incorrect.

5. **c.** Choice **c** restates information found in the second sentence of the paragraph, so it is the correct answer. Choices **a** and **e** contradict information found in the third sentence of the paragraph, so they are incorrect. Choices **b** and **d** contradict information found in the second sentence of the paragraph, so they are incorrect.

6. **d.** Choice **d** restates the information in the last sentence of the paragraph, and is the correct answer. Choice **b** contradicts the information that all the employees over 30 were working legally, so it is incorrect. Choices **a** and **c** rely on the assumption that there are workers under 30 from Bolivia who were legally employed, which the paragraph does not confirm. The paragraph does not state whether any of the Argentinean workers were over 30, so choice **e** is incorrect.

7. **a.** Since the paragraph states that most agents were assigned to the U.S.-Mexico border, it can be concluded that more agents are concentrated there than in Canada, so choice **a** is correct. Choices **b** and **c** rely on a false assumption that could not have been concluded from the information in the paragraph, so it is incorrect. Choice **d** contradicts information given in the last sentence of the paragraph, so it is incorrect. Because the correct answer is found in the choices, choice **e** is incorrect.

8. **e.** None of the answers presents conclusions that could not have been drawn from the information in the paragraph, so choice **e** is the correct answer. Choice **a** restates information found in the fourth sentence within the paragraph, so it is incorrect. Choice **b** restates information found in the first three sentences within the paragraph, so it is incorrect. Choices **c** and **d** restate information found in the first sentence within the paragraph, so they are incorrect.

9. b. Although if the signature is not notarized it would render the application incomplete, the opposite is not necessarily true, as there are other requirements that are necessary to complete the application; choice **b** is therefore the correct answer. Choices **a**, **d**, and **e** restate information found in the last sentence, so they are incorrect. Choice **c** restates information found in the second sentence, so it is incorrect.

10. e. None of the choices contains information that could be concluded from the paragraph, so choice **e** is the correct answer.

11. d. Choice **d** restates information found in the last sentence of the paragraph, so it is the correct answer. Choices **a**, **b**, and **c** are faulty conclusions that could not have been drawn from the paragraph, so they are incorrect. Because the correct response is found within the answers, choice **e** is incorrect.

12. d. The policy was passed in 1965 and led to sharp increases in the late 1960s, so the increase was almost immediate; therefore, choice **d** is correct. Choices **a**, **b**, and **c** misinterpret information found within the paragraph, so they are incorrect. Because the correct response is found within the answers, choice **e** is incorrect.

13. e. Choices **a**, **b**, **c**, and **d** misinterpret information found within the paragraph, so they are all incorrect conclusions. Therefore, choice **e** is the correct answer.

14. b. Choice **b** restates information given in the second and fourth sentences, so it is the correct answer. Choices **a**, **c**, **d**, and **e** confuse information given in the paragraph, so they are incorrect.

15. a. Although according to the paragraph permanent residents may not vote in elections limited to U.S. citizens, the opposite is not necessarily true; therefore choice **a** cannot be a valid conclusion and is the correct answer. Choices **b**, **c**, and **d** restate information found in the paragraph and are therefore incorrect answers. The correct response is found in the answers, so choice **e** is not the correct answer.

16. b. Choice **b** restates information found within the paragraph, so it is the correct answer. Choices **a** and **e** confuse the job duties of a GS-5 level agent with that of a GS-7 level agent, so they are incorrect. Choices **c** and **d** make faulty assumptions that could not have been concluded from the information in the paragraph, so they are incorrect.

Artificial Language

1. b. Only word 2 is correct, so the answer is **b**. *Questions* is translated by adding the suffix *-ot* to the stem (Rule 6) of *pafsur* (*to question*) since the verb is in the present tense and is singular. *Yevgid* is incorrect because the feminine suffix *-gid* has been added to *yev* (*he*), which would have been the correct form. Word 3 is incorrect because the suffix *-lek* has been added to the infinitive *bonsur* (*to guard*); instead, it should be added to the stem to form *bonlek*.

2. d. Words 1 and 3 are correct, so the answer is **d**. *Yevgid* is translated by adding the feminine suffix *-gid* (Rule 1) to *yev* (*he*). *Zellekgid* is formed by adding the suffix *-lek* to the stem (Rule 9) of *zelsur* (*to inspect*) in order to create a noun from a verb and then adding the feminine suffix *-gid*. Word 2 is incorrect because the plural verb suffix *-et* has been added to the stem of *synsur* (*to be*); instead, the singular suffix verb *-ot* should have been added to the stem to form *synot*.

PRACTICE TEST 6

3. c. Only word 3 is correct, so the answer is **c**. *Loyal* is translated as *inle*; this form is correct since *patrol* is gender neutral. Word 1 is incorrect because the correct translation of *the* in this case is *ric*; the feminine suffix *-gid* is unnecessary since *patrol* is gender neutral. Word 2 is incorrect because it, too, includes the feminine suffix *-gid*.

4. a. Only word 1 is correct, so the answer is **a**. *Women* is translated by adding the feminine suffix *-gid* (Rule 1) to *kaplek* (*man*) and then adding the plural suffix *-ol* (Rule 2). Word 2 is incorrect because it includes the suffixes *-gid* and *-ol*, which is not necessary for a verb. The correct word is formed by adding the suffixes *-rem* and *-et* to the stem (Rule 7) of *bonsur* (*to guard*) because the verb is in the past tense and is plural, to form *bonremet*. Word 3 is incorrect because it, too, includes the feminine suffix *-gid*; the correct form is simply *avelek* (*enemy*) since the word is gender neutral.

5. e. None of the numbered words is incorrect, so the answer is **e**. *Volle* means *this*; the correct word would be *velle*. Word 2 includes the infinitive; *is* should be translated by adding the suffix *-ot* to the stem (Rule 6) of *synsur* (*to be*). Word 3 is incorrect because *gonlek* (*danger*) is a noun; *dangerous* should be translated by changing the suffix *-lek* to *-le* (Rule 10) to form *gonle*.

6. d. All three words are correct, so the answer is **d**. *Girls* is translated by adding the feminine suffix *-gid* (Rule 1) to *ekaplek* (*boy*) and adding the plural suffix *-ol* (Rule 2). *Boys* is translated by adding the suffix *-ol* to *ekaplek*. *Identified* is translated by adding the suffixes *-rem* and *-et* to the stem (Rule 7) of *kalensur* (*to identify*) because the verb is in the past tense and is plural.

7. b. Only word 2 is correct, so the answer is **b**. *Questioned* is translated by adding the suffixes *-rem* and *-ot* to the stem (Rule 7) of *pafsur* (*to question*) because the verb is in the past tense and is singular. *Woman's* should be translated by adding the feminine suffix *-gid* (Rule 1) and the possessive suffix *-oe* (Rule 12) to *kaplek* (*man*) to form *kaplekgidoe*; instead the plural suffix *-ol* has been used. *Her* should be translated by adding the feminine suffix *-gid* (Rule 1) to *yev* (*him*) to form *yevgid*; the plural suffix *-ol* has been added unnecessarily.

8. d. Only words 1 and 2 are correct, so the answer is **d**. *That* is translated as *velle*. *Ru* is the correct translation of *on*. Word 3 is incorrect because *velle* means *that*; the correct translation of *this* would be *volle*.

9. a. Only word 1 is correct, so the answer is **a**. *These* is translated by adding the plural suffix *-ol* (Rule 2) to *volle* (*this*). *Legal*, in this case, should be translated by adding the plural suffix *-ol* to *colle* (*legal*) because it refers to a plural noun (*documents*) to form *colleol*. *Documents* should be translated by adding the suffix *-lek* to the stem (Rule 9) of *clegsur* (*to document*) and then adding the plural suffix *-ol* to form *cleglekol*; word 3 is incorrect because the suffix *-ol* has been added to the infinitive *clegsur*.

10. d. Only words 2 and 3 are correct, so the answer is **d**. *Are* is translated by adding the suffix *-et* to the stem (Rule 6) of *synsur* (*to be*) because the verb is in the present tense and is plural. *Unnecessary* is translated by adding the plural suffix *-ol* (Rule 2) to *munle* (*necessary*) and then adding the negative prefix *ja-* (Rule 13). Word 1 is incorrect because it includes the infinitive *fonsur*; *reports* should instead be translated by adding the suffix *-lek* to the stem (Rule 9) of *fonsur* (*to report*) and then adding the plural suffix *-ol* to form *fonlekol*.

11. e. None of the numbered words is correct, so the answer is **e**. In this case, *a* should be translated by adding the feminine suffix *-gid* (Rule 2) to *bex* (*a*) because the guard is female, to form *bexgid*. *Loyal* should be translated similarly, by adding the suffix *-gid* to *inle* (*loyal*) to form *inlegid*. *Guard* also should be translated by adding *-gid* to *bonlek* (*guard*), which has been formed by adding the suffix *-lek* to the stem (Rule 9) of *bonsur* (*to guard*) in order to create a noun from a verb.

12. c. Only word 3 is correct, so the correct answer is **c**. *Do not cross* is translated by adding the suffix *-et* to the stem (Rule 6) of *chonsur* (*to cross*) because the verb is in the present tense and is plural, and then adding the negative prefix *ja-* (Rule 13). *These* should be translated by adding the plural suffix *-ol* to *volle* (*this*) to form *volleol*; instead, the suffix *-lek* has been added unnecessarily. *Patrols* should be translated by adding the suffix *-lek* to the stem (Rule 9) of *linsur* (*to patrol*), and then adding the plural suffix *-ol* to form *linlekol*; instead, the suffixes have been added to the infinitive *linsur*.

13. e. None of the numbered words is correct, so the answer is **e**. *Has* should be translated by adding the suffix *-ot* to the stem (Rule 6) of *tulsur* (*to have*) because the verb is in the present tense and is singular to form *tulot*; instead, the suffix has been added to the infinitive, *tulsur*. *To arrest* should be translated simply as the infinitive *hodsur* (*to arrest*); instead, it has been translated as the verb *arrests*. *Illegal* should be translated by adding the plural suffix *-ol* to *colle* (*legal*) and then adding the negative prefix *ja-* to form *jacolleol*; word 3, however, lacks the plural suffix.

14. b. Only word 2 is correct, so the answer is **b**. *Those* is translated by adding the feminine suffix *-gid* (Rule 1) and the plural suffix *-ol* (Rule 2) to *velle* (*that*). *Inspector* should be translated by adding the suffix *-lek* to the stem (Rule 9) of *zelsur* (*to inspect*) to form *zellek*; instead, the suffix *-le* has been used. *Women* should be translated by adding the feminine suffix *-gid* and the plural suffix *-ol* to *kaplek* (*man*) to form *kaplekgidol*; the suffixes have instead been added to *ekaplek* (*boy*), forming the translation of *girls*.

15. d. Each of the numbered words is correct, so the answer is **d**. *Disloyally* is translated by adding the suffix *-de* (Rule 11) to form an adverb from the adjective *inle* (*loyal*) and then adding the negative prefix *ja-* (Rule 13). *Reported* is translated by adding the suffixes *-rem* and *-ot* because the verb is in the past tense and is singular (Rule 7). *His* is translated by adding the possessive suffix *-oe* (Rule 12) to *yev* (*he*).

16. d. Only words 1 and 2 are correct, so the answer is **d**. *Girls* is translated by adding the feminine suffix *-gid* (Rule 1), the plural suffix *-ol* (2), and the possessive suffix *-oe* (Rule 12) to *ekaplek* (*boy*). *Question* is translated by adding the suffix *-lek* to the stem (Rule 9) of *pafsur* (*to question*). *Intelligent* should be translated simply as *varle* since it refers to *question*, which is gender neutral; instead, it has been translated with the feminine suffix *-gid*.

17. a. Only word 1 is correct, so the answer is **a**. *Guards* is translated by adding the suffix *-lek* to the stem (Rule 9) of *bonsur* (*to guard*) and adding the plural suffix *-ol* (Rule 2). *Bravely* should be translated by adding the suffix *-de* to *gafle* (Rule 11) to form *gaflede*; the suffix, however, has not been used. *Crossed* should be translated by adding the suffixes *-rem* and *-et* to the stem (Rule 7) of *chonsur* (*to cross*) because it is in the past tense and is plural to form *chonremet*; instead, the suffix *-et* has not been added.

18. c. Only word 3 is correct, so the answer is **c**. *Arrested* is formed by adding the suffix *-to* to the stem (Rule 8) of *hodsur* (*to arrest*) since *arrested* functions as a predicate; the plural suffix *-ol* must then be added because the word refers to the plural *aliens*. Word 1 is wrong because *velle* means *that*; *the* should be translated by adding the plural suffix *-ol* (Rule 2) to *ric* (*the*) to form *ricol*. Word 2 is incorrect because *ric* means *the*; *that* should be translated as *velle*.

19. d. Only words 2 and 3 are correct, so the answer is **d**. *Arrested* is translated by added the suffixes *-rem* and *-et* to the stem (Rule 7) of *hodsur* (*to arrest*) because the verb is in the past tense and is plural. *Her* is translated by adding the feminine suffix *-gid* (Rule 1) to *yev* (*him*). *They* should be translated by adding the plural suffix *-ol* (Rule 2) to *yev* (*he*) to form *yevol*; instead, the feminine suffix *-gid* has been unnecessarily added to the gender-neutral word.

20. c. Only word 3 is correct, so the answer is **c**. *Patrolled* is translated by adding the suffix *-to* to the stem (Rule 8) of *linsur* (*to patrol*) because the word functions as a predicate; then the plural suffix *-ol* is added because it refers to *borders*, which is plural. *Dangerous* should be translated by changing the suffix *-lek* to *-le* (Rule 10) in *gonlek* (*danger*) in order to change the noun into an adjective and by adding the plural suffix *-ol* (Rule 2) to form *gonleol*; word 1 instead does not include the suffix *-ol*. *Borders* should be translated by adding the suffix *-lek* to the stem (Rule 9) of *regsur* (*to border*) in order to form a noun and then adding the plural suffix *-ol*, to form *reglekol*; word 2 instead includes the suffix *-le*.

21. e. This choice is correct because both *brave* and *intelligent* are translated by adding the plural suffix *-ol* (Rule 2) to *gafle* (*brave*) and *varle* (*intelligent*), respectively, since they both modify the plural *members*; *cre* is the correct translation of *and*. Choice **a** is incorrect because *brave* and *intelligent* have been translated using the feminine suffix *-gid*, whereas *members* is gender neutral. Choice **b** is incorrect because *brave* and *intelligent* have been translated using the suffix *-gid* and without being made plural. Choice **c** is incorrect because *brave* and *intelligent* have been translated using the suffix *-lek*, instead of *-le*, and without the plural suffix *-ol*. Choice **d** is incorrect because *brave* and *intelligent* have been translated without the plural suffix *-ol*. Don't be tricked into thinking that these words are modifying the singular *patrol*; they are referring to *members*.

22. d. This choice is correct because *their* is translated by adding the plural suffix *-ol* (Rule 2) to *yev* (*he*) and then adding the possessive suffix *-oe* (Rule 12); *dangerous* is formed by changing the suffix *-lek* (Rule 10) in *gonlek* (*danger*) to *-le*; and *work* is translated by adding the suffix *-lek* to the stem (Rule 9) of *frigsur* (*to work*) in order to make the noun from a verb. Choice **a** is incorrect because *their* has been translated without the plural suffix *-ol* or the possessive suffix *-oe*. Choice **b** is incorrect because *their* has been translated without the possessive suffix *-oe* and because *work* has been translated using the plural suffix *-ol*. Choice **c** is incorrect because *their* has been translated without the plural suffix *-ol*. Choice **e** is incorrect because *dangerous* and *work* have been translated using the plural suffix *-ol*.

23. a. This choice is correct because *the* is translated by adding the plural suffix *-ol* (Rule 2) to *ric* (*the*); *country's* is translated by adding the possessive suffix *-oe* (Rule 12) to *failek* (*country*); and *borders* is translated by adding the suffix *-lek* to the stem (Rule 9) of *regsur* (*to border*) to form the noun from a verb, followed by the addition of the plural suffix *-ol*. Choice **b** is incorrect because *country's* has been translated with the plural suffix *-ol*, whereas it is only possessive. Choice **c** is incorrect because *borders* has been translated using the suffix *-le*, instead of *-lek*. Choice **d** is incorrect because *the* has been translated in the singular; keep in mind that *the* modifies *borders*, not *country's*. Choice **e** is incorrect because *the* has been translated in the singular and because *country's* has been translated using the plural suffix *-ol*, instead of the possessive suffix *-oe*.

24. c. This choice is correct because *they* is translated by adding the plural suffix *-ol* (Rule 2) to *yev* (*he*); *loyally* is translated by adding the suffix *-de* (Rule 11) to *inle* (*loyal*) in order to form an adverb from an adjective; and *guard* is translated by adding the suffix *-et* to the stem (Rule 6) of *bonsur* (*to guard*) since the verb is in the present tense and is plural. Choice **a** is incorrect because *they* has not been translated in the plural and because *jainle* means *disloyal*. Choice **b** is incorrect because *they* has been translated with the feminine suffix *-gid*, whereas it is gender neutral, and it lacks the plural suffix *-ol*; *jainle* means *disloyal* and *guard* has been translated with the singular verb suffix *-ot*, instead of *-et*. Choice **d** is incorrect because *they* has been translated with the feminine suffix *-gid* and because *guard* has been translated with the singular verb suffix *-ot*. Choice **e** is incorrect because *they* has been translated with the feminine suffix *-gid*.

25. b. This choice is correct because *have* is translated by adding the suffix *-et* to the stem (Rule 6) of *tulsur* (*to have*) since the verb is in the present tense and is plural; and *to arrest* is translated as the infinitive *hodsur*. Choice **a** is incorrect because *have* has been translated using the singular verb suffix *-ot*, instead of *-et*. Choice **c** is incorrect because *have* has been translated using the singular verb suffix *-ot* and because *to arrest* has been translated into a present tense verb, whereas it should be in the infinitive form. Choice **d** is incorrect because *to arrest* has been translated into a present tense verb. Choice **e** is incorrect because *have* has been translated using the singular verb suffix *-ot* and *to arrest* has been translated as a past participle.

26. a. This choice is correct because *border* is translated, first, by adding the suffix *-lek* to the stem (Rule 9) of *regsur* (*to border*) to make a noun from a verb, then changing *-lek* to the suffix *-le* (Rule 10) since the word modifies *stations*, and, finally, by adding the plural suffix *-ol* (Rule 2). *Stations* is translated, first, by adding the suffix *-lek* to the stem of *lexsur* (*to station*), then adding the plural suffix *-ol*. Choice **b** is incorrect because *border* has been translated using the possessive suffix *-oe*. Choice **c** is incorrect because *border* has been translated using the suffix *-lek*, instead of *-le*. Choice **d** is incorrect because *border* has not been translated in the plural, which it must be since *stations* is plural. Choice **e** is incorrect because *border* has not been translated in the plural and because *stations* has been translated using the suffix *-le*, instead of *-lek*.

27. d. This choice is correct because *document* is translated by adding the suffix *-et* to the stem (Rule 6) of *clegsur* (*to document*) since the verb is in the present tense and is plural; and *aliens* is translated by adding the plural suffix *-ol* (Rule 2) to *huslek* (*alien*). Choice **a** is incorrect because *document* has been translated using the verb suffix *-rem*, putting it in the past tense. Choice **b** is incorrect because *document* has been translated using the singular verb suffix *-ot*, instead of *-et*, and because *aliens* has been translated using the feminine suffix *-gid*, whereas *aliens* is gender neutral. Choice **c** is incorrect because *document* has been translated using the verb suffix *-ot*. Choice **e** is incorrect because *aliens* has been translated using the feminine suffix *-gid*.

28. e. This choice is correct because *have* is translated by adding the suffix *-et* to the stem (Rule 6) of *tulsur* (*to have*) since the verb is in the present tense and is plural; and *crossed* is translated by adding the suffix *-to* to the stem (Rule 8) of *chonsur* (*to cross*) since it is a past participle used in a compound tense with *to have*. Choice **a** is incorrect because *crossed* has been translated using the plural suffix *-ol*, which is not used in a compound tense. Choice **b** is incorrect because *have* has been translated with the singular verb suffix *-ot*, and because *crossed* has been translated using the plural suffix *-ol*. Choice **c** is incorrect because *crossed* has been translated by adding the suffix *-to* to the infinitive *chonsur*, instead of to its stem. Choice **d** is incorrect because *have* has been translated with the singular verb suffix *-ot*.

29. c. This choice is correct because the first use of *these* is translated by adding the plural suffix *-ol* (Rule 2) to *volle* (*this*); *men* is translated by adding the plural suffix *-ol* to *kaplek* (*man*); *cre* is the correct translation of *and*; the second use of *these* is translated by adding the feminine suffix *-gid* (Rule 1) and the plural suffix *-ol* to *volle*; and *women* is translated by adding the feminine suffix *-gid* and the plural suffix *-ol* to *kaplek*. Choice **a** is incorrect because neither use of *volle* has the necessary suffixes and because neither *men* nor *women* has been translated in the plural. Choice **b** is incorrect because neither translation of *these* is in the plural. Choice **d** is incorrect because this translation means *these women and these men*. Choice **e** is incorrect because this translation means *those men and those women*.

30. b. This choice is correct because *unnecessary* is translated by adding the plural suffix *-ol* (Rule 2) to *munle* (*necessary*) since *mistakes* is plural, and then by adding the negative prefix *ja-* (Rule 13). Choice **a** is incorrect because the translation includes the feminine suffix *-gid*, whereas *mistakes* is gender-neutral. Choice **c** is incorrect because the translation does not include the plural suffix *-ol*. Choice **d** is incorrect because the translation does not include the plural suffix *-ol* and because the prefix *ja-* has been placed at the end of the word. Choice **e** is incorrect because the negative prefix *ja-* has been positioned in the wrong place in the word.

31. c. *Yevgidoe failekoe avelekol synremet ru ric reglek* means *Her country's enemies were on the border*. *Her* is translated by adding the feminine suffix *-gid* (Rule 1) and the possessive suffix *-oe* (Rule 12) to *yev* (*he*). *Country's* is translated by adding the possessive suffix *-oe* to *failek* (*country*). *Enemies* is translated by adding the plural suffix *-ol* (Rule 2) to *avelek* (*enemy*). Choice **a** is incorrect because *yev* means *he* and is missing the necessary suffixes; *enemies* has been translated using the possessive suffix *-oe*, instead of the plural suffix *-ol*. Choice **b** is incorrect because *her* has been translated without the possessive suffix *-oe*; *country's* has been translated using the suffix *-ol* instead of *-oe*; and *enemies* has been translated using the suffix *-gid*, even though the word is gender neutral. Choice **d** is incorrect because *country's* has been translated using the suffix *-ol* instead of *-oe*. Choice **e** is incorrect because *her* has been translated without the possessive suffix *-oe* and because *enemies* has been translated using the suffix *-gid*.

32. a. *Ricgid ekaplekgid gaflede chonremot ric browlek* means *The girl bravely crossed the river*. *Bravely* is translated by adding the suffix *-de* to *gafle* (*brave*) to create an adverb (Rule 11). *Crossed* is translated by adding the suffixes *-rem* and *-ot* to the stem (Rule 7) of *chonsur* (*to cross*) because the verb is in the past tense and is singular. Choice **b** is incorrect because *bravely* has been translated without the suffix *-de*. Choice **c** is incorrect because *bravely* has been translated with the suffix *-lek*, instead of *-le*. Choice **d** is incorrect because *bravely* has been translated with the suffix *-lek* and because *crossed* has been translated with the plural verb suffix *-et*, instead of *-ot*. Choice **e** is incorrect because *bravely* has been translated with the feminine suffix *-gid*, which is not necessary since the word is an adverb, and because *crossed* has been translated with the plural verb suffix *-et*.

33. d. *Yevoloe kometlekol mor velle failek tulet cleglekol* means *Their friends from that country have documents*. *Their* is translated by adding the plural suffix *-ol* (Rule 2) and the possessive suffix *-oe* (Rule 12) to *yev* (*he*). *Friends* is translated by adding the plural suffix *-ol* to *kometlek* (Rule 2). *From* translates as *mor*. *That* translates as *velle*. *Country* translates as *failek*. Choice **a** is incorrect because *their* has been translated without any of the necessary suffixes; *friends* and *country* have been translated using the suffix *-le*, instead of *-lek*; and *volle* means *this*. Choice **b** is incorrect because *their* has been translated without the plural suffix *-ol*; *friends* and *country* have been translated using the suffix *-le*; and *volle* means *this*. Choice **c** is incorrect because *their* has been translated without the possessive suffix *-oe* and because *volle* means *this*. Choice **e** is incorrect because *their* and *friends* have been translated using the feminine suffix *-gid*, whereas the words should be gender neutral.

34. e. *Vollegidol kaplekgidol bonremet ric ekaplek* means *These women guarded the boy*. *These* is translated by adding the feminine suffix *-gid* (Rule 1) and the plural suffix *-ol* (Rule 2) to *volle* (*this*). *Women* is translated by adding the suffixes *-gid* and *-ol* as well. *Guarded* is translated by adding the suffixes *-rem* and *-et* to the stem (Rule 7) of *bonsur* (*to guard*). Choice **a** is incorrect because *these* has been translated without either of the correct suffixes, using the possessive suffix *-oe* instead, and because *guarded* has been translated by adding the suffixes to the infinitive of *bonsur*, instead of to its stem. Choice **b** is incorrect because *these* and *women* have been translated without the feminine suffix *-gid* and because *guarded* has been translated by adding the suffixes to the infinitive of *bonsur*, instead of to its stem. Choice **c** is incorrect because *these* and *women* have been translated using the suffix *-oe*, instead of *-ol*. Choice **d** is incorrect because *guarded* has been translated using the singular verb suffix *-ot*, instead of the plural *-et*.

35. b. *Ricgib zellekgib jamunlede fonremot mor ric linle lexlek* means *The inspector [female] unnecessarily reported from the patrol station.* *Unnecessarily* is translated by first adding the suffix *-de* to *munle* (*necessary*) to create an adverb and then adding the negative prefix *ja-* (Rule 13). *Reported* is translated by adding the suffixes *-rem* and *-ot* to the stem (Rule 7) of *fonsur* (*to report*) because the verb is in the past tense and is singular. *From* translates as *mor*. *The* simply translates as the singular *ric*. *Patrol* is translated, first, by adding the suffix *-lek* to the stem (Rule 9) of *linsur* (*to patrol*) to form the noun, and then by changing *-lek* to the suffix *-le* because the word modifies *station* (Rule 10). Choice **a** is incorrect because *unnecessarily* is translated using the suffix *-lek*, instead of *-le*; *reported* has been translated using the plural verb suffix *-et*, instead of *-ot*; *patrol* has been translated with the suffix *-lek*, instead of *-le*. Choice **c** is incorrect because *unnecessarily* is translated without the suffix *-de*; *reported* has been translated using the plural verb suffix *-et*; and *patrol* has been translated with the suffix *-lek*. Choice **d** is incorrect because *unnecessarily* is translated without the suffix *-de* or the prefix *ja-*. Choice **e** is incorrect because *unnecessarily* is translated without the prefix *ja-*; *reported* has been translated using the plural verb suffix *-et*; and *patrol* has been translated with the suffix *-lek*.

36. b. *Ricol fonlekol ru ricol almanlekoe gonleol avelekol synremet paftool* means *The reports on the government's dangerous enemies were questioned.* The first use of *the* is translated by adding the plural suffix *-ol* (Rule 2) to *ric* (*the*). *Reports* is translated by, first, adding the suffix *-lek* to the stem (Rule 9) of *fonsur* (*to report*) to form the noun and then by adding the plural suffix *-ol*. *On* translates as *ru*. The second use of *the* is translated as *ricol* since it refers to the plural *enemies*. *Government's* is translated by adding the possessive suffix *-oe* (Rule 12) to *almanlek* (*government*). *Dangerous* is translated, first, by changing the suffix *-lek* in *gonlek* (Rule 10) to *-le* to create an adjective, and then by adding the plural suffix *-ol*. *Enemies* is translated by adding the plural suffix *-ol* to *avelek* (*enemy*). Choice **a** is incorrect because the first *the* has been translated without the plural suffix *-ol* and because *government's* has been translated using the plural suffix *-ol*, instead of the possessive suffix *-oe*. Choice **c** is incorrect because the first *the*, as well as the word *dangerous*, has been translated without the plural suffix *-ol*. Choice **d** is incorrect because *reports*, *government's*, and *enemies* have all been translated using the suffix *-le*, instead of *-lek*. Choice **e** is incorrect because the second *the* has been translated without using the plural suffix *-ol*; *government's* has been translated using the suffix *-ol*, instead of *-oe*; and *dangerous* has been translated without the plural suffix *-ol*.

37. a. *Volle regle linlek tulot chonto ric browlek* means *This border patrol has crossed the river.* *This* translates as *volle*. *Border* is translated, first, by adding the suffix *-lek* to the stem (Rule 9) of *regsur* (*to border*) to form the noun, and then by changing *-lek* to the suffix *-le* because the word modifies *patrol* (Rule 10). *Patrol* is translated by adding the suffix *-lek* to the stem of *linsur* (*to patrol*). Choice **b** is incorrect because *border* has been translated using the suffix *-lek*. Choice **c** is incorrect because *patrol* has been translated using the suffix *-le*. Choice **d** is incorrect because *velle* means *that*. Choice **e** is incorrect because *velle* means *that* and because *border* has been translated using the suffix *-lek*.

38. e. *Ric kaplek zelremot ricol cleglekol* means *The man inspected the documents.* *Inspected* is translated by adding the suffixes *-rem* and *-ot* to the stem (Rule 7) of *zelsur* (*to inspect*) because the verb is in the past tense and is singular. *The* is translated by adding the plural suffix *-ol* (Rule 2) to *ric* (*the*). *Documents* is translated by adding the suffix *-lek* to the stem (Rule 9) of *clegsur* (*to document*), and then adding the plural suffix *-ol*. Choice **a** is incorrect because *documents* has been translated by adding the suffixes to the infinitive of the verb, not its stem. Choice **b** is incorrect because *inspected* has been translated with the plural verb suffix *-et*, instead of *-ot*; *the* has been translated without the suffix *-ol*; and *documents* has been translated using the suffix *-le*, instead of *-lek*. Choice **c** is incorrect because *the* has been translated without the suffix *-ol*. Choice **d** is incorrect because *inspected* has been translated with the plural verb suffix *-et*, instead of *-ot*.

39. c. *Ric huslek synremot hodto cre bonto* means *The alien was arrested and guarded.* *Was* is translated by adding the suffixes *-rem* and *-ot* to the stem (Rule 7) of *synsur* (*to be*) because the verb is in the past tense and is singular. *Arrested* and *guarded* are translated by adding the suffix *-to* to the stem of *hodsur* (*to arrest*) and of *bonsur* (*to guard*) because both words function as a predicate after the verb *to be* (Rule 8). *And* is translated as *cre*. Choice **a** is incorrect because *arrested* and *guarded* have been translated by adding the suffix *-to* to the infinitives *hodsur* and *bonsur*, instead of to their stems. Choice **b** is incorrect because *was* has been translated using the plural verb suffix *-et*, instead of *-ot*, and because *bex* means *a*. Choice **d** is incorrect because *was* has been translated using the plural verb suffix *-et*, instead of *-ot*, and because *arrested* and *guarded* have been translated using the suffix *-de* (which is used to create adverbs) instead of *-to*. Choice **e** is incorrect because *arrested* and *guarded* have been translated using the suffix *-de*, instead of *-to*, and because *bex* means *a*.

40. d. *Ric bonlek pafremot ricgidol kaplekgidol cre ricol ekaplekol* means *The guard questioned the women and the boys.* The first use of *the* is translated by adding the feminine suffix *-gid* (Rule 1) and the plural suffix *-ol* (Rule 2) to *ric* (*the*). *Women* is translated by adding the suffixes *-gid* and *-ol* to *kaplek* (*men*). *And* is translated as *cre.* The second use of *the* is translated by adding the plural suffix *-ol* to *ric. Boys* is translated by adding the suffix *-ol* to *ekaplek* (*boy*). Choice **a** is incorrect because the first *the* lacks the suffixes *-gid* and *-ol* and the second *the* lacks the suffix *-ol.* Choice **b** is incorrect because the first *the* lacks the suffixes *-gid* and *-ol* and the second *the* lacks the suffix *-ol*; and because *women* has been translated without the feminine suffix *-gid.* Choice **c** is incorrect because the first *the* has been translated without the feminine suffix *-gid.* Choice **e** is incorrect because *the boys* has been translated using the feminine suffix *-gid* in each word, forming *the girls.*

41. c. *Ricol zellekol fonremet mor ric lexlek* means *The inspectors reported from the station. Reported* is translated by adding the suffixes *-rem* and *-et* to the stem (Rule 7) of *fonsur* (*to report*) because the verb is in the past tense and is plural. *From* translates as *mor. The* is translated simply as *ric* since it refers to the singular *station* (Rule 3). *Station* is translated by adding the suffix *-lek* to the stem (Rule 9) of *lexsur* (*to station*) because it is a noun formed from a verb. Choice **a** is incorrect because *reported* has been translated by adding the suffixes to the infinitive, instead of to the stem, and because *the station* has been translated by unnecessarily using the plural suffix *-ol*, forming *the stations.* Choice **b** is incorrect because *station* has been translated using the suffix *-le*, instead of *-lek.* Choice **d** is incorrect because *reported* has been translated using the singular verb suffix *-ot*, instead of the plural suffix *-et.* Choice **e** is incorrect because *reported* has been translated using the singular verb suffix *-ot* and because *station* has been translated using the suffix *-le*, instead of *-lek.*

42. b. *Ricol kaplekol synremet ru ricol bontool reglekol* means *The men were on the guarded borders*. *The* is translated by adding the plural suffix *-ol* (Rule 2) to *ric* (*the*). *Guarded* is translated by, first, adding the suffix *-to* to the stem of *bonsur* (*to guard*) because the word is a past participle functioning as an adjective, and then by adding the plural suffix *-ol* (Rule 8). *Borders* is translated by adding the suffix *-lek* to the stem (Rule 9) of *regsur* (*to border*) because the word is a noun formed from a verb. Choice **a** is incorrect because *the* and *guarded* have been translated without the plural suffix *-ol*. Choice **c** is incorrect because *the* has been translated without the plural suffix *-ol*; *guarded* has been translated by adding the suffix *-to* to the infinitive of *bonsur* (instead of its stem) and also lacks the suffix *-ol*; and *borders* has been translated by adding the suffixes to the infinitive of *regsur*, instead of its stem. Choice **d** is incorrect because *the* has been translated without the plural suffix *-ol*. Choice **e** is incorrect because *guarded* and *borders* have been translated by adding the suffixes to their infinitives, instead of their stems. Also, *guarded* is missing the *-to* suffix.

43. d. *Ricgidol ekaplekgidol synremet kometlek* means *The girls were friendly*. *Friendly* is translated by, first, changing the suffix *-lek* in *kometlek* (*friend*) to *-le* to form an adjective (Rule 10), and then by adding the feminine suffix *-gid* and the plural suffix *-ol*. Choice **a** is incorrect because it lacks the suffixes *-gid* and *-ol*. Choice **b** is incorrect because it lacks the suffix *-gid*. Choice **c** is incorrect because it lacks the suffix *-ol*. Choice **e** is incorrect because the suffix *-lek* has not been replaced by *-le*.

44. a. *Vellegid ekaplekgid synremot gaflegid* means *The girl was brave*. *Was* is translated by adding the suffixes *-rem* and *-ot* to the stem (Rule 7) of *synsur* (*to be*) because the verb is in the past tense and is singular. *Brave* is translated by adding the feminine suffix *-gid* (Rule 1) to *gafle* (*brave*). Choice **b** is incorrect because *was* has been translated using the plural verb suffix *-et*, instead of *-ot*. Choice **c** is incorrect because *brave* has been translated without the feminine suffix *-gid*. Choice **d** is incorrect because *was* has been translated using the plural verb suffix *-et* and because *brave* has been translated without the feminine suffix *-gid*. Choice **e** is incorrect because *was* has been translated without the past tense suffix *-rem* and because *brave* has been translated without the feminine suffix *-gid*.

45. e. *Yevol jainlede fonremet yevoloe kometlekol* means *They disloyally reported their friends*. *Disloyally* is translated, first, by adding the suffix *-de* to *inle* to form an adverb (Rule 11), and then by adding the negative prefix *ja-* (Rule 13). Choice **a** is incorrect because the word includes the suffix *-lek* and because *ja-* has been put at the end of the word. Choice **b** is incorrect because the positions of *-de* and *ja-* have been reversed. Choice **c** is incorrect because *-de* has been placed at the beginning of the word. Choice **d** is incorrect because the word includes the suffix *-lek*.

46. d. *Ricgidol lexlegidol bonlekgidol synremet kometlekgidol* means *The station guards were friends*. *Station* is translated, first, by adding the suffix *-lek* to the stem of *lexsur* (*to station*) to create a noun (Rule 9); *-lek* is then changed to the suffix *-le* because *station* modifies *guards* (Rule 10); then the feminine suffix *-gid* (Rule 1) and the plural suffix *-ol* (Rule 2) are added. *Friends* is translated by adding the feminine suffix *-gid* and the plural suffix *-ol* to *kometlek* (*friend*). Choice **a** is incorrect because *station* has been translated without changing the suffix *-lek* to *-le* (and is also missing the suffixes *-gid* and *-ol*), and because *friends* has been translated without the feminine suffix *-gid*. Choice **b** is incorrect because *station* has been translated without the feminine suffix *-gid* or the plural suffix *-ol*, and because *friends* has been translated without the feminine suffix *-gid*. Choice **c** is incorrect because *station* and *friends* have been translated without the feminine suffix *-gid*. Choice **e** is incorrect because *station* has been translated without changing the suffix *-lek* to *-le*.

47. a. *Ricol frigremet ru ric fonlek* means *They worked on the report*. *Worked* is translated by adding the suffixes *-rem* and *-et* to the stem (Rule 7) of *frigsur* (*to work*) because the verb is in the past tense and is plural. *Report* is translated by adding the suffix *-lek* to the stem (Rule 9) of *fonsur* (*to report*). Choice **b** is incorrect because *worked* has been translated without the suffix *-rem* and because *report* has been translated using that suffix. Choice **c** is incorrect because *worked* has been translated using the singular verb suffix *-ot*, instead of *-et*. Choice **d** is incorrect because *worked* has been translated only using the singular verb suffix *-ot* and because *report* has been translated using the suffix *-rem*. Choice **e** is incorrect because *report* has been translated using the suffix *-le*, instead of *-lek*.

48. c. *Ricol hodlekol synremet jacolleol* means *The arrests were illegal*. *Arrests* is translated by adding the suffix *-lek* to the stem (Rule 9) of *hodsur* (*to arrest*) to make a noun from the verb, and then by adding the plural suffix *-ol*. *Illegal* is translated by adding the negative prefix *ja-* (Rule 13) and the plural suffix *-ol* (Rule 2) to *colle* (*legal*). Choice **a** is incorrect because *arrests* has been translated using the suffix *-le* instead of *-lek*, and because *illegal* has been translated using the suffix *-de*, instead of *-ol*. Choice **b** is incorrect because *arrest* has been translated by adding the incorrect suffix *-ol* (instead of *-lek*) to the infinitive *hodsur*, instead of its stem, and because *illegal* has been translated using the suffix *-de*. Choice **d** is incorrect because *illegal* has been translated without the plural suffix *-ol*. Choice **e** is incorrect because *arrests* has been translated by adding the suffixes to the infinitive *hodsur* and because *illegal* has been translated without the plural suffix *-ol*.

49. e. *Yevgidoe paflekol synremet gonleol* means *Her questions were dangerous. Her* is translated by adding the feminine suffix *-gid* (Rule 1) and the possessive suffix *-oe* (Rule 12) to *yev* (*he*). *Dangerous* is translated by, first, changing the suffix *-lek* in *gonlek* (*danger*) to *-le* in order to form an adjective (Rule 10), and then by adding the plural suffix *-ol* (Rule 2). Choice **a** is incorrect because *her* has been translated using the plural suffix *-ol*, instead of the possessive suffix *-oe*, and because *dangerous* has been translated without changing the suffix *-lek* to *-le*. Choice **b** is incorrect because *her* has been translated without the feminine suffix *-gid* and *dangerous* has been translated by using the suffix *-oe*, instead of *-ol*. Choice **c** is incorrect because *dangerous* has been translated by using the suffix *-oe*. Choice **d** is incorrect because *her* has been translated by adding the plural suffix *-ol* to *yev*; it is missing the feminine suffix *-gid* and possessive suffix *-oe*.

50. b. *Ricgidol jakometlegidol bonlekgidol jatulremet ric fonlek* means *The unfriendly guards did not have the report. The* is translated by adding the feminine suffix *-gid* (Rule 1) and the plural suffix *-ol* (Rule 2) to *ric* (*the*). *Unfriendly* is translated by, first, changing the suffix *-lek* in *kometlek* to *-!e* in order to form an adjective (Rule 10), and then by adding the feminine suffix *-gid*, the plural suffix *-ol*, and the negative prefix *ja-* (Rule 13). *Did not have* is translated by, first, adding the suffixes *-rem* and *-et* to the stem (Rule 7) of *tulsur* (*to have*) because the verb is in the past tense and is singular, and then adding the negative prefix *ja-*. Choice **a** is incorrect because *the* and *unfriendly* have been translated without the feminine suffix *-gid*, and because *did not have* has been translated without the negative suffix *ja-*. Choice **c** is incorrect because *the* has been translated without any of the needed suffixes; *unfriendly* has been translated without the feminine suffix, the plural suffix, or the negative prefix; and *did not have* has been translated without the negative prefix *ja-*. Choice **d** is incorrect because both *unfriendly* and *did not have* have been translated without the negative prefix *ja-*. Choice **e** is incorrect because *the* has been translated without any of the needed suffixes, and because *unfriendly* has been translated without the plural suffix *-ol*.

Practice Test 6: Scoring and Diagnostic Chart

To evaluate how you did on this practice exam, start by totaling the number of correct responses on the two sections of this practice exam. First, find the number of questions you got right in each part. Questions you skipped or got wrong don't count; just add up the number of correct answers.

If at least 70% of your responses on the two parts are correct (47 correct), you are most likely prepared to pass the Border Patrol Exam. However, because the entrance process is competitive, you may need a higher score on the official exam to get accepted into the Border Patrol Academy.

In addition to seeing how you performed overall, you can use the following scoring chart to help diagnose your strengths and weaknesses in the different skills assessed on the exam, to better focus your study preparation.

LOGICAL REASONING SECTION	
SKILL	QUESTION
Reasoning about Groups and Categories	1–8
Reasoning about Events or Situations	9–16

ARTIFICIAL LANGUAGE SECTION	
SKILL	QUESTION
Artificial Language I	1, 2, 3, 4, 5, 6, 7, 8, 9, 10, 11, 12, 13, 14, 15, 16, 17, 18, 19, 20
Artificial Language II	21, 22, 23, 24, 25, 26, 27, 28, 29, 30
Artificial Language III	31, 32, 33, 34, 35, 36, 37, 38, 39, 40, 41, 42
Artificial Language IV	43, 44, 45, 46, 47, 48, 49, 50

ADDITIONAL ONLINE PRACTICE

Whether you need help building basic skills or preparing for an exam, visit LearningExpress Practice Center! On this site, you can access additional practice materials. Using the code below, you'll be able to log in and get additional practice. This online practice will also provide you with:

- **Immediate scoring**
- **Detailed answer explanations**
- **Personalized recommendations for further practice and study**

Log into the LearningExpress Practice Center by using the URL: **www.learnatest.com/practice**

This is your Access Code: **9032**

Follow the steps online to redeem your access code. After you've used your access code to register with the site, you will be prompted to create a username and password. For easy reference, record them here:

Username: _____ **Password:** _____

With your username and password, you can log in and answer these practice questions as many times as you like. If you have any questions or problems, please contact LearningExpress customer service at 1-800-295-9556 ext. 2, or e-mail us at **customerservice@learningexpressllc.com**.